THE PUPPETEER

Ajit Menon—author, philanthrope, and a unique nation builder in his own right—has worked in very senior leadership roles in five different industries, before deciding to follow his passion, storytelling. He was rated amongst the 'Top 12 inspiring writers of 2023' by *Mid-Day*. Ajit and his family run an NGO called Anugraha Foundation, which funds homes for abandoned and destitute senior citizens. Ajit lives in Gurgaon with his family.

Anil Verma is a well-known lyricist, screenplay writer and ad man. His songs are blockbuster hits, and he is known for his patriotic lyrics. He travelled extensively across India to understand the authentic Indian way of life, which is now reflected in his songs and film scripts. Anil thinks in his mother tongue; hence, he prefers to express himself in Hindi. However, he has partnered with Ajit to co-author this book in English. He was recently recognised as the 'Emerging Lyricist of the Year' by *Tycoon Global*. Anil and his family live in Mumbai.

Praise for *The Panther's Ghosts*

'A compelling espionage thriller that does not border on didacticism or sensationalism'

telegraphindia.com

'The fictionalised version of what transpires in the real world'

abplive.in

'Ajit's thrillers take you on an absolute rollercoaster ride through different countries, situations, and scenes even as they unveil one mystery after another'

lokmattimes.com

THE PANTHER'S GHOSTS SERIES

THE
PUPPETEER

AJIT & ANIL

First published by Westland Books, a division of Nasadiya
Technologies Private Limited, in 2023

No. 269/2B, First Floor, 'Irai Arul', Vimalraj Street, Nethaji Nagar,
Alapakkam Main Road, Maduravoyal, Chennai 600095

Westland and the Westland logo are the trademarks of Nasadiya
Technologies Private Limited, or its affiliates.

ISBN: 9789395767996

10 9 8 7 6 5 4 3 2 1

This is a work of fiction. Names, characters, organisations, places,
events and incidents are either products of the author's imagination
or used fictitiously.

Typeset by R. Ajith Kumar, Delhi

Printed at HT Media Ltd, Greater Noida

'If God is a reality, then man is a slave, a puppet.
All the strings are in his hands, even your life.
Then there is no question of any enlightenment.
Then there is no question of there being any Gautam
the Buddha, because there is no freedom at all. He pulls
the strings, you dance; he pulls the strings, you cry;
he pulls the strings, you start murders, suicide, war.
You are just a puppet and he is the puppeteer.'

—Osho, *God Is a Puppeteer*

CONTENTS

सत्यमेव जयते

राज्यपाल, पश्चिम वंगाल
Governor of West Bengal
রাজ্যপাল, পশ্চিমবঙ্গ

FOREWORD

The Puppeteer, second book in 'The Panther's Ghosts' series, of the rarest of the rare genre—the murky world of cloak and dagger espionage—is thrilling, arresting, exciting and like the classical Greek tragedies, leads to catharsis in the readers.

This world where magic weds realism, where evil guards good and untruth provides a shield for truth, is digested by the reading public because the authors, Ajit & Anil, have been able to create a willing suspension of disbelief—which Coleridge in his *Biographia Literaria* described as the ultimate in imaginative creativity.

Treading on the hills and dales of the secret service, the Panthers and the puppets are truth masquerading as untruth and good camouflaged as evil. Trust, affection, honesty and candour are all anathema to the world of spy kingdoms. Success is the end and any means, how so ever meanly employed, does not mean bad for the nocturnal wizards of the spy-world.

Creating pity and fear, loathe and love within the readers as they go along the trail of crime and punishment, intrigue and investigation—every word in this book gives you Goosebumps.

Here we will see the strange visual of Watson teaching Holmes, Hercule Poirot holding hands with Miss Marple and James Bond's tricky bond with Agatha—an imaginative world where impossible becomes possible, night becomes day and both sink into the black hole of mystery.

How to create an illusionary world of suspense and suspicion, and make it look real is an I art which calls for creative dexterity and imaginative craft. The authors, who have carved out a niche for themselves, in the genre of suspense thrillers and imaginative jugglers have graduated into another plane where the reader gets a feeling that he 'on honeydew hath fed and drunk the milk of Paradise'.

This realism of illusions is a paradox which lends itself to extreme manoeuvrability in the hands of the seasoned authors.

As Dryden said about the characters of Chaucer, it can be said about this book—'here is God's plenty'. Human emotions, intellect and intrigue, stealth sans sentiments, sense sans sensibility and success being the only reality, this book is an interesting, intriguing, puzzling, enigmatic and novel reading experience, hitherto unknown in contemporary literary history.

I wish Ajit and Anil hazy failure, which—in the milieu of the book—can be termed sterling success.

Here is a book where opposites reconcile, night and day rolls into one and you will see the 'new moon on the full moon's lap'.

So sharpen your brain and your pencil, and get ready to join the dots.

Dr CV Ananda Bose
Honourable Governor of West Bengal.

PROLOGUE

THE THURAYA SATELLITE PHONE BUZZED briefly and then fell silent. The blue-lit screen shone brightly for a few seconds, displaying the day, the date and a message, before going dark again. It was 20 February, 2020.

ISI agent Abdul Qadir examined his bruised knuckles, and then fixed his gaze on the hooded figure, bound at his waist, to a plain, folding aluminium chair in front of him. His hands were zip-tied behind the chair. Blood seeped through the black sack shrouding the man's face. He was about to smash his fist against the man's face again, but a gruff voice came from behind him, making him pause.

'Check the message on the phone, idiot.' It was Major Khan of the ISI.

Qadir nodded and picked up the Thuraya. He was about to hand it over to the major, when Khan said, 'Read it out loud so that our friend can hear it too.'

Complying, Qadir read: *If you have finished your Kathmandu romance, please return immediately. Mom.*

Major Khan turned to his captive and asked, 'And who is "your mom"?'

'My mom is a beautiful, sophisticated, kind lady. Not the poor woman who regrets producing you,' murmured the man, chuckling. His head drooped, blood dripping from below the hood onto his chest, a testament to the innumerable cuts and bruises he had received at Qadir's hands. His split, bleeding lips, hidden beneath the black hood, made speaking difficult.

'Who are you romancing in Kathmandu?' asked Major Khan, seething at the insult. The hooded man mumbled something.

'I cannot understand what he is saying,' barked Major Khan to Qadir.

Qadir repeated the question. The hooded man mumbled again in response.

'What? Speak up,' said Qadir, lifting the hood up just enough to expose the captive's lips. He stooped to bring his left ear close to the man's mouth.

'I am romancing a bunch of circumcised pricks,' the man whispered.

Before Qadir could take a step back, strong teeth clamped down on his left ear. Qadir screamed in agony, trying to pull away from the man's vice-like jaws, but the teeth only dug further into his ear. Realising what was happening, Major Khan held Qadir by his waist and gave a desperate tug. Qadir's screams filled the room, as felt his left ear rip off from his face. The two staggered back, and crashed on the seat where Major Khan, was sitting. Qadir's body weight and the sudden impact of his head on the aluminium chair and then the floor, knocked Major Khan out for a few minutes. With trembling hands, Qadir touched the side of his head and found only a bleeding stub. He looked down to find the hood and his ear on the floor. Faint with pain, Qadir locked eyes with the man who had done this to him.

Now that the hood was off, he could see the wry smile on the captive's bloody face.

As he scrambled to get off the major, Qadir heard a roar come from the captive as he jumped four feet in the air. The captive's recent training in kalaripayattu, the martial art that originated in Kerala, had clearly paid off. He was still tied to the aluminium chair as he came crashing into them with his bent knees, ramming into Qadir's chest. Qadir's rib cage cracked, puncturing his heart and lungs, killing him instantly.

A dazed Major Khan wriggled out from beneath Qadir's now limp body and tried to stand on wobbly legs, but the man headbutted him in the face, breaking his nose and drawing blood. Before Major Khan could regain his balance, the man swiped with his left leg, making contact with Major Khan's ankle. The major's body flipped, parallel to the ground for a brief moment, before crashing to the concrete floor. The force of the impact caused his body to bounce before it hit the floor a second time. A scream escaped his lips as his neck broke. His head rocked back once and finally lolled forward onto his chest. Major Khan had died a painful death.

The crash from a four feet height had broken the aluminium chair into multiple pieces. The man expanded his chest as much as he could and then let out the air making the rope around his waist loosen. Then he backed towards the broken aluminium chair and started grazing the rope against the jagged edge of a broken piece of the leg. A few minutes later, the ropes around his wrists gave way. His hands freed, he quickly pushed the binding ropes around his waist down and stepped out of them.

The man stood up and removed the broken pieces of aluminium that had dug into his forearms and then made for the tap in the corner of the room, his body swaying, his legs unsteady. He turned the tap on and put his head under it, welcoming the ice-cold water that washed away the blood from his face and revived him a little. He let the water flow till the throbbing pain in his head subsided. Then he took off his bloody clothes, unbuttoned Major Khan's shirt and trousers, and pulled them on instead. He grabbed the holster and Glock from Qadir's dead body and snapped it around his waist. Next was the Thuraya phone, lying on the floor. The man punched the code; 31164 which primed a detonator and set an automatic timer.

As he exited the building, he spotted a black Toyota SUV parked nearby. A ranger from the Pakistan Army stood next to it, chewing tobacco and facing the road. The ranger, hearing the door shut, turned around. The moment he saw the man, his hand darted towards his hip holster, but the intruder was faster. In a flash, Major Khan's Glock appeared in his right hand. He pulled the trigger twice and the ranger's chest exploded in crimson.

'I didn't want to kill you,' he murmured, 'but you saw my face.' He pushed the ranger's body onto the footpath, climbed into the Toyota, started the engine and began to speed away.

Thirty seconds later, the left wing of the KAS Institute for Humanity and Cultural Studies in Sonbarsa, Nepal, exploded.

The strategically placed C4s had brought the wing down

like a house of cards, and with it, the entire surveillance set-up of the building, the weapons cache, the GPS monitoring system, and the ISI and jihadi training materials that were housed in the institute. Seven terrorist instructors and fifty-six jihadis, all waiting for infiltration into India via Bihar, were killed instantly, buried under the debris. A second explosion rocked the institute when the flames from the first blast spread to the explosives and ammunition storage in the right wing. In a matter of minutes, the night sky glowed orange, lighting up the quiet hamlet like a Diwali evening.

As the Toyota hit National Highway 77, the 142-kilometre stretch that connects Sonbarsa at the India–Nepal border to Hajipur in Bihar, the man pulled out his Thuraya phone and dialled a number. On the other end was Ajit Dhariwal, the National Security Advisor, or NSA, of India.

'Where are you, Raj?' Dhariwal asked.

'On my way. I'm in Janakpur in Nepal. I'll be reaching Khutauna in two hours,' replied Raj.

'Are you planning to enter India through Sonbarsa?'

Raj chuckled. 'Wow. Aren't you quite the Nostradamus. How did you know?'

'Save the sarcasm for another time will you? Listen, you'll soon get to Gamhariya Roundabout in Rautahat district. Look for a white Hyundai i10 with the number plate GAB0123. You'll find it parked in front of a sweet shop called Natto Sweets. Leave your car there and get into the i10. The driver will bring you to the border. We'll have someone there to bring you back. Once you are on Indian soil, the Panther would like to meet you,' said Dhariwal.

'Is he upset?' asked Raj.

'Come and see for yourself,' came Dhariwal's terse response.

'Sure. See you soon, sir,' said Raj, pressing his foot down on the accelerator.

⌘

The Prime Minister of India, Damodar Das, was known to many as DD. To the team that protected him, the Special Protection Group, or the SPG, he was 'the Panther'. DD believed that diplomacy, geopolitics and governmental procedures were obstacles to his chosen doctrine of 'defensive offence'.

The defensive offence doctrine was a policy where India would have a proactive strategy against anything—nations, organisations or radical beliefs—that posed a threat to national security. Offensive action was taken to defend the country against these foreign threats. Rather than a typical act of war, this policy first identified the threat, then broadcasted it globally and finally took offensive measures against it.

But DD's doctrine had a small twist—while he too identified the threat first, he avoided public announcements. Instead, he would deploy a team of covert operatives, unknown to the general public, to go on the offensive and eradicate that threat. DD's other revision was to have every offensive action orchestrated as a false flag operation, where the covert operatives were never given credit after execution. The result was always attributed to a third party. This ensured the confidentiality of both the mission and the operatives.

NSA Ajit Dhariwal, a close confidant of DD, had been assigned the formidable task of forming a special unit to carry out these covert operations. This unit comprised six people recruited from the SPG and Special Forces. Once recruited, these operatives were discreetly pulled from active service, their identities erased from all records, unbeknownst to even their families, leaving them untraceable. With no official connection to the government or the armed forces, they operated as 'Ghosts'.

The current team of six Ghosts blended seamlessly into society, indistinguishable from civilians. They had families and held regular office jobs. Whenever summoned for a mission, they would leave their homes under the pretext of a work trip and report to NSA Dhariwal. Each mission was termed a 'Strike', followed by a sequential number indicating its order. Since the Ghosts belonged to the Panther, they were aptly named the 'Panther's Ghosts', and they had successfully completed Strike 1 and Strike 2 a couple of years ago.

One of these six Ghosts was Raj Pratap Rana. His peers were Arvind Menon, aka Sniper, Ram Madhav Lala, Ashok Vashisht, Shiv Kumar Raju and Geeta Rathode.

At sixty-seven, Arvind Menon was the oldest member of the Panther's Ghosts. He was six feet two inches tall, broad shouldered with flowing grey hair. His body was tough and battle hardened. He was an ace shooter, with over sixty kills to his name, including six assassinations executed from a staggering distance of 2,000 yards using his custom M24 rifle. This prowess earned him the name 'Sniper'.

Sniper's past was marred by tragedy. During a mission years ago, he had been betrayed by a corrupt Indian police officer, Rajiv Prasad, or RP. Driven by greed, RP, who had financial links with the Pakistan-based gangster Don Mohammed Adnan, had leaked Sniper's whereabouts in Pakistan to the don. The don in turn passed on this piece of information to the international terrorist Hafiz Salahuddin, the notorious head of the terrorist organisation Lashkar-e-Taiba (LeT) who was carrying a US bounty on his head.

Acting on this intelligence, Pakistan's ISI nabbed Sniper and handed him over to the LeT, who imprisoned him in a Quetta dungeon, where he was subjected to torture. The LeT then sent an ultimatum to the Indian government: release the terrorist Mazour Assad, who was lodged in a jail in India, in exchange for Sniper. When the Indian government refused, the LeT employed their Indian counterpart, the Indian Mujahideen, a local terrorist unit founded by two militant brothers working for the Al Qaeda. The group abducted Arvind's three sons when they were on their way to school. Following another refusal from the Indian government, the three children were ruthlessly killed, and the images of their lifeless bodies were uploaded to the internet. When Sniper, who had by then escaped from the Quetta prison, learnt about the death of his children, he unleashed his vengeance. He returned to Quetta and, in a span of eleven days, killed eight ISI officers, eight of Hafiz's mercenaries and a pivotal ISI major—the orchestrator of the plot against his sons.

When Dhariwal learnt that Sniper was setting his sights on Hafiz next, he tried to involve Raj's father, Veer Pratap Rana who was the then Mumbai Police Commissioner in Sniper's extraction from Quetta. Recognising the high risk of the Ghosts being exposed and considering Veer's background as a former para commando and SPG, Dhariwal believed he was perfect for the task. But the Indian government refused again to allow Veer to go. It was then that Dhariwal reached out to his trusted friend across the border, Safi Doha, a Pakistani industrialist whom Dhariwal often turned to for logistical support and mission funding during covert operations in Pakistan. Doha smuggled Arvind out of Quetta to Mumbai via Afghanistan and Iran. On his return, Sniper retired and settled down in the foothills near Yashwant Wadi in Pune with his wife, Bhavani.

But in 2017, Dhariwal coaxed Sniper out of retirement for two missions, Strikes 1 and 2, as one of the Panther's Ghosts. The following year, Dhariwal gave Sniper an opportunity to exact his revenge and sent him to Quetta. Sniper targeted Hafiz Salahuddin in his own house in Quetta and used his favourite M24 rifle to execute the man. Done from a sand dune over 1,000 yards away, it was his sixty-first kill.

Ram Madhav Lala, standing at five feet and eleven inches, was in his mid-fifties. He was born in Punjab to a Sikh family and was the youngest of three children, all of whom had dedicated their lives to the nation. Unmarried, the three brothers never thought of starting a family—the nation was their true family. Lala faced devastation when his two elder brothers were martyred in the Kargil War against Pakistan. Before the grief had settled, he lost his parents a year later, both within a span of two months. All of a sudden, at the age of forty-eight, he was alone and working as a Ghost for the Panther. He stayed with Raj in a secluded independent house on a hillock facing a dam in Mulshi Taluk of Pune. The house was called Veer's Bungalow and it doubled up as the headquarters of the Ghosts. Lala was more like a brother than a colleague to Raj, and was always around to protect him and keep a close eye on him. He found family in Raj and his mother, Shanti. During Strike 1, which was Raj's inaugural mission, Lala helped him exact revenge for his father Veer Pratap Rana's death. And in Strike 2, he was the lookout and the getaway driver out of Pakistan.

Ashok Vashisht, or AV, came from Maharashtra. He was five feet nine inches tall, extremely fair and well-built, and had a receding hairline. His glasses lent him a scholarly air. In reality, he was an outdoors person and a strong nationalist. Married to Ameeta from Pune, AV had two sons, who were studying abroad. AV joined the police academy along with Veer and trained with him in the Special Forces. Later he worked for the SPG for a few years, till they were enrolled into active police duty by Commissioner Sivanandan. While Veer was sent to Mumbai, AV was posted in Pune, eventually rising to the position of DCP for Crime in Pune. He played an instrumental role in helping Veer gather intel on Don Mohammed Adnan during the initial attempt to capture him. After Veer's death, it was AV who convinced Raj to join the Panther's Ghosts and helped him nab the don in 2017.

Shiv Kumar Raju, dark complexioned, five feet ten inches tall, barrel chested and strong as a bull was from Andhra Pradesh. He was a member of the SPG, and DD's personal bodyguard, living in 7, Lok Kalyan Marg, New Delhi. In the line of duty, he had had to sacrifice his wife Leela while saving Raj's mother, Shanti. When Raj's father, Veer, had still been alive, Shiva received information that Shanti was going to be kidnapped on her way to the airport—a move that would jeopardise Strike 1. Shiva took a desperate measure: he had his own wife take Shanti's place in the car, hoping the kidnappers would release her when they discovered their mistake. Instead, in anger, they mortally shot her. Shiva was shattered by Leela's death. Seeing his condition, DD gave him a special post of 'personal body guard' and kept him close to him in Delhi. Over the years, when he doubled up as a Ghost, he started slowly getting out of his depression and was now a strong asset in the team. He was the spotter for Sniper in Strike 2 and also did a fantastic job in rescuing Raj from Quetta along with Sniper.

Geeta Rathode, was from Himachal and was the daughter of Major Indrajit Rathode, aka IR, a former comrade of Veer's who was currently employed as the head of security of the tech company Raj had founded, Info Dynamics, or ID. Geeta was striking, a tall, slim and dusky-complexioned woman of thirty. She had green eyes and an oval face, and a dimple appeared on her left cheek with every smile. She was the epitome of beauty and brains. Inspired by Veer and her father, she completed her 1 para commando training before joining the Panther's Ghosts. Growing up without a mother, she was particularly close to her father; the two shared everything. To the rest of the world, Geeta Rathode was a freelance crime reporter who wrote for different publications, most often for the popular English newspaper *India Times*. For the longest time, Raj had had no clue that Geeta was Indrajit's daughter. In fact no one, including Geeta knew much about her mother. Other than that her name was Kiran Iyer, she was a singer and had died in a car accident when Geeta was two years old. It was only after Strike 2 that Lala told Raj about her and Indrajit. Though Indrajit was not an active member of the Panther's Ghosts, he was called in by Dhariwal to help whenever needed.

Before Raj, his father, Veer Pratap Rana, former Deputy Commissioner of Mumbai, had been the sixth Panther's Ghost. When Veer was assassinated during Strike 1, Raj assumed his role and completed the mission. Raj mirrored his father, in both appearance and behaviour. When Veer was killed, Raj had been in Paris. A year after Veer's death, when his mother told him that his father had been betrayed by his own commissioner, Rajiv Prasad, and had been killed by 'Kalia Rafa', the bodyguard of Don Mohammed Adnan, an enraged Raj swore to take revenge.

The moment NSA Dhariwal set his eyes on Raj, he knew he had found a younger version of Veer. When Dhariwal discovered that Raj was going solo after the very same villains he was after, he explained that Don Mohammed Adnan and Rajiv were all part of a larger conspiracy, and invited Raj to join their collective pursuit. Raj accepted the invitation. Despite being the head of ID, he handed over the reins to his second-in-command, Shankar Narayanan, and became the last of the Panther's Ghosts.

Though Raj was a martial arts expert in kalaripayattu and a third-degree Shaolin kung fu graduate, Dhariwal ensured that he was trained in guerrilla warfare and covert operations. Alongside his martial prowess, Raj had an MBA from Paris—he had always had a strong business sense. Patriotic and decisive, Raj also possessed a strategic approach and an ability to easily influence others, which proved advantageous during Strikes 1 and 2. He also had

Highly Superior Autobiographical Memory, or HSAM, wherein he could recall past events in great detail, along with the exact dates when they occurred. Raj had not been aware of his unique talent until a few years ago, when he returned to India with an abdominal injury he had sustained while executing Strike 2 in Quetta. It was while he was recovering post-surgery that the doctors noticed him sketching people and places from the two strikes in exceptional, even abnormal, detail. Subsequent HSAM testing confirmed their suspicion. The newest—and most rebellious—of the Panther's Ghosts, Raj was also the most liked in the group. Because of his ability to influence people, the Ghosts nicknamed him 'The Puppeteer'.

◎⫯⫯∽

The i10 Dhariwal had mentioned was parked next to Nattoo Sweets near Gamhariya Roundabout. Raj parked the Toyota, walked up to the white car and rapped on the driver's side window. A short Nepali driver stepped out with a smile.

'Raj Pratap Rana?' he asked.

'Yes, and you?' asked Raj.

'I am just Rana,' the driver said.

'Ha, funny,' said Raj drily.

'Please give me your car keys. After dropping you to your destination, I will come back for the Toyota,' said Rana, his hand outstretched.

Raj handed over the keys and got into the back seat of the i10. 'Where are we going?' he asked as Rana pulled the car on to the main highway.

'My instructions are to drop you in Birgunj. From there someone will pick you up and take you to ICP Jogbani.'

ICP Jogbani was on the international border between India and Nepal and was about 325 kilometres from Patna, the capital of Bihar. Jogbani in India and Birgunj in Nepal were connected by a vital trading route. Over one lakh trucks plied this route, conducting trade amounting to over 5,500 crore rupees. The integrated checkpost, or ICP, was spread across 186 acres, with the Indian side housing a helipad.

Raj typed out a message to Dhariwal telling him of the plan, before leaning back and going to sleep. This was a habit he had picked up from his role model, Sniper. 'No day is so bad it can't be fixed with a nap,' he would say. Like his father, Veer, Raj greatly respected Sniper and often looked to him for advice. Safi Doha and Pavak Dahiya were two others he held in high esteem. Since the strikes were being conducted without the knowledge of the Indian government, Dhariwal was helped by these two industrialist brothers—Safi who lived in Karachi and Pavak, who resided in Delhi. They funded all the strikes across the globe and also helped with logistics and documentation. Safi Doha and Pavak Dahiya were related and were actually cousins living on both sides of the border because of their ancestors' choices during the Partition. Safi's side of the family decided to stay back in Karachi because they had business there. Everything was okay for a few years but then, by the time Safi was born, the authorities started putting pressure on conversion. When the army took over Pakistan in 1999, life for the Hindus in Pakistan became hell. Safi's grandfather had no choice but to convert to Islam, a decision which was hated by the family, especially Safi. When Safi took over the business, he got close to Pavak who believed that one day, Pakistan and India would reunite. Safi was a hundred percent Indian in his mind, so when Pavak asked him to join him in this mission, he willingly agreed. If caught, he would be hung for treason but that was the risk Safi had chosen to take. Raj could not believe that such patriotic people even existed across the border.

When the i10 entered Birgunj, Rana stopped the car and gently shook Raj awake. 'We're here sir,' he said.

Out of the window, Raj spotted a white Mahindra Scorpio parked on the side of the road. The driver's head was wrapped in a black scarf, only his eyes remaining visible. Raj squinted for a second—the eyes seemed familiar, but he couldn't quite place them. He got out of the i10 and shook Rana's hand, slipping him a hundred-dollar bill, before walking over to the Scorpio and getting into the front seat.

When the Scorpio started moving, Raj asked the driver, 'And who might you be?'

The man, slowly unravelling the scarf, said sarcastically, 'Your father-in-law.'

Raj broke out in a grin. 'Lala,' he said, laughing. He reached over to hug his best friend.

The friends had so much to catch up on that they scarcely realised that the drive to ICP Jogbani was three hours long.

'How did the Puppeteer land up in Nepal? Weren't you supposed to be in London surveilling the Pakistani Ambassador to Nepal, Haji Ali?' asked Lala as he drove. He was careful to maintain the highway speed of 80 kmph, lest he attract the attention of the local police.

'Yes, brother. As per the intel from RAW, Haji was to be in London to meet Raul, the bomb maker from Syria, correct?' Raj asked.

'Absolutely. Your job was to keep an eye on his movements and report back, which you did for five days, before disappearing. It's only when your mom contacted me from Earl's Court that I knew you had left for Nepal. She asked me to keep it confidential for a while, so I did. Dhariwal tried to trace you, but after a week-long radio silence we heard about the KAS explosion this morning and knew you were there. I was about to leave for Kathmandu, but then you happened to call Dhariwal. Luckily, when Dhariwal called me, I was in Patna, so he asked me to take an IAF chopper to ICP Jogbani and wait for you in Birgunj. En route, I called Rana, organised your pickup and told Dhariwal to pass on the message to you as I wasn't carrying my Thuraya. But forget all that—why the KAS?' asked Lala.

'Okay, let me explain. You see, to the world, Kapilavastu Agricultural Society in Naoganga, Nepal, was a society set up eight years ago to develop organic farming in the country. It was funded and run by an NGO that went by the name Pakistan Agro Ltd. To justify the large number of people coming into KAS regularly, they added the Humanity & Cultural angle to KAS and now it is called KAS Institue of Humanities and Cultural Studies. This allowed them to give visas to people without being questioned by Nepalese authorities. In reality, KAS was an LeT training and holding base run by the ISI. After completing physical training in Pakistan, the jihadis were sent to the KAS to receive training in navigation, drone operations and bomb making, among other things, and then pushed into India across the Bihar border.

'Following the Indian surgical strikes in PoK in response to the Uri attack, the ISI decided not to keep all their terror bases in PoK, so they shifted a few to the Indo-Nepal border. For the past two years, they've been smuggling terrorists through Bihar, disguising them as traders. Fifty-six jihadis with over a 100 kilos of C4 finished their training this month and were ready to infiltrate six Indian states. Imagine what would have happened if they had succeeded. How many 26/11s do you think would have happened?' Raj asked.

'My God, how did you come to know all this?' asked Lala.

'Remember when I went trekking to Naoganga with three of my Nepali friends last year? They told me that the locals were talking about a large number of suspicious-looking foreigners who were Muslim in the KAS. That perked up my ears, and I decided to investigate. Posing as an admirer of organic farming and a potential research donor, I approached the KAS. They took the bait and took me on a site tour. The moment I entered their research labs, I detected the strong smell of C4. During my interactions with the so called staff and research students, I realised that this was all a front and none of them knew anything about agriculture. And none of the students there knew anything about organic farming. I secretly recorded my findings during the visit, and that night I returned and scaled the institute walls for a quick recce. During my search, I found a large stockpile of ammunition and C4 bricks stored in the basement of the right wing, as well as several weapons, mostly AK47s and Chinese pistols. I decided to come back the next Friday and do a detailed search when everybody was at the local mosque, but Dhariwal called me and told me to rush to London to check on Haji. I had no choice but to park the KAS investigations for a short while.

'I had every intention of telling you all about this after wrapping up my probe. But on my fifth day in London, while I was trailing Haji, he met someone at Trafalgar Square who gave him a note. With digital footprints being traced easily, terrorists have gone back to old-school methods like exchanging physical notes in busy places. After reading the note, Haji threw it into a bin and then left. I retrieved the note before resuming my surveillance and saw two words in bold: "Activate KAS". Below that were the names of six Indian states and a date—the very next day. I would have briefed you all immediately, but then Haji left Trafalgar Square and I followed him all the way to the airport. I called Mom and told her I was going to Nepal on urgent business and then tried your number, but your Thuraya kept ringing. You know I always carry all six of my passports with me, so when I saw him board an Emirates flight to Nepal, I followed him using my Pakistani passport. On landing, he went straight to the KAS. Now I was convinced that there was something big brewing.'

'You could have at least called us then,' said Lala.

Raj smiled sheepishly. 'I could have, but I got busy planning and forgot everything else.'

'Don't bullshit me with excuses like your Thuraya rang and no one answered, or "I got busy". You did this on purpose. You decided to go alone because you weren't patient enough to wait for reinforcement. You're not a team player,

Raj; you're a loner—just like your father. He made the same mistake and paid a price for it,' scolded Lala.

Brushing him off, Raj said, 'Okay, okay, I have my father's traits. I can't change my genes, can I? But I promise I'll work on being a team player, okay? Anyway, I scaled the walls again that night and when I went through the office drawers, I saw the blueprint of the attacks in one of them. The jihadis were planning to leave for India the next night. Since there was no time to plan, I made an executive decision. I used their own C4 on them. I packed the bricks in the left wing, where all the jihadis were, because I wanted to eliminate them first. I knew the explosions in the left wing would ultimately travel to the right.'

'And then you got caught,' said Lala flatly.

'Precisely. How did you know? Are you secretly my twin?' Raj said, expecting a laugh.

'Can we just get on with the story?' asked Lala, rolling his eyes.

'Once I finished setting the charges and the timer, I was just about to vault the wall again, when I got caught. The bloody dog chose to sleep right where I chose to put my foot. He yelped and they hit me with the floodlights,' said Raj.

After waiting for a few seconds for Raj to continue and then noticing that his friend was busy admiring the greenery outside, Lala nudged, 'And then?'

'Oh, right! And then they took me to the basement to interrogate me. But they got nothing out of me. The fools were novices and I dealt with them easily. That's the story. Now tell me what I did wrong,' Raj said innocently.

'You decide to leave London without informing

Dhariwal. You take the executive decision of blowing up a terror launchpad with fifty-six jihadis using 100 kilos of C4. Then you justify it by saying all this was an executive decision you took, and then you have the audacity to ask me where you went wrong? I think you've lost your mind,' said Lala, pressing harder on the accelerator.

After a few seconds of silence, Lala, glancing sideways at Raj, asked, 'By the way, how did you get so familiar with the layout of the KAS to know exactly where to plant the C4?'

Raj gave Lala an exasperated look, but before he could respond, Lala cut him off. 'Let me guess, your HSAM kicked in. The previous trip has been etched in your memory, right?' asked Lala sarcastically.

'Now I'm convinced you really are my twin,' said Raj with a smile.

'*I* may be your twin, but Dhariwal isn't. He's pissed off, and I think this time he'll ground you for sure.'

'No, brother. If you tell him, he'll listen and see the wisdom in what I have done,' pleaded Raj.

'One day, you're going to get me into trouble,' snapped Lala.

But Lala knew Raj was right. Dhariwal wouldn't even give Raj a chance to justify his actions. He would have to brief Dhariwal in advance so that, hopefully, he would calm down by the time they reached his office in New Delhi.

As the Scorpio rounded the final turn, they saw ICP Jogbani 200 yards away. Lala pulled the car over and made a call. In response, an elderly Nepali officer stepped out of his cabin at the checkpost and waited for them next to the boom barrier.

Lala drew up to the checkpoint, stopped the car and got out. The Nepali officer hugged him and said, 'Ram Madhav again.' Then he peeped inside the Scorpio and gave Raj a warm, open smile. 'So this is your package?' he asked Lala.

'Yes, meet Raj Pratap Rana,' said Lala. Turning to Raj, he said, 'This is my good friend Ravinder Thapa. He has helped me—and Veer—many times before.'

'I'm deeply grateful,' said Raj with folded hands.

Ravinder Thapa appreciated the respect and gratitude shown to him by Raj. 'I already like you. You look exactly like my friend Veer,' he said, before signalling to the guards at the gate to open the barrier and let the duo through.

STRIKE 3

THE DRAGON'S FALL

FEBRUARY 2020

FEBRUARY IS A BEAUTIFUL TIME to be in New Delhi. As the bone-chilling winter of January thaws, tourists start flocking to the city's historic sites, while locals busy themselves with shopping and frequenting their favourite restaurants. Parks and private gardens come alive with spring flowers, and there is a gentle warmth that gradually drives away the last vestiges of winter as the light February breeze tousles your hair.

Unfortunately, none of these were having any effect on the National Security Advisor of India, Ajit Dhariwal. Instead, here was a man who was deeply upset. The reasons were twofold. One, a global crisis had arisen due to the emergence of the deadly coronavirus from China. Two, he had just realised that the only viable agent for the new mission in Albania was the rebel Ghost, Raj Pratap Rana, the Puppeteer.

1

AJIT DHARIWAL, AT SIXTY YEARS old, had a thick moustache, meticulously styled hair and piercing black eyes. A former director of RAW, the Indian intelligence wing, he had dedicated years to combating insurgency operations throughout the country and had spent many years in the Indian High Commission in Islamabad. In 1990, he persuaded militants in Kashmir to become counter insurgents targeting hard-line anti-India terrorists funded by Pakistan.

Now, as India's seventh National Security Advisor, he was orchestrating covert, false flag operations in and around the nation on behalf of the Panther, with the Ghost operatives under his command. They followed his rules to the letter—everyone except Raj, who, to Dhariwal's frustration, had a mind of his own. But since he was the son of Veer and Shanti, the others couldn't help but have a soft corner for him. He was exactly like Veer—fearless and stubborn. And that is what Dhariwal feared. The last thing he wanted was for Raj to end up dead in a mangrove like Veer. He had given Shanti his word that her son would always be protected, and it was only on this condition that she had allowed Raj's entry into the Panther's Ghosts. Dhariwal was also answerable to Sniper, who viewed Raj as his own son and had warned

Dhariwal and Lala that if anything happened to Raj, he would skin them alive.

'Let him come,' Dhariwal muttered to himself as he paced the room, waiting for Lala to bring Raj to him. 'I'll kick his arse and ground him this time.' Despite Lala having thoroughly briefed him, his nerves were shot. As he took a drag from his cigarette, seeking respite, Lala walked in with a smile.

'Good morning, sir,' Lala said.

Dhariwal looked past Lala's shoulder with a scowl on his face and asked, 'Where is the rebel?'

On cue, Raj walked in, a big, boyish smile on his face. He swiftly approached Dhariwal and enveloped him in a bear hug before his boss could say anything.

'If you think this elaborate show of affection is going to melt my heart and make me pardon you, you're mistaken,' Dhariwal murmured through gritted teeth.

Raj, not having let go of the man, whispered back, 'This isn't for show, sir. If there was one person I missed all these days, it was you.'

Dhariwal could see right through Raj's attempt at swaying his emotions, but he also knew he was a sucker for Raj's boyish charm and could never stay angry with him for more than a few minutes. Predictably, he softened and hugged him back tightly. 'I was scared I had lost you this time. Never do this again,' Dhariwal said softly.

'Never,' Raj promised.

Lala, sensing the need to refocus the conversation, cleared his throat. 'If the two of you have finished expressing your love for each other, can we get down to business?' he asked.

Dhariwal laughed and settled into his chair behind the big mahogany table while Raj sat next to Lala on a brown leather sofa.

Pressing the intercom, Dhariwal instructed, 'Please send AV and Geeta in.'

A smile spread across Raj's face at the mention of Geeta. Their connection was anything but ordinary. Raj took every opportunity to openly express his undying love for her, but she rebuffed him time and again. It was not that Geeta didn't harbour deep feelings for him. She held a profound love for him—so deep that she'd sacrifice her life for him. But she believed that an emotional attachment with Raj would make him weak. And a weak Raj would be a liability for the Panther's Ghosts.

The door swung open as AV and Geeta walked in. Raj jumped up from his seat, hugged Geeta tightly and kissed her on both cheeks. 'I missed this warmth so much in Kathmandu.'

'Don't push your luck,' said Geeta returning his hug and then pushing him off her playfully.

When Raj hugged AV, he returned the hug warmly and whispered, 'Heard you put up quite a show in Nepal.'

'Yeah, I had a blast there,' laughed Raj, sitting down next to Lala again.

'A blast, is it?' asked Geeta, who had overheard them. She picked up a copy of the *India Times* that lay on the table and started reading aloud: 'KAS blown to smithereens. Pakistani ambassador's links to terror exposed.

'Kathmandu finally decides to crack the whip on terrorism. The terror hub KAS was brought down today

by the Nepal Intelligence Bureau (NIB). The NIB had reliable intel that KAS was being used as a training and launching pad for jihadis from Pakistan. In a late evening raid yesterday, the NIB used the jihadis' explosives to bring down their lair of terror. Fifty-six jihadis and their trainers were killed in the explosion, but the biggest embarrassment for Pakistan came when the body of the Pakistani ambassador to Nepal was found buried with the terrorists in the debris. Numerous documents and pieces of training material corroborated KAS's reputation as a terror nexus. The Nepal Home Ministry has restricted travel for all officials in the Pakistani embassy and has initiated a probe into this. The Prime Minister of Nepal, Udham Singh, expressed pride in the NIB's efforts and congratulated the Home Ministry and the police for their impeccable work.' She dropped the paper back on the table and looked at Raj.

'All's well that ends well,' said Raj with a sheepish look.

'Really? My dear, it ended well only because of this article that got published thanks to Pavak Dahiya, who managed the media. The NIB and their PM were initially shocked by the news, but with the world congratulating them, they seem to be taking credit for your false flag operation without batting an eyelid,' said Geeta. Though she tried to hide it, there was an undertone of concern in her voice—she had been worried about Raj's disappearance.

'You know I love it when you call me "my dear",' said Raj impishly. But when he saw the look in everyone's eyes, he quickly apologised. 'All right, all right, I agree I shouldn't have gone solo. It's just that when a situation pops up, I forget the teamwork part. It's a work in progress.'

'So finally, Lucifer apologises for his sins,' said AV with a wry smile. 'Now, Raj, would you care to educate all of us on what actually transpired?'

Raj filled them in on everything that had happened from London to Kathmandu, ending with an apology to them all. Dhariwal, who was eager to shift gears to another pressing issue, said, 'Okay, Ghosts, there's a crucial matter to discuss.' He pulled out a file from his drawer.

'Not so fast,' said Geeta, looking at Raj pointedly.

Turning to Dhariwal, she said, 'He still hasn't explained his sudden need to go to the Balkans last year for a six-month course in Albanian culture studies held by the University of New York, Tirana. He went there before he left for his so-called "trek" in Nepal.'

Raj explained, 'Sorry, I missed that out. Tirana is going to be an important economic and political centre in the Balkans. It's pegged to be declared the European Youth Capital by 2024, and has initiated some of the biggest technology projects in Europe. The Albanian technology drive is being led by a gentleman called Hector Dekovi—he's a tech billionaire and also the country's opposition leader. Last year, my company, ID—learnt of a new concept of Hector's. It's called "Digital Tirana". It's an online platform developed by Tirana city innovation team, a government body that focuses solely on innovation in city administration. It brings together new digital start-up companies from across the globe to work towards a larger tech and innovation objective in Europe. Hector had invited many entrepreneurs from all over the world to invest in Tirana, and I was one of them.'

'So you're investing in Digital Tirana?' asked Geeta.

'I'm not, but ID is. ID got shortlisted to work on two projects with Digital Tirana. While my team is dealing directly with the Digital Tirana CEO, as the promoter of ID, I was among the twenty-five global promoters invited to a dinner with Hector Dekovi. At the dinner, I met an enterprising gentleman who told me that film production in Albania is a lucrative business and that he had invested in it. I was curious, so I travelled with him to various shoot locations across Albania, and in the end, I fell in love with the country. With nothing to do for a year, I decided to learn the Albanian language and its culture. I finished the course in six months and went off to Nepal for the trek after that.'

'So now you're investing in film production in Tirana?' Geeta probed further.

'Yes. I was always interested in film production, but never found an opportunity before, so I've invested some money alongside this person I met,' explained Raj.

'A person you met once at a dinner?' said Geeta. Realising that her questions were getting uncomfortably intrusive, she pivoted, 'Well, it's your money and your call.' Though she was trying to act nonchalant, it was evident to the room that she was concerned about Raj, which left her feeling flustered.

But Lala jumped in to save the day for her. 'Raj, I know you told me about all this before getting into it, but I think Geeta is right. You should have done a lot of due diligence before you invested anywhere.'

'I agree,' Dhariwal said, winking at Geeta.

Geeta turned to AV and asked softly, 'Were *you* aware of this?'

'Not fully. Because of Covid, everyone was kind of

isolated and in their own bubble. None of us were meeting anyone regularly. I think Lala knew about it because he lives with Raj. Dhariwal knew because Raj would have had to take permission from him to leave the country,' AV said quietly.

Geeta shot Dhariwal a questioning look, but he was saved by the sound of an incoming message on his phone. Seeing that it was a message from the PMO asking them to come in, he stood up and said, 'All right, guys, please wait here while I take Raj to the Panther.'

'He's going to take your arse this time,' said Geeta as Raj and Dhariwal passed her on their way out to meet Prime Minister Damodar Das.

In response, Raj gave her a wink before walking out behind Dhariwal.

2

DD, WAS FIVE FEET AND eleven inches tall and stoutly built, with white hair and a matching white beard, which presented a contrast to his piercing black eyes that missed nothing.

DD had had humble beginnings, born into a family of grocers in the small village of Aloda in Mehsana, 15 kilometres away from the city of Gandhinagar in Gujarat. While Mehsana became famous due to the arrival of the Oil and Natural Gas Corporation of India, which had found oil reserves in the district, Aloda became famous for giving India its first 'Other Backward Class' Prime Minister. After his move to New Delhi on becoming the Prime Minister, the only remaining family he had in Aloda was his ninety-five-year-old mother, who lived in a small one-bedroom house surrounded by paddy fields. The only child of his parents, DD had lost his father to lung disease when he was five years old.

DD cherished his quarterly visits to his mother's house. The rest of the year, he lived in Bungalow 5 and worked out of Bungalow 7, Lok Kalyan Marg, the Indian Prime Minister's residence and office in New Delhi.

He had just finished talking to Defence Minister Rajneesh Singh, when Dhariwal walked in with Raj. The morning news played on the wall-mounted TV, and the Kathmandu incident was spotlighted when they entered the office.

'Good morning, sir,' said Dhariwal

DD muted the television and gestured for Dhariwal to take a seat. Then he pointed at Raj and asked Dhariwal, 'Have you briefed him on Albania?'

'Yes, sir, I have, on the way,' replied Dhariwal, presenting DD with a file.

'And you're fine with his maverick behaviour?' asked DD, keeping his voice low.

Dhariwal hesitated for a moment. 'Not really, sir, but the outcome has been favourable this time. He has managed to thwart potential terror attacks in twenty-five cities.'

'And who would have saved him if anything had happened to him? I've told you this before—we don't need Rambos in our team.' DD's voice was getting noticeably louder.

'Yes, you have, sir,' said Dhariwal.

Pointing at the TV, the Prime Minister continued, 'And now, after all this, you still think he should go to Albania?'

'He knows the country, the language and the culture. He's also on good terms with Hector Dekovi. I think he's right for the Albanian job,' said Dhariwal gently.

DD shook his head in frustration, then looked at Raj and asked, 'In which language should we communicate to you the importance of each of our assignments, Raj?'

'Good morning, sir,' said Raj.

DD scowled. 'Oh, so now you're trying to teach me courtesy, is it?'

'No, sir. Just wishing you a good morning. That's all, sir,' Raj replied with an innocent look on his face.

'I give up,' said DD, glaring at Dhariwal. Then he turned to Raj and asked slowly, 'What were your instructions when you were asked to be in London?'

'To follow Ambassador Haji, sir.'

'Did you do that?'

'Yes, sir.'

'Then how did you land up in Nepal?'

'I realised Haji was travelling there, so I followed him.'

'Did you inform Dhariwal that you were going to Nepal?'

'No. I wasn't given that instruction, sir,' replied Raj, sneaking a mischievous glance at Dhariwal.

'Do you think you're funny?' snapped DD. Addressing Dhariwal, he said, 'I respect the patriotism and all that, but if he is part of a team, then he needs to be a team player. You better make sure he understands that.'

Before Dhariwal could respond, Raj interjected, 'Every situation is unique, and we need to act accordingly, but the goal should always be to protect our country. The nation always comes first, sir.'

'Well done on repeating what I said in my Independence Day speech of 2013 when I was CM,' said DD, 'but I never gave my PM this much cause for concern.'

'Sir, after the Gujarat riots, the then-PM was upset with your independent decisions and even advised you to maintain *Raj dharam*,' pointed out Raj.

'And I told him my so-called independent decisions maintained just that,' retorted DD.

'I believe I have maintained that, sir,' said Raj.

DD rubbed his forehead in frustration and asked, 'What if you had got caught? Worse still, what if you had been killed? What would I have said to Shanti?'

'You would have told her that her son followed in his father's footsteps and died fighting for his country, sir,' Raj said solemnly. 'But I recognise the distress I've caused you all, sir. I'm sorry. It won't happen again.'

DD could not help but admire the man standing before him. Raj was fiercely loyal to his country, just like his father, but DD knew he had to punish him for insubordination. 'No more assignments for him until the adrenaline rush subsides,' he said to Dhariwal.

'But, sir—' Raj began.

'No means no. You're grounded,' said DD.

After Raj had been dismissed from the room, Dhariwal addressed the Prime Minister. 'That was harsh.'

'It's for his own good.'

Dhariwal did not argue. He knew it was the wrong time to push Raj's case. Instead, he inserted a memory stick into the USB port of the television and unmuted it. A recording from a recent news broadcast on the Hindi channel Naya Bharat started playing. The ticker running on the bottom of the screen read 'Indian industrialists, the Sandesars, become Albanian citizens.'

The anchor began, 'Today, one of India's most ostentatiously affluent families have become Albanian citizens. The Sandesar brothers, owners of Sterling Technologies, boarded their private jet at Albania's Tirana International Airport. Sources say they are en route to Nigeria and China for meetings with the trade and commerce ministers in both countries. Notably, the Sandesar brothers have had ties with the Communist Party of China for over two decades, and have even been the subject of suspicion of espionage. Recent investigations by the NIA in India have unearthed wire transactions that indicate they have been on the PRC payroll for an extended period of time. When the Indian intelligence wing, RAW, started closing in on them, they flew out of India to the UK, and from there to Albania, adopting the country's citizenship. The Sandesar brothers have been on the run for the last few years. RAW reports accuse them of selling confidential information on Indian ports, harbours and other maritime facilities to China. Furthermore, India's Economic Offences Wing has accused them of defrauding local banks out of loans worth over 700 million dollars. The fugitives have now not only become citizens of Albania but also been allowed to invest large sums of money in construction projects across Albania and other Balkan countries.'

The camera focused on the Sandesar brothers as they breezed through the airport security gates brandishing new Albanian passports specially awarded by the President of the Republic of Albania, Tefik Metta.

Dhariwal paused the recording. 'The Organised Crime and Corruption Reporting Project investigation has established the fact that high-ranking Albanian and Nigerian officials are helping the Sandesar brothers evade our attempts to extradite them. All the reports show that the brothers and their families are allowed to move freely and continue to run their businesses without any obstruction, not only in Albania but also in countries that are aligned with China.'

'So our analysis was right. China is involved,' said DD.

'Yes. Our source in Albania confirmed that the Dragon is personally involved in this decision,' said Dhariwal.

The Dragon was the code name for the Chairman of the People's Republic of China, Xi Wang. The source that Dhariwal was referring to was Adia Markova, the personal secretary of the head of the Albanian Army, General Beqir Hoxha, and Dhariwal's most trusted informant in the Balkans.

After pondering silently, DD said, 'The Sandesars are just pawns in the larger game. We're talking national security, Ajit. Tefik has already signed the OPOR agreement. If Tefik stays for one more year, the OPOR will become a reality in the entire Balkan region and the Chinese will have us encircled.'

China's One Path One Road initiative, or OPOR, was Xi Wang's brainchild. He envisioned having a single superhighway connecting Xinyang to Europe. He had already convinced forty-five countries along the route to pledge their commitment. In return, China was giving them huge loans to bolster their infrastructure projects. The member countries believed that these projects would create more jobs and improve their economic condition. Covid had intensified the need for most developing countries to borrow money to survive. The Chinese had signed lucrative deals for themselves with most of these nations. While the interest on the loans seemed very low, what the member countries did not realise was that China had made them sign over a 20 per cent share in the commercial establishments for a fixed period as well. The onus of infrastructure development, employment generation, business creation and loan repayment rested on these countries. A default in payments could lead to China claiming full ownership of these ventures.

While many nations were confident of profiting from this deal and of being able to finance the loans, India knew very well that China had already deployed this strategy in a few neighbouring countries, like Pakistan and Sri Lanka, which were now in a debt trap and on the verge of losing their land and the projects to the Chinese. China–Pakistan Business Corridor, CPBC in Pakistan, which was phase one of the OPOR was one such project and the second was the Hambantota Port in Sri Lanka which was completely in the hands of the Chinese.

More than OPOR entering Albania, what worried DD was the fact that Tefik was in the process of convincing the other Balkan nations to sign up too. If that happened, China would have free access to the Balkan nations, and soon, they would set up their military bases there. The Americans were also aware of this Chinese threat. Hence, they supported India in opposing OPOR.

India was already battling CPBC. The CPBC was being built through Gilgit-Baltistan, which was a disputed territory and belonged to India but was illegally occupied by Pakistan. In the fight against the CPBC, India had found an ally in the Baluch rebel army. Every time the Chinese completed 10 kilometres of the highway, the Baluch rebel army would blow it up using C4s, which caused the Chinese to incur big losses. China was frustrated that after five years, they had not progressed at all on the CPBC. The Chinese and the ISI suspected that the Baluch rebel army was being funded and armed by RAW.

As DD continued, Dhariwal listened intently. 'While I agree we need to secure the Sandesars' return to India before the general elections in 2024 to counter any political backlash, our larger problem is OPOR. With the CPBC in the doldrums, the Chinese are focusing on the Balkans so that they can threaten us from there. We need to stop OPOR from becoming a reality in the Balkans, Ajit.'

'I know, sir. But, like you said, as long as Tefik is in power, that will be difficult,' replied Dhariwal.

'Absolutely. Tefik needs to go, but his departure will only stall OPOR. Whoever comes next will again fall prey to the Chinese bribes, and then we will be back at square one. We need to find a permanent solution to the Albanian issue,' DD said.

'Our first step should be to replace Tefik with Hector Dekovi. He will be an India-friendly President. Not only will he not allow Chinese influence, but he will also partner with us in the long term. One option is to wait for the Albanian presidential elections and see how we can get Hector to take over. But that is a long shot,' said Dhariwal.

'And I guess the other option is to move forward with the Albanian job,' said DD.

'I know we have never orchestrated a coup before, sir, but this time around, we have to break the mould and try something different.'

'If it is through elections, we can discuss it with some of the saner voices in the opposition and get their support. But if you're really suggesting a coup, we can't discuss this with anyone.'

'The saner voices may support us, but you know that there will be plenty of others who will go to their US and Chinese masters and create international scrutiny. We have so much on our plate already, sir. The last thing we need is global involvement. As discussed earlier, I recommend that we use our Ghosts to facilitate this coup. We will get it executed from within Albania using someone powerful, someone who wants Tefik to be ousted as much as we do: General Beqir Hoxha,' said Dhariwal.

'You think the General will be willing to walk down that road?' asked DD.

'According to Hector, the General has been eyeing the vacant Albanian NSA's post for a long time. If Hector can promise him that, he will be incentivised to do it.'

'But Hector cannot approach him directly. It will amount to treason if the General decides to change his mind and inform Tefik. And the shrewd General is capable of using this to curry favour with Tefik and get the NSA post.'

'That crossed my mind as well. I suggest we go with Gef Bajrami, the arms dealer whom we helped long ago in Iraq. He shifted to Albania a while ago and is pretty close to the General, he also harbours a deep resentment for the Chinese. Remember they tried to help the President's brother-in-law, Misha Perci take over his business? Luckily General Beqir interfered and stalled the attempt. Misha wanted to acquire Gef's business and be the one and only arms dealer for Albania. This way he would continue to have control of the mafia in Albania. Gef and Misha Perci don't get along at all. If Gef speaks to the General and convinces him that Tefik is planning to make Misha the NSA, the General will action the coup,' said Dhariwal.

'Is that true? Is Tefik trying to make Misha the NSA?' asked DD.

'It's not official, but Misha has been angling for it, Beqir is aware and not very happy about that. Gef can use this to create further insecurity in Beqir's mind.'

'Hmm … and who will talk to Gef and convince him?'

'I will. But then, like I suggested earlier, Raj Pratap Rana should lead this mission,' said Dhariwal.

'What? No. I've just grounded him,' snapped DD.

'I'm aware of that, sir. But objectively speaking, we need someone who knows the place, speaks the language, and can deal with Hector and Gef. Right now, Raj ticks all the boxes. He spent over six months in Tirana. You know he has HSAM. By now, every nook and corner of the place is etched in his memory. He and Hector Dekovi are friends, as it is his company ID that is running two of Hector's Digital Tirana projects. And the man with whom he is partnering for his film production venture is Gef Bajrami. Raj met him at a dinner Hector had organised.'

'Too much of a coincidence, Ajit,' said DD.

'I agree. It really is. I never knew Gef was involved in film production. But I see this as divine intervention—we now have a man who has connections and contacts. We should not let Raj's personality dictate our larger goal, sir.'

DD was hesitant, but he finally caved, though it came with a condition. 'Send Geeta along with him. She will make sure he toes the line. He won't refuse her either. But remember, Ajit, at the end of the day, he is your responsibility. If he goes Rambo on us again, it's your head on the chopping block. Don't say I didn't warn you.'

'Thank you, sir,' said Dhariwal, and left. The moment he entered his office, he fixed his gaze on the Panther's Ghosts and said, 'Listen up, folks. We've got a new assignment.'

3

DHARIWAL TOOK THE NEXT HOUR to outline the intricacies of OPOR, the CPBC, the Dragon's long-term plans and the coup to the Ghosts. Addressing Raj, he said, 'You will be leading the Albanian job. You have a few months to plan this entire operation. Geeta will assist you.' Then, as an afterthought, he added, 'I know you need to be with your mom for her eye surgery in Pune. I have factored that in. That's why I'm giving you a few months to plan and execute.'

Raj nodded. 'Who will be assisting us on ground?'

'Your film production partner, Gef Bajrami,' said Dhariwal. Noticing the puzzled expressions around the room, he said, 'The Panther and I know him well. He is an arms dealer who is also our ally.'

Focusing on Raj again, he continued, 'I know it comes across as too much of a coincidence that your partner in Tirana is known to us and is helping us with the coup, but let me assure you, it *is* just a massive coincidence. We had no idea he was interested in the movie business or that you would partner with him.'

'With Raj, nothing is a coincidence. Tell us the truth. What is your connection with Gef?' asked Geeta.

'I swear I wasn't aware of this connection,' said Raj,

turning to Dhariwal helplessly when he saw the sceptical looks on everyone's faces.

Dhariwal came to his rescue. 'It's true, guys. Raj was not aware of our connection with Gef. Anyway, now that you all know, let's worry about the job ahead and forget Gef for the moment.' He handed Raj and Geeta a folder each and said, 'Read it and destroy it. It has everything you need to know.'

Raj looked into the file, smiled and turned to Geeta. 'You shall accompany me to Tirana as my wife,' he said, grinning. 'We're film producers and are in Tirana to make a travel documentary on Albania. We will use Gef's crew for our shoot and also find time to romance in the Albanian Alps.'

'You okay with this?' Dhariwal asked Geeta.

'No, not by any stretch of the imagination, but I will suffer this man for the country, sir,' said Geeta.

'We will leave at the end of May, darling. Till then I will be busy in Pune with your mother-in-law. You're more than welcome to join me,' said Raj, thoroughly enjoying himself.

'I will come and pay my respects to her, not as her daughter-in-law but as a colleague of her son's who has been entrusted with saving his arse.'

The others chuckled. AV put his hand on Raj's shoulder and said, 'Give my love to Mom.'

'I will,' said Raj.

Lala was thrilled that Raj's mom, Shanti, was coming to Pune. It had been almost a year since she had come to India, as she now lived in Earl's Court, London. 'Let me know when you're coming,' he said to Geeta as she and AV moved for the door. 'I'll organise a party—nothing too big.'

'I will,' Geeta said over her shoulder as she and AV left.

'Raj, I'll wait for you in the car,' Lala said before walking out, leaving Raj and Dhariwal alone.

'Gef will wonder how I came to be involved in a coup. He thinks I'm just a businessman,' said Raj.

'To Gef, you are still a film producer. He does not know you are involved. He assumes, I am orchestrating it through him who in turn is using General Beqir to execute it. That is Plan A,' Dhariwal replied.

'In that case, what is our role?' asked Raj.

'You are Plan B. If Plan A fails, then you need to come up with Plan B,' said Dhariwal.

'What is Plan B?' asked Raj

'The assasination of Metta.'

There was a few seconds of silence as Raj absorbed the statement. Then Raj said, 'I can plan that only after reaching Tirana and studying the situation on the ground. Any plan we make here will be just theoretical.'

'I agree. Take your time,' said Dhariwal. The two shared a hug before Raj left. Outside, Lala was waiting for him in the white Scorpio. 'I wish I were coming with you to Tirana,' said Lala as the driver took them to the airport. 'By the way, what happened to Shantiji's eye?'

'Remember how both Nana and Mom contracted Covid last December? While Nana never recovered and finally succumbed to the virus, Mom came out of it, but ever since then, her left eye has been very weak. The doctor has recommended surgery. Once her operation is over, I'll take her to Chitrakoot—that's the family ashram. She wants to spend time with our guru, Swami Sai. With me away in Tirana, she will need you, brother,' Raj said.

'You know I'll be with her,' said Lala as the car hit the highway that led to the airport.

On the two-hour flight to Pune, Lala chose to catch up on sleep; he hadn't slept for two nights in a row. Raj decided to go through the folder Dhariwal had given him in detail. The first page of the document read: 'The President of the Republic of Albania is the head of state and the commander-in-chief of the military. The president is elected through a secret parliamentary vote by a three-fifths majority. He is elected for a five-year term, similar to India.'

Raj flipped the page. The second sheet had a photograph of the president, Tefik Metta. Raj read on.

'Sixty-five-year-old President Tefik Metta is also the leader of the Socialist Movement for Progress (SMP), which was created by the fifteen most influential mafia families in Albania. While Metta was never the popular choice among the country's citizens, he came to power with the help of Chinese funding and the muscle power of the SMP. Hector Dekovi, head of the Opposition, spearheaded two unsuccessful impeachment attempts against Metta. The President lives with his wife Teuta Metta in Tirana's presidential palace. Formerly called the Royal Palace, it is now known as the Palace of Brigades. He has no children, and, therefore, intends to pass on his legacy to his brother-in-law, Misha Perci, against the wishes of General Beqir Hoxha. His political funding comes from the budget of the People's Liberation Army, the PLA, but his personal funding comes from Misha Perci, who controls the mafia and their drug business.

'Though Metta was often sponsored by Gef Bajrami, and Teuta Metta had invested in Gef Bajrami's films, Metta began to slowly get Misha Perci involved in the arms and ammunition business with the help of the Chinese so that he had complete control of all the profitable businesses in Albania. Aware that Gef would resist and possibly counteract, he tried not to let Gef see his manoeuvre to transition the arms dominance to Misha. However, Gef grew suspicious and harboured resentment for his deceit.'

Raj moved to the third page and found a photograph of Gef Bajrami. Below it was a detailed write-up. Raj read: 'Gef Bajrami; original name Benjamin Jefferson; born on 10 December 1985. He is a former American arms dealer and runs a company called BJ Arms Incorporated, BJA Inc for short.'

In his early career, he was a major weapons contractor for the United States Department of Defence. But following a scandal in which he provided subpar, unusable Chinese ammunition rebranded for American troops in Afghanistan, BJA Inc. faced a US ban and he was jailed.

In prison, Jefferson's entrepreneurial spirit and gift of the gab enabled him to forge connections, especially with the drug dealers. Soon, he brokered a deal with Ruff Rogers, aka 'Cooker' as he cooked his own Methamphetamine. Cooker was one of the biggest drug dealers in America. Jeff offered him money laundering services through his arms trade in exchange for a commission. On his release, Jefferson fulfilled his promise to 'Cooker', profiting from the deal but also coming under the radar of the Federal Bureau of Investigation. With the FBI on his tail, Jefferson knew he had to leave America, so he sought help from the Cooker who introduced him to an Albanian arms dealer,

Yuri Pinari. Yuri and Jefferson soon became good friends as they had common interests. With Yuri's help, Benjamin Jefferson changed his name to Gef Bajrami and became a citizen of Albania. Soon, they started a company called PGA Inc. (Pinari Gef Arms Incorporated). Gef and Yuri did well in Albania and, after a few years, Yuri decided to focus on the business in Albania and Afghanistan, while Gef homed in on Europe.

In early 2000, an ammunition stockpile amassed by Yuri exploded and wiped out an entire Albanian village. When Yuri was caught, tried and incarcerated in one of the country's most notorious prisons, Burrel, he entrusted Gef with the running of their operations, and Gef did not disappoint him. He not only looked after the business but also cared for Yuri's family as if they were his own. Prioritising their well-being, Gef bought 20 acres of land in Tirana in the name of Yuri's wife, Svetlana. On this plot, he built a massive mansion for the Pinaris, equipping it with advanced surveillance equipment and round-the-clock security guards. He sent Yuri's two daughters to the best school in the country and then to university. Currently, both daughters were doctors at Tirana District Hospital, one a heart surgeon and the other a paediatrician. When Gef decided to diversify and venture into film production, he asked Yuri's son, Gregory, to head it as he did not want him to be in the arms business. Moreover Gregory was the creative kind and had majored in Communication. Gef lived alone in a small single-room apartment right outside the Pinari estate to keep an eye on the family. For Yuri, Gef was godsent.

Over the years, Gef and Yuri's firm, PGA Inc, pivoted away from supplying arms and ammunition to global terrorists. Instead, they catered to both local and international mafia and rebel groups. Misha Perci found an opportunity here and filled the vacuum by starting his own arms company with a Chinese partner to supply weapons to global terror groups. Gradually, Misha began encroaching on the local mafia's arms trade, jeopardising Gef's stronghold. Over the next year, Misha and Gef became sworn enemies. Gef feared that if Misha became the NSA, his sweeping power would be detrimental to his business. In his mind, he prayed for Tefik and Misha's downfall. When Gef realised that General Beqir Hoxha also harboured similar feelings, since Misha was a threat to him as well, he decided to get close to the General. On a personal front, Gef and Beqir knew that Misha did not trust them, and it wouldn't be long before he would strike. So both busied themselves with creating safe havens for their wealth while building highly secure safe houses within the country and across the world for themselves.

Raj smiled as he read about Gef. He recollected meeting him at Hector Dekovi's dinner party. During their conversation, Gef had spoken at length on his film production business and how the Indian film industry could make a killing in Albania. Raj had smelled an opportunity, invested in Gef's film production business and become a 50 per cent partner. Beyond business, the two developed a bond, sharing their life struggles, though they held back some personal details. Gregory's involvement in a film funded by Tefik's wife, Teuta Metta, granted him frequent invitations to Tefik's estate and central functions at the royal palace. He would often take along Gef and Raj, which allowed Raj to familiarise himself with the palace and Tirana's landscape over half a year.

Raj reached the fourth page of the folder. Looking back at him was a photo of a blond man in his mid-forties. Below the picture were details on the Albanian mafia and Misha Perci. It read: 'The typical structure of the Albanian mafia is hierarchical. A family clan is referred to as a *fis* or a *fare*. Every family has an executive committee known as a *bajrak* that selects a high-ranking member for each unit. A unit is led by a *krye*, or boss. Currently, Misha Perci dominates this underworld, effectively controlling the entire drug business. He exercises control over all fifteen kryes. The kryes buy narcotics from Afghanistan, Cuba, Columbia and Pakistan and sell these to Misha, who in turn uses the Nigerian infrastructure and network to push the drugs into Europe and Central America. And for this, Misha has the blessings of the President of Nigeria: Sani Abdullah. Misha's distribution system operates through a logistics firm, LogiQ, owned by Nitin and Chetan Sandesar. To ensure allegiance, Misha compensates Sani, the kryes and the Sandesars handsomely, supplemented with a profit-share. Beyond narcotics, Misha owns the biggest chain of hotels in Albania, Acapulco Hotels. He lives in and operates his drug business out of a suite on the thirtieth floor of the Acapulco Grande in Tirana. When Gef and Yuri stopped supplying arms and ammunition to global terrorists, Misha took that spot with a Chinese partner, and is now eyeing the vacant NSA post.'

'Hmm, so that's why the Sandesars have been given Albanian citizenship. And that's why Dhariwal is confident that Gef will convince Beqir to go through with the coup,' Raj murmured to himself as he closed the folder and looked out of the window.

The Pune skyline was fast approaching. He nudged Lala awake. 'We're about to land.'

MARCH 2020

SPRING HAD ARRIVED IN BEIJING, yet a chill from winter remained, with the daily temperature oscillating between -1 °C and 11 °C. Formerly called the Imperial Garden within the Imperial City, Zhongnanhai was the headquarters of the Communist Party of China and the state council, or central government, of China. It also housed the office of the Chairman of the People's Republic of China (PRC)— Xi Wang.

Born shortly after the Second World War, he was the third son of a Chinese Communist stalwart Wang Xiu. Xi went on to marry Paitoon Luan, the daughter of the head of the powerful Central Committee, Peng Luan, and rose through the political establishment quickly to become the Chairman of the country.

As the Chairman and General Secretary of the Communist Party of China, President of the PRC, Chairman of the Central Military Commission, head of state and China's 'Paramount Leader', Xi had recently changed the constitution to ensure that he had a never-ending tenure—he would rule China for as long as he lived.

Following the death of Wang Xiu, under Xi's regime,

China's claims in the South China Sea increased. Xi was going against the wishes of Peng Luan with the intent of creating a 'Greater China', one that included half of Europe and all of Asia.

Central to realising this dream was the success of the OPOR project. But thanks to Damodar Das and the President of America, Hussain Akhmu, the project was currently in tatters and losing its charm to the rest of the world. The spreading of the Corona virus had done enough damage to his country's reputation, and to top it all off, most of his allies were slowly pulling out of OPOR.

And for this, Xi hated Damodar Das and Akhmu.

4

AT ZHONGNANHAI, XI WAS SO engrossed in his thoughts of DD that he did not register the shrill ring of the hotline. His wife, Paitoon, who was in the room writing an email to her father, Peng Luan, drew his attention to the blue phone on the table and said, 'You have a call, Xi.'

Jolted back to reality, Xi looked at the number flashing on the screen for a moment, and then hit the speaker button.

'Yes, Tony?' Xi asked.

Dongsun Tony was the head of the Chinese intelligence wing, the MSS. The MSS was a combination of three functions—intelligence, security and secret police.

'President Sani's office reached out. As per your directives, Nitin and Chetan Sandesar have aborted their trip to China. They're now stationed in one of President Sani's conference rooms at the presidential suite, awaiting a virtual meeting with you,' relayed Tony.

The Sandesars had owned Sterling Infra Ltd, a colossal business conglomerate dealing in real estate, infrastructure, technology and logistics. The conglomerate had an Albanian partner: Misha Perci. Following Misha's foray into arms dealing, Sterling Infra Ltd partnered with him in the transportation of arms and ammunition to global terrorist groups. While their ventures back home in India had done well, particularly in infrastructure and real estate, their greed led them down a dangerous path. They decided to siphon off a 700-million-dollar business loan they had taken for corporate expansion from a consortium of Indian banks. When Sterling started defaulting on payments, the consortium lodged a complaint with the Indian Economic Offences Wing, the EOW, which investigated the conglomerate and unearthed the troubling truth: apart from their legitimate ventures in real estate, infrastructure and logistics, most entities under the Sterling Technologies banner were non-performing assets and mere shells.

The EOW informed the Enforcement Directorate, which swung into action and sent the company a summons. The very next day, the Sandesar family fled the country to Albania. But luck wasn't in their favour this time. A one-hour stopover in Dubai led to them being detained at the Dubai International Airport at the request of the Indian Ministry of External Affairs.

A worried Nitin called his partner, Misha Perci, who in turn contacted the Chinese ambassador stationed in Dubai. The ambassador immediately reached out to an airport shift supervisor who was on his payroll. Thanks to the supervisor, the Sandesars boarded the flight to Tirana. By the time the officials from the Indian embassy arrived to take the brothers back to India, they were already 30,000 feet in the air and on their way to Albania. On landing, the Sandesars were greeted warmly by Misha's team and escorted to a meeting with Tefik Metta. A fortnight later, they were made citizens of Albania.

'Is Misha with them?' Xi asked Tony. It was to avoid media scrutiny, especially during COVID that he had made the Sandesars cancel their trip to China.

'No, sir. He is at the Sheraton in Lagos.'

'Good. Send Chetan Sandesar to the Sheraton to meet Misha. I will have the meeting with only Nitin.' Xi disconnected the call and was about to leave for the video meeting with Nitin, when he noticed Paitoon staring at him.

'What is it?' asked Xi.

'So what I heard is correct,' Paitoon said.

'Depends on what you heard and whom you heard it from,' said Xi as he pulled on his jacket.

'You are using the Sandesars for your cyber war on India. I heard it from Chin, and he doesn't lie.'

'Oh! The in-house spy, Mao Chin Luan, your head of security and your dear brother. He's on borrowed time,' said Xi as he combed his hair.

'Yes, Chin is my security chief and my brother, but he is no spy. Remember he is the proud son of Peng Luan, the man who put you in this chair. You touch him, and you will have to deal with both my father and me,' said Paitoon sharply. Without waiting for Xi's response, she stormed out of the room.

Xi was furious. Everything he planned somehow found its way to Chin's ears. He was sure that this would now make its way to Peng Luan. To add to his frustration, the younger Sandesar had become a pain in the arse.

'That bungling fool Chetan talks too much. Misha will deal with him in Lagos,' Xi thought as he walked to his library for the Zoom call. Just the previous day, despite

COVID restrictions, President Sani Abdullah had extended an invitation to the Sandesars for a private party in Lagos. Coincidentally, Chin, who had been in Lagos on an unrelated business, was also invited. The younger Sandesar, Chetan, having had far too much to drink, bragged to Sani and Chin about their collaboration with the PLA's cyber hackers, TAG-1, to plant malware in the administrative program of the Mumbai electric grid the previous year. He also alluded to their potential involvement in another cyber-attack alongside TAG-2.

TAG-1 hackers employed a US-based firm, Techtron Technologies, for the malware installation in the Mumbai electric grid. They used the Trojan to black out the entire city of Mumbai for over twenty-four hours, inflicting losses of millions of dollars on the Indian state of Maharashtra. Owned by the Sandesars, Techtron Technologies conveniently shut shop post the cyber-attack.

The conference call was already set up when Xi walked into the library. Tony waited for Xi to sit before the screen, unmuted the call and then quietly left the room. Xi looked at a visibly nervous Nitin Sandesar and smiled. Nitin Sandesar, chartered accountant, entrepreneur and head of Sterling Infra Ltd, was tall, fair and heavyset. When Chetan had been escorted to the Sheraton by one of Misha's men, Nitin had known that it was the last time he would be seeing his brother. And now, when he saw Xi, a thin layer of sweat appeared on his forehead. He wiped it away with a crumpled handkerchief, licked his dry lips and managed a weak smile underneath the white mask.

Xi studied his Montblanc pen before addressing Nitin.

'I got you all out of India not because I was obligated to do so. I did it because of our long-standing relationship and, most importantly, your confidentiality and absolute loyalty to me. Unfortunately, your brother had different inclinations. He has caused me irreversible damage. Chin, Sani and Mrs Wang know about the TAG-1 project, and it won't be long before it reaches the ears of Damodar Das too. Chetan's indiscretion has made him expendable. I am a generous man, though, Nitin. I will take care of Chetan's family. But you need to be aware that my generosity should not be misconstrued as my weakness.'

It only took a wave of his hand for Xi to close the chapter on Chetan.

Nitin nodded, his eyes brimming with tears for the loss of his beloved younger brother.

Xi noticed, and quickly pacified him with praise and promises. 'Nitin, you manoeuvred the TAG-1 project extremely well. I recognise and value that. I have great plans for you. When the Chinese history will be rewritten, your name will be mentioned as a loyal foot soldier who played a critical role in the making of our new legacy. But for that I want you to promise me your undying loyalty. Can you do that, Nitin?' he asked.

Xi's implied menace wasn't lost on the petrified Nitin, who responded in a feeble voice, 'Yes, sir. I promise.' He wiped the sweat from his forehead and the tears from his eyes with the handkerchief.

'All right! On that happy note, let us talk about the future. As we've discussed, our next project is to hit India's pride: BARC—Bhabha Atomic Research Centre.'

Established in January 1954 to drive India's nuclear programme, BARC was the country's premier nuclear research facility. Based in Trombay, Mumbai, BARC came under the Department of Atomic Energy and was directly overseen by the Prime Minister of India. This massive multi-disciplinary research centre, which boasted extensive infrastructure and cutting-edge tools and expertise for advanced research and development covering the entire nuclear science spectrum, served as the research bedrock for the Indian nuclear programme. BARC operated several research reactors across the country, and its core mandate was to produce peaceful applications of nuclear energy for domestic use. Instructed by Xi, the Chinese PLA hackers, TAG-2, intended on collaborating with Softnett for the BARC operation. Headquartered in Vancouver, Softnett was owned by a Canadian techie but funded by one of the Sandesars' shell companies in the Cayman Islands.

'Yes, sir, b-but there is one issue,' said Nitin, his voice shaky.

'And what is that?' asked Xi.

'BARC is a high-security zone and comes under the protection of the central agencies. I'm not sure how TAG-2 can hack Trombay.'

'TAG-2 will not be hacking Trombay directly. They will hack one of the seven new facilities under it that are responsible for the nuclear submarine programme and enter Trombay via this facility.'

'But, sir, unlike the Maharashtra State Electricity Board in Mumbai, where we bribed the officials and got the contract for the city grid's administrative software upgradation, the new facilities responsible for the nuclear submarine programme are all under the direct supervision of central agencies,' said Nitin.

'Except in Kerala, where it is still under the state, and they have filed a petition in the Kerala High Court against the central agency takeover. The case is pending for hearing, so it is not with the central agency yet,' said Xi.

'The court hearing is next month, and from what I have heard, the state will lose the case. So by the end of May this year, the facility responsible for the nuclear submarine programme in Kerala will also come under the central agencies.'

'I know. Hence time is of the essence, Nitin,' Xi said sharply. 'We have just one month to install our Trojan—the "Cobra"— which is a type A malware that will download automatically into the nuclear submarine programme during their routine monthly sanitisation program. Disguised as a software component, it will lie dormant in the facility software till TAG-2 uses it to extract data. Once we have all the information on the submarine programme, we will use this malware to hack into the main frame and enter Trombay.'

'In that case, I think it's possible, sir. The facility in Kerala has floated a tender for a new CRM. I'll get one of my contacts in India to apply for it. Once they win the contract, they will coordinate with Softnett, which will install the Trojan for TAG-2. The team will then first take control of the facility handling the nuclear programme and then enter Trombay.'

CRM or Customer Relationship Management is a

software which sits on top of the hardware, through which the engineers operate or execute their commands.

Xi smiled. 'If RAW can sabotage my CPBC, I will show them even I can sabotage their nuclear programme.'

'But if you think Mr Damodar Das will soon learn about TAG-1, then the chances are that he will also find out about TAG-2. Their entire cyber team will be on high alert,' Nitin pointed out.

'Precisely. That's why we need to make sure that this time we route our work through different companies so that the Indians get lost in the maze. By the time they sort themselves out, we will have done the job and dissolved all the companies,' Xi responded.

'How do you suggest we do this?'

'We will route Softnett through a Pakistani company, which in turn will route it through a company in Tirana, which will then speak to your Indian contact who will bag the contract.'

'Who will do all this routing? And which companies do we have in mind?'

'You will do it. First, I want a tech company set up in Pakistan. Tony will help you by speaking to the Pakistan Army Chief, General Qamar Javed Khan. Softnett will operate solely through this Pakistani company. Now, this Pakistani firm will operate through another firm in Albania, which Misha will set up. The Albanian firm will then work through the Indian IT firm that you are talking about. The Indian IT firm will pitch for the CRM tender. And you need to ensure this Indian IT firm wins the contract,' said Xi.

'So who will TAG-2 speak to?' asked Nitin.

'All the CRM work will be done by the Indian IT firm, granting access to the Albanian firm. They will then give access to the Pakistani tech company. TAG-2 will speak to this Pakistani tech company.'

'Then what is Softnett's role?'

'To prepare the Trojan and hand it over to the Pakistani tech company.'

Nitin realised that Xi was creating a firewall to protect himself. If ever anything was discovered, all fingers would finally point at Pakistan. In essence, he would have access to all the programmes in Trombay, but Pakistan would be the fall guy. Though he admired Xi's cunning, he was petrified by the casualness with which Xi was willing to betray an ally, Pakistan, which had always stood by China. He cursed the day he joined forces with Xi and Tefik—but it was too late now.

'I will start work on TAG-2 immediately, sir,' Nitin said, eager to leave Xi's presence. As soon as their call ended, Nitin navigated to a photo of Chetan on his iPhone. Staring at his brother's radiant smile, he gently traced the image, tears flowing freely.

After the call, Xi summoned Tony to discuss details, going on to instruct him to speak to the Pakistani Army Chief, General Qamar Javed Khan.

After seeing off Xi, Tony returned to his office and called the General. General Khan was in his office in Rawalpindi when his phone rang. Before answering the call, he told his aide Shaukat Ali, who was pouring tea for him, to leave the room and close the door behind him. General Khan, removed his white mask, pulled out a pad of paper and a pen to take notes and then hit the speaker button. 'Good morning, Mr Dongsun. How can I help you?' he said.

Tony did not miss the happiness in the General's voice. And why wouldn't he be? Every call Tony had made to the General in the past few years had always been followed up with the delivery of a packet of dollars to his residence. The General was expecting a similar reward after this call too.

Tony brought General Khan up to speed on everything, including the TAG-2 project, and said, 'I need you to set up a tech firm in Pakistan that Nitin Sandesar can use to collect the Softnett Trojan. The TAG-2 hackers will be operating from your facility. We'll cover expenses for the space and the personnel.'

'Consider it done. I will coordinate with Nitin on the specifics,' said General Khan

'Thank you, General,' said Tony.

Just as Tony was about to disconnect, General Khan cleared his throat. 'And, uh, about the payment…'

'It will reach you by tonight,' said Tony before ending the call.

General Khan called the ISI chief, Lt General Nadeem Ali, briefed him on his conversation with Tony and told him to organise the tech company. 'I want it ready and operational within a week,' he instructed. After the call, he stretched his legs, looked out of the window to admire the greenery and rang the bell for Shaukat Ali.

Shaukat Ali had been standing right outside General Khan's cabin, eavesdropping. He walked in quickly with a fresh pot of hot tea.

'You seem to be in a good mood, sir,' said Ali as he poured

a cup for the General.

'I am, Ali. Indeed I am. I'll be leaving early today so tell the driver to be ready in an hour.' said General Khan as he lifted the cup of tea to his lips.

MARCH 2020

UNLIKE IN BEIJING, WINTER HAD more or less left Islamabad in the last week of March. The days were warm, but the mornings were cold enough to prompt the city's residents to don a sweater or at least wrap a shawl around themselves. The three-storeyed greystone mansion, Rajwad Palace, glistened in the morning dew. Rajwad Palace, found at No. 10, F-8/3, Islamabad, was the residence of Shehbaz Sharafat, the leader of the Opposition in Pakistan and brother of the former Pakistani Prime Minister, Naved Sharafat. After the death of his wife, Mariam, Naved vacated Rajwad Palace and moved to his luxurious Mayfair Gardens apartment in London, where he lived alone. The real reason for Naved's exit from Pakistan was to evade incarceration by the new Prime Minister of Pakistan, Imran Masood, on charges of corruption.

Shehbaz, a mere five feet two inches in stature but with ambitions dwarfing Pakistan's highest mountains, lived with his second wife, Rihanna Durrani. Unknown to Naved, Shehbaz nurtured a secret desire to be the Prime Minister of Pakistan one day. Given Pakistan's high inflation, rampant poverty and growing unemployment across the country, the current Prime Minister, Imran Masood, was struggling to keep Pakistan together, and Shehbaz knew that it was only a matter of time before Imran's government fell and he became the PM.

Despite a deep-seated hatred for General Qamar Javed Khan and the ISI Chief, Lt General Nadeem Ali, Shehbaz maintained cordial relationships with the two, concealing his true sentiments, so as not to let them know his real feelings for them. He also kept in regular touch with Chairman Xi Wang—if he ever became the PM, he would need China's help to get out of the financial mess Pakistan was currently in.

By nature, the Sharafat brothers were insecure and mistrustful. But Shehbaz had found a way to counter his insecurity. He planted spies strategically in the offices and homes of all his opponents. He had a diverse group: cooks, butlers, aides, drivers and assistants. And for their services, Shehbaz paid them handsomely. His current network included Shaukat Ali monitoring Qamar, a driver shadowing Nadeem and a cook observing Imran, with other minor operatives stationed in various ministerial settings. It was by being this shrewd and cunning that he kept Naved happy, sharing information selectively with him, and enjoying his trust.

5

IT WAS 6.45 A.M. IN ISLAMABAD, and Shehbaz Sharafat was drinking tea with his wife Rihanna in the Rajwad Palace gardens, when Shaukat Ali called and briefed him on what had transpired between Xi Wang, Tony, General Khan and Nadeem. Shehbaz thanked Ali and dialled Naved. 'Good morning, bhaijan. How is the situation with Covid in London?'

'The situation is bad. Everything is shut here,' said Naved. 'What makes you call so early, brother?'

Without wasting a moment, Shehbaz briefed Naved. 'Xi Wang is planning a cyber-attack on BARC in Trombay, India. The Indians were right when they said that the Mumbai electric grid disruption was orchestrated by the Chinese. I believe the Chinese PLA hackers, operating under the code name TAG, did it. The hackers who broke into the Mumbai electric grid and brought Mubai to its knees were called TAG-1, and now the BARC attack will be done by a new set of hackers called TAG-2.'

'How does this affect us?' asked Naved. 'While we were not involved in the Mumbai electric grid hacking, the TAG-2 hackers who are going to hit BARC are going to be operating from Pakistan. If the Indians discover this, which I know they will sooner or later, another surgical strike is inevitable. And trust me, this time it will be worse than anything we've faced. Damodar Das is waiting for a reason to reclaim PoK, and there cannot be a bigger reason than this. Even the US won't support us. And knowing Xi, he will turn the other way.'

Naved sighed. 'Well, this is worrying. What does Imran have to say about this?'

'Imran doesn't know anything. This is between Tony and Qamar.'

'Then inform Imran,' said Naved.

'And what will he do? He'll just nod and keep quiet,' Shehbaz retorted. Then, as an afterthought, he added, 'The silver lining here is that if Xi is not speaking to Imran about this, it means he has lost faith in him.'

'But the bad news is that Xi is using Pakistan because he wants us to be the fall guy if it fails. And we tell the world that we are all-weather friends,' scoffed Naved.

'Xi cannot be trusted any more, bhaijan. We need to take matters into our own hands,' said Shehbaz, knowing very well that Naved would turn to DD for help as he had always done before.

Such a course of action suited Shehbaz's plan. If DD retaliated, China would lose respect in the eyes of the world. A weak China was good for Pakistan. Pakistan could use this as an excuse and pivot from the Chinese alliance to get closer to the US bloc. With the US on its side, the International Monetary Fund and the World Bank would resume giving the country loans, both of which had currently stopped their support. As the leader of the Opposition, Shehbaz could bury Imran by telling the people of Pakistan that their current prime minister was spying on India for China. His party would lose faith in him and abandon him for not taking them into confidence. And then he would bring in the no-confidence motion to oust Imran from office. With Naved still in London, this could well be his chance to finally become the Prime Minister.

'You need to do something quickly, brother,' Shehbaz told Naved, steering him the way he wanted.

And it worked.

Naved's chest puffed up with pride. 'Leave this with me. I will handle it,' he said. After ending the call with Shehbaz, Naved pulled out his satellite phone.

'Good morning, janaab,' said Naved.

'Good morning, Mr Prime Minister. It's an honour to receive a call from you, sir,' said Dhariwal.

Naved loved Dhariwal's deference in addressing him as Mr Prime Minister. He briefed Dhariwal on his conversation with Shehbaz and warned him of the impending cyber-attack on BARC.

'I will inform the Prime Minister immediately. Thank you for your unwavering support and friendship, Mr Prime Minister,' said Dhariwal before disconnecting.

At Rajwad Palace, the beautiful Rihanna, who had discreetly listened to the entire conversation between the two brothers and was already dreaming of becoming the prime minister's wife, looked at her husband lovingly and said, 'You are a cunning fox, darling.'

In London, Naved studied himself in the mirror, a smile playing on his lips. 'The Indians treat me with far more respect than my own people,' he said to his reflection. 'Once DD deals with Xi, I will deal with Imran.'

A few hundred miles away in New Delhi, winter had given way to scorching heat in the last week of March. The temperature had already touched 42 °C, and in the office of the Prime Minister of India, at 7, Lok Kalyan Marg, three air conditioners battled to keep the room cool. But despite that, with masks on their faces, everyone was sweating a little.

Dhariwal did not want to disturb DD early in the morning with partial details. So after his conversation with Naved, he spoke to the chiefs of the Intelligence Bureau, the National Intelligence Agency and RAW, gathering all the information he needed. At noon, he walked into DD's office.

DD was authorising provisions for 80 crore people in India to ensure them free food, water and basic necessities to tide over the pandemic. Seeing DD busy, Dhariwal waited patiently for him in the PM's library. A few minutes later, DD joined him.

'Why are you sitting here? You could have joined me in my office,' DD said.

'Not an issue, sir. I have some confidential information to share,' said Dhariwal, ensuring the door to the room was shut.

'I'm all ears,' said DD.

Dhariwal recounted his conversation with Naved and handed DD a folder.

'What's this?' asked the Prime Minister.

'The follow-up report on the Mumbai electric grid incident from the NIA, sir. The first report pointed towards the PLA's hackers, TAG-1. "TAG" stands for "Technical Advisory Group", with "1" representing the hack count.

But now, this report gives us details on the company that the electricity board, the MSEB, contracted for the upgradation of their grid administrative software. The company is called Techtron Technologies—they installed the Trojan.'

'Is this Techtron Technologies an Indian company?'

'It's a US-based company that had a branch in India till a few months ago.'

'What do you mean "till a few months ago"?'

'It does not exist any more. But the NIA used its resources in the US and connected the dots. Techtron Technologies was owned by Jagjit Singh, a second-generation Sikh American & the son of Ripudman Singh, the Khalistani who is accused of involvement in the terrorist bombing of flight AI182 on June 23, 1985, which took the lives of 329 passengers and crew who were on board. However, he was acquitted by a Canadian court in 2005. I had AV and Lala look into the company's finances. The trail led to a shell company in the Cayman Islands.

'AV's contacts in the Caymans discovered that the shell company, whose registered office was nothing but a three-digit mailbox, was owned by none other than the Sandesars. Interestingly, Techtron Technologies was set up exactly one year before they signed the contract with MSEB and shut down a week after the attack,' said Dhariwal.

'And the MSEB's commercial team handed over the contract to a one-year-old company because some corrupt officials got bribed,' surmised DD.

'Exactly. Now the impending attack on BARC will be carried out by a hacker team called TAG-2. We know the malware they call the Cobra is being created by a Canadian company called Softnett. AV and Lala are investigating the firm as we speak. But our issues do not end there.'

'Of course not. Unless we know the name of the Pakistani tech company and the Albanian one, we are nowhere close to preventing the attack.'

'That's right, sir.'

'Who else knows of this impending attack?' asked DD.

'Only us and the Ghosts. I briefed all of them already,' Dhariwal replied.

'No NIA or RAW?'

'No, sir.'

'Then keep it that way. If RAW or the NIA get involved in this, it will become an official project, which will have to then be recorded in the files. And then we would have to inform the select committee on Indo-China operations. That would mean too much exposure and more chances of a leak. We will have to keep this strictly confidential. No one in the government or in the Opposition should even get a whiff of it till we have handled it completely. Once things have been taken care, you can leak it to the American press. Let the world hear from America. If anyone asks us to clarify, we will say we have no comment on anything related to national security. The Opposition will make some noise for a week and then it will die down,' said DD.

'Shall I delegate this to AV and Lala?' asked Dhariwal.

'Please do,' said DD.

'I'll tell the Ghosts that Strike 3 is officially on,' said Dhariwal.

DD nodded. 'How long do you anticipate the Ghosts will need to wrap this up?'

'With international investigations involved, probably a month.'

'Good. Do what you have to do but stay two steps ahead of the Dragon,' DD cautioned.

APRIL 2020

AV AND LALA SPENT HALF of April running a thorough investigation into Softnett, using both their resources in India and abroad. Although AV's sources from the darknet highlighted TAG-2's active presence, Softnett's Pakistani connection remained a mystery, so they decided to do some reverse engineering. They already knew that Techtron Technologies, based in the US, was the front of TAG-1. So Lala contacted his friend Pritam Patel, a Gujarati American beat cop in New Jersey, and asked him for all the details on the company. Pritam's investigation, along with information from an FBI associate, came up with some crucial findings. A year ago, the FBI had started cracking down on Khalistanis in America. Fearing arrests, most of them fled the US to Canada. Two of these were Ripudman Singh and his son Jagjit Singh, both of whom have featured in the FBI list of wanted Khalistanis. A few inquiries in Canada revealed that Ripudman Singh was living a quiet life but his son Jagjit Singh, now living in Vancouver under the name Harry Singh, had converted to Christianity with the Church of Peter. The church had aided their migration to Canada. Now a member of the church's finance team, he was married to a Canadian techie called Maurice Cooper, who was a devout Christian. Maurice, a software engineer, was the owner of Softnett.

With the help of his darknet contact, AV hacked into Harry Singh's email but found nothing of interest there. It was when they hacked into Maurice Cooper's account that they found a piece of correspondence between her and a man named Aslam Sheikh, who owned a tech company—Aslam Tech—in Karachi. It was the only mail from her computer to someone in Pakistan, and it read: 'Transfer complete. Sent USB as well by courier.' A little digging confirmed that someone had not only downloaded a program on to a USB drive but had also used a customised Windows Easy transfer cable, to transfer data. An Easy Transfer Cable is a type of cable that helps transfer data from one computer to another. The transfer itself is done using a special software program that uses the cable to transfer your files. Once, these were special cables, usually USB cables but now everyone uses the Ethernet cables or what is normally called Network cables.

AV's darknet source uncovered something else. Based on Maurice's travel itinerary, the day the mail was sent, she was on a Catholic retreat in an isolated Quebecois city, Iqaluit, which had no internet or mobile tower facilities. This meant someone who knew her password had accessed her computer and sent the mail from there. Having a strong hunch that Aslam Tech was the front for Softnett in Pakistan and that Harry Singh had sent the mail, AV called Safi Doha to get more details on Aslam Tech.

Safi's Pakistani contacts reported that Aslam Tech was a recently set-up firm—it was hardly a few weeks old—and specialised in coding, app creation and software programs.

Interestingly, the firm had a recent alliance with an Albanian tech firm, Zuari Techwire, about which details were scarce. AV asked Safi to get everything possible on Maurice Cooper. Then he turned to his darknet friend yet again for details on Zuari Techwire. But no information on the company existed on the net. With the investigation having hit a wall, AV and Lala turned to Dhariwal for help.

Three days later, Dhariwal called for a meeting with the two of them.

6

'I KNOW WHY YOUR DARKNET friend could not find anything on Zuari Techwire,' said Dhariwal, pouring himself a steaming cup of coffee and returning to his seat behind the mahogany table. AV looked at Lala and then at Dhariwal. The three were gathered in the NSA's office in New Delhi.

'And why is that?' asked AV.

'Zuari Techwire is a shell company owned by Misha Perci. It does nothing, it has no people and there are no physical assets. It has only a PO box for its address,' explained Dhariwal.

'So we're at a dead end again, I guess,' said Lala.

'Not entirely,' said Dhariwal. After a pause, he resumed. 'Zuari Techwire may be a shell company, but the company registration department in Tirana noted that the firm has recently aligned with a software company in Chennai.'

'What's the name of this Chennai company?' asked an excited Lala.

'Aster Bridge Holdings Pvt. Ltd,' said Dhariwal with a hint of a smile.

'I've heard this name before,' said AV, drumming his fingers on his chair's armrest.

'Me too,' said Lala.

'Of course you have. Aster Bridge Holdings is owned by the infamous Karthi Chettiar. He's under investigation by the CBI and the Enforcement Directorate for money laundering and financial fraud,' said Dhariwal.

'Oh, he's the son of ex-finance minister Palaniyappan Chettiar. Isn't he also being investigated by the ED?' AV asked.

'Yes. Our very own PC and KC,' said Dhariwal.

'They're under investigation and they're still doing business with criminals? These guys have guts,' commented Lala.

'These guys have solid reach in the police department and with the judiciary boys. They're not the type to be scared of an investigation. PC is an eminent lawyer and a master at creating alibis and tampering with evidence. Pinning them down or securing a conviction is no small feat. But back to our discussion—there's more news to share,' said Dhariwal.

'What is it?' asked AV.

'Aster Bridge Holdings has just secured the CRM software upgradation contract for the Kerala facility handling our nuclear submarine programme,' Dhariwal disclosed.

'I'll be damned. PC's from Kerala. He has connections in the state government, and he's a Xi Wang supporter too,' said AV softly.

'Looks like they planned it well this time,' said Lala.

Dhariwal nodded in agreement and then looked at the calendar on his table. 'According to the facility head, Aster is starting work in fifteen days.' He paused before adding, 'The Panther wants you two to handle it, but there's a condition. He does not want India to expose China.'

'Why?' asked AV.

'He wants the American media to expose China. In his view, the impact will be far better, and it'll keep us out of all this. There's an underlying strategy here, but I can't share that just yet. Pavak Dahiya will handle the American media leak,' said Dhariwal.

'How is the Panther planning to keep this away from the Indian media? It's bloody well happening in India. And how will RAW react if they discover the BARC operation is being carried out by us?' asked Lala.

'To start with, I'm naming this Strike 3 so that there is no mention of BARC going forward. Here's the plan: I'll liaise with Dr B.B. Vyas, the director of BARC, and brief him on a possible cyber-attack on the Kerala facility. He'll discreetly create a dummy CRM for the facility, which will sit over the current original CRM program. Aster will start working on the dummy CRM, assuming it's the original, and give access to TAG-2, who will hack into the CRM interface software and plant their Trojan. The moment they do that, we will launch a counter Trojan that will infiltrate the TAG-2 computer and from there worm its way into the PLA military computer mainframe. Since the PLA will be observing the hack in real-time, we anticipate a seamless transition,' Dhariwal laid out.

'Won't the facility team realise that it's a front?' asked Lala.

'They won't initially, as the dummy will mirror the original system perfectly but will be sitting on another server. But yes, they'll catch on eventually, but then B.B. Vyas will say it was created as fire wall during installation time,' said Dhariwal.

'I'm playing devil's advocate here, so bear with me. What if they realise within twenty-four hours of the work starting that they are working on a dummy?' asked AV.

'That's enough time for BB's team to corrupt the dummy system using their own malware and embed a Trojan in the PLA computers,' explained Dhariwal.

'But if the dummy program gets corrupted, won't Aster and TAG-2 deduce their Trojan's malfunction? They'll immediately retreat and wipe all traces of entry,' said AV.

'It's possible. But by then we will have planted our Trojan. We'll be inside their domain, and from then on, whatever they do, we can see. Every time they try to launch a Trojan in the future, we will know. This is why DD does not want us to expose China. If China realises we knew about this, they'll assume we've been up to something and sanitise their software. Our Trojan will get exposed,' said Dhariwal.

'Brilliant. When Aster discovers that they have failed, they'll panic, make up an excuse and pull out of the deal, rather than end up in another investigation. But this won't sit well with the Kerala facility team. Those who have taken bribes will become adversaries, and they'll likely pursue legal action against Aster for breach of contract. This will inevitably capture media attention,' said Lala.

'Yes. It will be a fight between the Kerala facility and Aster over a simple breach of contract. The involvement of local police and the CID will lead to the unearthing of Zuari Techwire's connection. Given the international implications, the NIA will be called and they will start investigations. PC and KC's connections with Misha Perci will be spotlighted, and the Indian media will have a field day spinning conspiracy theories,' said Dhariwal.

'That's all well and good. And I'm sure that when news of this disaster reaches Xi Wang, he'll pray that the Indian media doesn't drag the Chinese into it. And I'm equally sure that the Indian media will find no connection between Aster, Zuari and the Chinese. But what happens to TAG-2, Aslam Tech and Zuari?' asked Lala.

'To understand that, we need to go by the Panther's decision of informing the American media. And that's where Pavak Dahiya steps in. Leveraging his connections, he will ensure the ANN (American News Network) gets a packet with evidence that Misha Perci's Zuari Techwire bought a Trojan from Aslam Tech in Pakistan, and that this Trojan was bought from Softnett, which is funded by the Sandesars, who work for the PLA hackers, TAG-2. The packet will also contain an additional page, which will talk about TAG-2 planning to install Trojans in the NASA programs as well. This will shake the Americans,' said Dhariwal.

'This'll create panic across America!' said Lala.

Dhariwal nodded. 'The CIA will spring into action. They'll take assistance from the Canadian National Cyber Crime Force and go after Softnett. Harry and Maurice will be interrogated, and they will expose Nitin. Then the CIA in Tirana will close in on Nitin, who will talk too. Eventually, all trails will point to Xi ,' said Dhariwal.

'And the narrative stems from the American perspective, not us, so we'll be out of the limelight,' said AV.

Lala smirked. 'I'd love to see Imran's face when President

Akhmu confronts him and tells him that he is freezing every single penny from the WHO and the IMF for his involvement in waging a cyber war on America and India.'

'Imran won't bat an eyelid before sacrificing the promoters of Aslam Tech, General Khan and ISI Chief Ali. He'll use the opportunity to not only please Akhmu but also to appoint a new general and an ISI chief who will toe his line,' said AV.

'But he'll surely be unhappy that Xi kept him in the dark about all this and spoke directly to his general,' said AV.

'Yes, but he won't have the courage to question Xi. More importantly, realising Xi is the mastermind behind all this, Akhmu will deploy the formidable American NSA, Robert Sullivan to address the issue. Bob and the American media will ensure Xi's portrayal as an international villain. This is bound to affect his OPOR. Also, if I persuade Hector Dekovi in Albania to insinuate that General Beqir Hoxha had a role to play in framing Misha in all this, Misha will go after Beqir,' said Dhariwal.

'Gef can use this to convince Beqir to execute the coup,' said Lala excitedly.

'Gentlemen, with one stone we're going to kill several birds.'

The next day, Dhariwal flew to Trombay to brief Dr B.B. Vyas on the plan. A week later, under BB's supervision, a five-man team discreetly created a firewall around the current facility CRM software in Kerala. Then they created a dummy CRM on a separate server, layered over the original. The facility remained unaware. On the fifteenth day, at 9 a.m., when Aster engineers commenced their work on the

CRM, the Trombay team, acting as the Kerala facility team, remotely guided the Aster engineers to the dummy CRM. By 11 a.m., TAG-2 had installed the Trojan, Cobra, in the dummy CRM, and by 4.30 p.m., the Trombay team had tracked and removed the Cobra.

Utilising a custom virus, the Trombay team corrupted the program files of the dummy, leading TAG-2 to presume their Trojan was malfunctioning. As TAG-2 hastily retreated, the Trombay team's own Trojan infiltrated the PLA's 'Border Military' computers. This malware could embed itself within the Chinese PLA systems, impersonating real, operational programs. Once the Trojan was inside their system, it sat idly on their computers waiting for further instructions from the Trombay team.

The Trojan had also uploaded additional malware on to the Chinese computers by bypassing their security settings while the TAG-2 and Aster teams were busy disabling themselves and wiping their digital foot print.

By 5.30 p.m., every email being sent by the PLA could be seen by the five man team in Trombay. By 6 p.m., the Indians had completed mirroring the PLA computers and handed access over to Dhariwal, who firewalled it with an exclusive password. Now the Trombay team was out of everything and the NSA had taken charge.

At 12.30 a.m., Dr B.B. Vyas called Dhariwal. 'I have connected three of our computers to the ones in your NSA war room, sir. You can see everything now, so my team and I are signing off. After all, we're peace-loving scientists, not experts in cyber warfare,' said BB with a touch of irony.

'Magnificent work,' said Dhariwal. 'Remember, BB, our secret dies with us.'

'Absolutely,' said BB as he disconnected.

Dhariwal looked up at the ceiling as he lay in bed that night, thoughts flitting through his mind. Then, he sent a message to AV and Lala. 'Strike 3 complete. Shutting down operation.' He sent another message to Pavak Dahiya: 'Send one packet to ANN and another to the CIA in Tirana immediately after the media breaks it.'

Setting his phone aside, he stretched languidly and closed his eyes. Within five minutes, he had succumbed to a deep sleep.

No day is so bad it can't be fixed with a nap.

APRIL 2020

THE STATE CAPITAL OF MARYLAND, Annapolis, lies 30 miles south of Baltimore and 33 miles northeast of the White House at 1600 Pennsylvania Avenue NW, Washington D.C. But the US National Security Advisor, Robert Sullivan, had decided to build his private residence in Annapolis, a fifty-minute drive away from the White House, seeking respite from the bustling D.C.

Sixty-seven-year-old Robert Sullivan didn't warm to people easily, earning him the nickname 'Lone Wolf' within the White House. As the head of the US National Security Agency, his primary role was to advise the President on vital national security issues. A staunch patriot, Robert prioritised the country above all, sidelining his personal life. He would readily sacrifice whatever it took for America.

But surprises, especially those from the President, were not to his liking.

On this Tuesday, Robert had unusually decided to go to bed early. He was just setting his morning alarm when President Akhmu called him and instructed him to tune into ANN.

Switching on the TV, Robert watched ANN break the

news about Misha Perci's Zuari Techwire, Aslam Tech and Softnett. How had the media received access to this information that had bypassed even his team?

As the report transitioned to the topic of TAG-2, the broadcaster declared, 'Our sources indicate that the PLA hackers, who go by the name TAG-2, had plans to install Trojan malware in the NASA programs. We are yet to confirm this with the NASA team, but given the circumstances, a comprehensive security review on their part seems prudent.'

The clock fell from Robert's hand as he jumped out of bed and dialled Bob Neilson, NASA's administrator. 'Have you seen the news? How much truth is there to it?' When Neilson told him to expect a call from him in ten minutes as he needed to check with his team, Robert hurriedly dressed for work.

Neilson returned the call while Robert was in the car, his chauffer's foot firmly on the accelerator, headed for the office. 'My team is running a safety audit to check the validity of the news, but they haven't found anything yet. Just so you know, the teams have been complaining that the programs have been running a bit slowly the last few days.'

He was a half-hour away from the White House when his phone rang again. It was the head of the CIA from Tirana. The frustration in his voice palpable, Robert snapped, 'You're a little late. The news beat you to it.' Just as he was about to disconnect, he saw he had another call waiting to get through—it was General Beqir Hoxha.

7

DAWN WAS BREAKING IN THE VILLAGE of Lin, Albania, when General Beqir Hoxha called Robert. 'Good morning, General. How can I help you?' Robert asked as his Cadillac sped towards the White House.

'I called to finish the conversation we started yesterday. It's weighing on me, Bob. I need a decision—quick,' said Beqir.

Robert was in no mood to talk to Beqir, but he knew a tactful response was important. After all, the man was planning a coup in Albania.

'Let's review what we spoke about, General, before I share my decision. You want to execute a coup and replace Tefik Metta with the opposition leader, Hector Dekovi. You feel, in return, Hector will make you the NSA of Albania, which is the most powerful position after the President. And this plan was suggested by your good friend Gef Bajrami, the arms dealer. Is that right?' asked Robert.

Beqir's reply was curt. 'Yes.'

'What is Gef's stake in this?' probed Robert.

'You asked me the same question yesterday, Robert, and I told you Gef is my well-wisher. Moreover, I've shared these sentiments with Gef many times before. My interest is his interest. Tefik is Xi's puppet, and if we don't replace him soon, Albania will end up as a Chinese colony.'

'Sorry to be a wet blanket here, but any position won through a coup will be accepted by neither the world nor your people. To win respect and acceptance, you have to earn your place democratically. This won't work,' said Robert frankly.

Beqir's patience was clearly running out. 'You have a better suggestion, Mr Sullivan?'

'Yes. You can still become the NSA but under Tefik,' said Robert.

'Not acceptable. Tefik has to go,' said Beqir.

'Serve as his NSA for six months. In the next elections, we will make you the President instead of Hector,' said Robert.

The General took the bait. 'And how would we do that?' he asked.

'Starting immediately, instil fear in Tefik's mind that you have enough intel on an imminent threat to his Presidency. Tell him an enemy state is planning a coup.'

'Which enemy state?' Before Robert could answer, Beqir suggested, 'It will have to be one of the Indians. Tefik hates India and its people.'

'Good. Once he buys into it, throw some random Indians under the bus. Your interrogation methods are effective. Get a few Indians arrested and make them confess. Let the media create a spectacle. Paint yourself as the saviour of the nation—you'll be a hero. That's when you demand the vacant NSA chair,' said Robert.

'Tefik has reserved that for Misha,' said Beqir.

'Then plant a doubt in Tefik's mind about Misha.'

'Not a bad plan, Robert. And I know who to throw under the bus. Gef's Indian partner in the film industry. He told me that the partner and his wife are coming to Tirana soon. I'll detain them and convince Gef that his associate is a RAW agent. But we'll need some documented evidence to show Tefik and Gef that the Indians are linked to RAW.'

'Give me the details of the Indians, and my people will fabricate a trail that will prove their affiliation with RAW,' said Robert.

'Tefik might be swayed, but Gef and the Indian are close. I'm not sure he'll buy into the story,' said Beqir.

'Whether Gef buys into it or not is immaterial. Once you have decided, he cannot do anything about it, General. Start thinking for yourself. A happy Tefik will make you the NSA of Albania. After all, you're doing this for the greater good of the country, aren't you? Think about it: President Beqir Hoxha.'

Robert's words had their intended effect on the General. 'Create the paper trail and I will do the rest,' he said.

'Done. But make sure you don't kill the Indians,' said Robert.

'Why not?' asked Beqir.

Robert sidestepped the question. 'Put the Indians in jail for a year. Next year, when you become President, pardon them and send them back to India. Dhariwal will be grateful and support you.'

'Bob, I thought Dhariwal was a close ally,' said Beqir.

'Of course he is,' said Robert.

'Yet you're advising me to sacrifice Indian civilians here.'

'For the greater good. That's what you get with

geopolitics. You will learn its nuances when you become the president. All the best, General.' Robert hung up before the guilt of betraying Dhariwal gnawed at him too much. When the car dropped him off, he walked over to the Oval Office.

The Oval Office, the main workspace of the President of the United States, is found in the West Wing of the White House. Its distinctive oval design showcases three large windows behind the President's desk and a fireplace across from it. It has four entrances: one to the Rose Garden, another to a dining room, the third to the main corridor of the West Wing, and the fourth to the President's secretarial office. Four secretaries assisted the President, working in shifts.

Robert entered the presidential lounge and walked over to Ann Wayne, one of Hussain Akhmu's secretaries. 'I need to speak with the President, please. It's urgent.'

Ann was wrapping up her last night shift of the month and was looking forward to the day shift starting again. Ann was an Indian American, born to a Gujarati Indian mother, whose family was close to DD, and a Californian father. At five feet seven inches tall and with long raven hair and brilliant white teeth, she epitomised what many term 'Indian beauty'. Ann lived alone in D.C. in a studio apartment but had a Russian boyfriend, Steven Petrov, who lived in New York. Steven was a painter by profession, a well-known one at that. But he always dreamt of returning to Moscow with Ann and starting a studio there. But Steven's hesitation stemmed from believing she'd sacrifice a great job just for him.

What Steven didn't know was that Ann wasn't just a secretary of the President. She was an Indian RAW agent in the White House.

Ann walked over to the Oval Office and addressed the President. 'Advisor Sullivan is here to meet you, Mr President.'

The President looked upset when he responded. 'Tell him I'll see him in the study.'

Ann walked back to Robert, who had been waiting for her. 'The President will meet you in the study, Mr Sullivan. If you could wait a moment, I'll prepare the room.' With an amiable smile, she walked over to her cabin, pulled out a small gadget from the desk drawer and made her way to the study.

Once inside, she positioned the device right below the CCTV camera, making sure to remain concealed from its view as she did. The gadget was a mini WiFi-enabled HD spy IP camera equipped with a microphone, night vision and a sound sensor that initiated recording upon detecting speech. She walked back to Robert and escorted him into the study. After serving him a cup of his favourite Cuban coffee, she said, 'President Akhmu will join you shortly.'

Hussain Akhmu was the first African American Muslim President of the USA. His ascension to the White House had been a controversial one, with accusations of direct voter fraud and poll rigging. Though the results were procedurally contested and protested nationwide by a large majority of Americans, technicalities eventually ushered him into the Oval Office. Standing at a poised five feet eleven inches, President Akhmu bore a wheatish complexion and short curly hair. Deep-seated insecurities, stemming from societal prejudices against him, sometimes surfaced when dealing with his white counterparts.

NSA Robert Sullivan was not a great fan of Hussain Akhmu. In fact, like many of the incumbent senators, he was not a fan of Muslims in general. But having worked with Akhmu for a few months, he had figured out that the only thing the President was interested in was being in the news and leading popularity metrics. Robert exploited both weaknesses. He ensured that Akhmu's name appeared in the papers continuously and kept giving him credit for security policies that he had drafted. This made the President happy. He also kept Akhmu busy with frequent foreign sojourns, permitting Robert to effectively run the government.

A few minutes later, President Akhmu walked in, his brows furrowed in concern. 'The news on ANN is unsettling. We need to get the CIA to go to the bottom of this and fast,' he said.

'I'm on it, Mr President, don't bother anyone at the moment' said Robert, not wanting anyone else to spoil his control over the President. 'I spoke to Bob Neilson, and for the moment I don't think we need to panic. But we should use this opportunity to conduct a thorough probe and see where it leads us. Mr President, I suggest addressing the ANN report on Twitter and making it clear that you have asked the NSA to investigate this. This will deflect all questions my way.'

Before Akhmu could venture further down that topic, Robert deftly guided the discussion towards Albania. He recapped his conversation with Beqir, detailing his recommendations. The President, clearly pleased with this update, expresed his gratitude to Robert.

'Issues will keep popping up in a large nation like ours, Mr President, but what the average Joe on the street wants to see is how their president is dealing with these problems. Your tweet will tell everyone that you hold their best interest in mind. I will handle the rest,' said Robert.

Once the President had left, Robert called the Director of the CIA, Justin Cole, summoning him to his office right away. When they convened, he instructed Director Cole, 'Contact the Canadians and get everything on this Softnett. I want everyone rounded up and singing like canaries in the next forty-eight hours.'

8

AS INSTRUCTED, THANKS TO THE Canadian Intelligence team, forty-eight hours later, Jagjit Singh and Maurice Cooper were picked up and flown to a secure location in Washington D.C. A ten-minute interrogation, including some coercive tactics on Jagjit, swiftly extracted what they needed. When Director Cole called Robert, he had all the information with him.

'Softnett is owned by Maurice Cooper, wife of Jagjit Singh. She seems to be innocent, but this guy Jagjit is the architect of the Trojan called Cobra. It seems Nitin Sandesar commissioned him to create the Trojan and hand it over to Aslam Tech. With Maurice in the dark, Jagjit used her computer to relay Cobra to Aslam Tech, whose directors are Pakistani General Khan and ISI Chief Ali. The Trojan was then transferred to a shell company owned by Misha Perci, Zuari Techwire, which in turn handed it over to their Indian partner, Aster Bridge Holdings. Aster was tasked with helping the PLA hackers. TAG-2, who then inserted the Trojan into the nuclear facility CRM in the Indian state of Kerala. Apparently, something went wrong with the Trojan and it corrupted the CRM software. The Indians came to know about it, but had no clue that it was a Chinese Trojan,' said Cole.

He continued, 'Aster is owned by Karthi Chettiar, the son of the ex-finance minister of India, P. Chettiar. Aster screwed it up and ended up corrupting the CRM program instead. Strangely, the facility program head said this wasn't an issue because there was a dual program running and the one that got corrupted was on a separate server. But even the facility software engineers were unaware of this dual program set-up. Something fishy here but we haven't been able to figure out what it is.

'According to Jagjit Singh, there was nothing wrong with the Trojan. He thinks that the screw-up could have happened when TAG-2 tried to use the Trojan to mirror the facility computers with the PLA comps. The hackers never expected a dual CRM set-up—it's the first of its kind. If they had been successful, the hackers would have bypassed the security system in the Trombay facility, as they were planning to lodge the Trojan in the main nuclear facility administrative software, through which all communications pass. But luckily for the Indians, just then the entire thing collapsed.'

'And?' asked Robert.'And nothing. The hackers scrambled out and tried to clear all trace of them but failed. Investigations have been ordered on Aster by the local police. They don't have all the information we have yet,' said the director.

'You suspect anyone?' asked Robert.

'I suspect an insider at Zuari knew about all this and re-programmed the Trojan before it went to India. Zuari is owned by Misha, and his only enemy is General Beqir Hoxha. Don't ask me how, but I suspect the General had a hand in tampering with the Trojan,' said Cole.

'Damn. I spoke to the bastard an hour ago and he didn't say a word about all this. Has anyone spoken to Nitin?' asked Robert.

'Our team in Tirana was ready to interrogate him, but he came clean without any pressure. He confessed that he got his instructions from Xi Wang himself and that this is his brainchild. We have it on record and in our recordings, both audio and video.'

There was pin-drop silence as Robert processed the revelations. Then he asked, lowering his voice, 'Was Xi planning an attack on NASA?'

'We don't know. Nitin said Xi did not talk to him about NASA but feels he may have given the job to someone else,' replied the director.

'Why was Nitin so eager to share information? Was he scared of the interrogation?' asked Robert.

'I don't think so. He said Xi had his brother, Chetan, killed through Misha Perci, and it was time for payback.'

'What do you plan to do with this guy Nitin now?' asked Robert. 'We don't need to do anything. He's aware that the MSS will be after him and Tefik will not give him any protection. I suspect he'll go into hiding if he values his life. One thing I know is that he has already sent his family back to India.'

Robert congratulated Director Cole on his meticulous efforts and then asked him to compile a detailed report, to be submitted for Robert's review the next morning.

After Cole's departure, he called the Press Secretary. 'Organise an interview with the ANN's Jeanette Smith tomorrow. I'll see her in the reporters' lounge at 10. Tell her the agenda is to brief her on the news she broke today.'

MAY 2020

EVER SINCE ZHONGNANHAI BECAME THE central government compound, it has been largely inaccessible to the general public. After the 1989 protest in Tiananmen Square, security around the compound tripled. This escalation made many party leaders feel imprisoned, prompting them to move. Many relocated to Jade Spring Hill, and some shifted to the countryside. But when Xi Wang became Chairman of the PRC, he chose to stay within the compound.

From Xi's bedroom window, he could see the primary entrance to the compound—the Xinhua Gate, or 'Gate of New China', flanked by two slogans: 'Long Live the Great Chinese Communist Party' and 'Long Live the Invincible Mao Zedong Thought'.

Dawn had just broken, and the morning sun filtered through the satin drapes, casting an orange glow across the room's floor and walls. This serenity was a stark contrast to Xi Wang's emotional state. After listening to the ANN report the previous night, he'd felt humiliated and furious.

He looked out of the window at the mountain ranges in the distance and saw dark clouds forming over the peaks.

His present feeling was that of the captain of a sinking ship—desperate, frustrated and panicking.

He walked back to the coffee table in his room and picked up the American newspaper, *The Morning Post*. The front page read: 'Xi Fails in Hack Attack'. Accompanying the headline was a cartoon of the famous FBI 'Wanted' poster, featuring a caricature of Xi Wang, captioned: 'Wanted for Cybercrime'.

9

XI DIALLED PRESIDENT TEFIK METTA'S number. It was the second time he was trying. This time he waited, and seven rings later Tefik finally answered.

'Where the hell have you been?' Xi snapped.

'I was in a meeting. My phone was on silent,' Tefik replied curtly.

Taken aback by Tefik's brusque tone, he collected himself and said gently, 'Tefik, the information I have is that the Trojan got re-programmed in Tirana. Misha failed, and now *I* am on a wanted poster in an American newspaper.'

'My information suggests otherwise. According to Zuari's timestamps, the interval between receiving the program by cable from Aslam Tech and sending it to Aster was barely thirteen minutes, and I don't need to educate you that no program can be reworked in such a short time, especially a Trojan like Cobra. I feel the Indians knew about this well in advance,' said Tefik.

'Bullshit. Very few people knew about it. My sources say Beqir did this to screw Misha,' retorted Xi.

'Perhaps too few people knew about this. The Prime Minister of Pakistan and the President of Albania were not aware that their countries were being used for cyber war by the Chairman of the PRC,' Tefik said. He couldn't believe he had been kept in the dark on this by Misha.

Xi Wang knew his authority was being questioned, but it was true that he had kept the two national leaders out of the loop. He admitted, 'We all make mistakes. But Beqir is the one behind this sabotage.'

'Once more for the record: General Beqir Hoxha has nothing to do with this.' Without further ado, Tefik disconnected.

Xi walked back to the window and looked out of it, unable to focus on anything. A knock on the door interrupted his contemplation. It was Tony.

'Supreme Leader, NSA Robert Sullivan is currently discussing you on ANN.' He walked into the bedroom and switched on the television, tuning into ANN. Robert was being interviewed by Jeanette Smith. 'TAG-2, the Chinese PLA hackers, failed to hack the Indian nuclear programme only because of India's luck. The Indians had no clue that TAG-2 had embedded a Trojan in their facility found in the southern state of Kerala. It's regrettable that they didn't learn from the TAG-1 attack in Mumbai last year, where the electric grid of the city was hacked. The western state of Maharashtra lost millions of dollars in just one night. The FBI had sounded alarm bells even back then, yet India took it lightly and paid a hefty price. We've put all the pieces of the jigsaw puzzle together and know how the Trojan travelled from Canada to Pakistan to Albania and then India. While the Indian police are questioning the former finance minister, P. Chettiar, and his son, Karthi Chettiar, who own Aster Bridge Holdings, we have the architect of the Trojan in our custody,' said Robert.

Jeanette leaned in slightly. 'Who is the mastermind behind all this?'

'It's yet to be definitively confirmed, but our detainees have indicated the PLA is involved. We are still investigating said Robert.

'Has there been a confirmed attempt by these Chinese hackers to compromise NASA?' asked Jeanette.

'There was an attempt, but we were well prepared,' came Robert's response.

'You bloody liar!' screamed Xi Wang as he threw the teacup in his hand at the television set. It missed, smashing against the wall instead.

'Compose yourself, Supreme Leader,' said Tony as he held Xi, who was shaking with anger. 'That bastard is lying! How could he have forewarned India? He had absolutely no clue about TAG-2. And we haven't touched NASA. He's using this opportunity to belittle me and drum up anti-China support. He's lying!' repeated Xi. Noticing Xi's laboured breathing, Tony guided him to an armchair and fetched a glass of water.

'These Americans are famous for lying. They lied about Iraq having WMDs as an excuse to attack them. They invaded Iran, claiming that it was retaliation for the Iranian mining of areas of the Persian Gulf as part of the Iran–Iraq War. Now they're lying about me and China. They're planning a war, Tony,' said Xi. Tony saw that the Chairman's eyes were bloodshot, the veins in his forehead throbbing.

'America is planning to form a coalition of seven nations to fight such cyber-attacks. To start with, we will be bringing this to the United Nations Security Council and asking for barring nations that do such acts from the council,' said Robert on screen. 'I told you, Tony. The bastards are preparing to attack us. These Americans and their allies will now attack us. They'll all land up in Taiwan and use it as their base. We need to prepare, Tony. We need to...' His voice wavered, his mouth now parched. He had broken out into a cold sweat.

Tony hit the emergency call switch, summoning the house doctor.

'We have a spy among us, Tony. Someone who has leaked everything to the Americans,' whispered Xi, his strength ebbing.

'Who do you think is the spy, Supreme Leader?' asked Tony, flicking the switch repeatedly.

'It is Chin Luan. Arrest him.' Xi's eyes rolled back in his head.

Feeling the chilling touch of Xi's hand, Tony realised he was having a seizure. The door burst open, and the medical team came rushing in. As they attended to Xi, Tony called the MSS team. 'Detain Chin Luan on charges of treason.'

10

IT WAS 8 P.M. IN NEW DELHI. Inside 7, Lok Kalyan Marg, AV and Lala sat on a sofa in the foyer outside DD's office, waiting for Dhariwal. Ten minutes later, he joined the two.

'Is the Panther busy?' asked Dhariwal.

'He's on the phone with Paitoon Wang,' said Lala.

'Must be talking to her about Xi Wang's heart attack. Luckily the MSS chief, Tony was there, so he managed to rush Xi to the hospital,' said Dhariwal. AV was about to add to the conversation, when Shiva stepped out to tell them DD was ready for them.

DD was still on the phone when they entered. He gestured for them to take a seat on the sofas.

Two minutes later, DD joined the conversation. 'Sorry to keep you waiting. It was Paitoon Wang. On the one hand, Xi is hospitalised, and on the other, her brother, Chin Luan, has been arrested by the MSS for treason. I think they suspect him of leaking plans to the Americans,' he said with a wry smile.

'I saw Robert's interview. He claims he had warned us about TAG-2. The man can certainly lie with a straight face. It's Chin Luan's bad luck that he went to the US to meet his wife and son just last week. He and Paitoon have always been against Xi's devious strategies, so Xi must have put two and two together,' said Dhariwal.

'Yes, but this time an innocent man has been put behind bars and...'

The room was filled with anticipation as everyone waited for DD to speak. He looked down at his hands and said, 'Paitoon Wang needs our help in getting Chin Luan out of jail. She wants us to drum up international pressure on Xi to have him released. She suggested I speak with President Akhmu and get Robert to release a statement that will deflect any suspicion from Chin.'

'So the idea is to suggest they got the hacking intel from a source other than Chin?' asked Dhariwal.

DD nodded. 'I can speak to Robert, but knowing the Americans, they'll politicise it for their own benefit, and it'll backfire. Where is Chin now?' asked Dhariwal.

'In Qincheng Prison,' said DD. He paused, seeming to reflect, then said, 'I'll think of something. The good thing is Xi is out of action for now, and Peng Luan is acting Chairman. Let me speak to him and see what can be done. And on a different note, congratulations to the three of you. Strike 3 went off flawlessly.' Turning to AV and Lala, he said, 'Take a break, boys. Spend time at home with family.'

'Thank you, sir,' said AV and Lala.

Leaning towards AV, Lala murmured, 'Raj's mom will be happy to see me. She's getting bored in Pune.'

Hearing Lala mention Raj's name, DD, as they approached the door, asked Dhariwal, 'What news from Raj and Geeta?'

'Both left for Tirana yesterday. Geeta called me from the airport. Gef was there to receive them and escort them to the Sheraton. I believe they rested up yesterday and today, and are planning on meeting Gef at 9 tomorrow morning,' said Dhariwal.

'Good. Keep me posted,' responded DD.

After seeing them off, DD freshened up and then sat down for dinner. The butler was about to serve him, when he said, 'Please ask Mr Raju to come see me.'

Three minutes later, the butler returned with Shiva.

'Have you had dinner?' asked DD.

'No, I was just about to,' said Shiva.

DD instructed the butler to set another plate and then said to Shiva, 'Join me. I have to discuss something with you.'

Once the butler had served them and left, DD said to Shiva, 'You know the situation in Zhongyang, correct?'

'Yes. Xi is in hospital, Peng Luan is in charge and Chin is in Qincheng, though I don't think Chin is capable of treason. I think Xi may have done this purposely to get Paitoon under control,' said Shiva.

DD shook his head. 'I think he suspects Paitoon more than Chin. I'm pretty positive that he thinks Paitoon leaked the news, but since he cannot do anything to her, he did the next best thing—arrest her brother, who is her security head, and send him to Qincheng. He's sending a message to Paitoon and Peng that he is capable of anything, and if they think he has become weak due to his failed project in India, they are mistaken.'

'That's an angle I hadn't thought of,' said Shiva.

'If we manage to get Chin out of Qincheng, it will be a big body blow to Xi. He'll realise that Paitoon and Peng have a stronger support system than him. He'll be rattled. It'll also embolden Peng to act against Xi for his failed cyber-attack. The Central Committee convenes in March 2025. Though he's elected for life, there's a clause that says the Central Committee can review his candidacy after a term ends and reverse their decision if they find that his leadership is affecting national security. If we free Chin, Peng can influence the Central Committee to vote in a new chairman. With Chin in jail, Peng Luan is a weak man,' said DD.

'What shall I do?' asked Shiva.

'Take two weeks to visit China and gather intel. Once you're back, we will put together an extraction plan for Chin. This isn't just about helping Paitoon—it's an opportunity to unseat Xi Wang,' said DD.

After dinner, Shiva left and DD retired to his bedroom. By the time he had finished reading and had drifted into slumber, it was thirty minutes past midnight.

⊙∰∼

In Tirana, 5,300 kilometres away, it was 9 a.m. Raj and Geeta had landed the day before, 31 May 2020, Gef and his team had received them at the airport, and escorted them to the Hotel. Now, as per plan, Raj & Geeta waited in the entryway of the Sheraton for Gef to pick them up.

'Dhariwal updated me,' Geeta said to Raj. 'Strike 3 is officially closed, and the Ghosts have planned a small celebration before leaving for their homes. It's just unfortunate that Chin Luan is in Qincheng Prison.'

Raj looked at Geeta gravely. 'The Ghosts are celebrating

the Dragon's downfall. But an innocent man rots in Qincheng for us.' He tried to change his tone to a more optimistic one. 'I'm sure the Panther will do something about it.'

Geeta's head turned. She had caught the hum of an approaching car. Gef's black Mercedes van rolled in.

Two men who were with Gef the previous day to receive them from the airport stepped out, greeted Raj and Geeta, and gestured for them to get in the van.

Gef couldn't make it?' asked Geeta as she got into the middle seat.

'He's caught up in a last minute meeting. He'll meet you later,' said one of them as he guided Raj towards the rear seats. The men got in and the van sped off.

Raj quickly sensed that something was wrong, so he asked them directly in Albanian, 'Is this an abduction?'

The man who had been speaking to the two replied, 'You're being escorted.'

'Where to?' asked Raj.

'To Beqir Mansion in Lin. General Beqir Hoxha wants to meet you.'

'Will Gef be there?' asked Raj.

The man's reply was succinct. 'No.'

While Geeta did not understand most of the Albanian exchange, she gathered that they were being taken to Lin. 'Your friend betrayed us,' she told Raj in Hindi.

Raj replied, conviction in his voice, 'Gef would never betray me.'

JUNE 2020

ALBANIA AND MACEDONIA ARE SEPARATED by the beautiful Lake Ohrid. Its western shores, characterised by its sandy and pebble-strewn beaches, are home to the picturesque village of Lin, dotted with meadows, brooks and gurgling streams. On one end of the lake lie the Ohrid Mountains.

On the other, overlooking the Black Mountains, was Beqir Mansion, a fortified three-storeyed structure with two wings—the home of the head of the Albanian Army, General Beqir Hoxha.

Constructed in the 1800s, Beqir Mansion was reminiscent of the Ottoman architectural style. The mansion was originally designed as a two-tower structure, known as a *kullë* in Albanian. One was the residential tower, where the General lived, and the other housed his office, a large interrogation room, a few cabins on the first floor, guest rooms on the second floor and a penthouse with a wraparound balcony on the third.

All the rooms in the residential tower also had balconies. The grand living room, library, bar, dining area and kitchen were on the ground floor, and three bedrooms were spread over the second and third floors. Both towers overlooked a man-made lake—Liqeni i Krokodilëve which meant Crocodile Lake. Locals called it Liqeni Kroko

Liqeni Kroko got its name from the four extremely aggressive pet Nile crocodiles that Beqir kept in the lake. Nile crocodiles are capable of taking down an animal four times their size. Their powerful jaws can rip apart an entire human body in minutes. Perpetually hungry, they have to be fed constantly.

Although water from the Ohrid fed into Liqeni Kroko, the moment it entered the lake, it took on a darker shade because of the black soil bed beneath, giving the lake an eerie aura come nightfall. Another strange thing was that the lake was permanently still, giving no indication of the deadly crocodiles that lay in wait for a prey in the depths.

11

IT WAS 5 P.M. THE EVENING SUN stretched its rays over the still waters of Liqeni Kroko, casting long, dark shadows. Occasionally, the surface of the lake would shudder when the Nile crocs moved about.

General Beqir Hoxha sat on a steel chair in the white-walled interrogation room, facing the bay windows. He watched the evening sun throw its fading light on the black waters and smiled. The anchored boat and its jetty shimmered, almost as if gilded in gold.

His gaze travelled to the far right of the jetty, where the guard barracks were located. Eight of the guards were chopping firewood. Behind the General, in the interrogation room, two tall, well-built bodyguards kept watch over their captive in the middle of the room: Raj knelt on the floor, his wrists cuffed behind his back with zip ties. His shirt was soaked in the blood that dripped down from his nose and a nasty cut on his right eyebrow. Despite Gef Bajrami telling General Beqir Hoxha that Raj was his friend and partner, following Robert Sullivan's advise, he had used Gef's team to bring the two of them to the Beqir mansion under the pretext that they were RAW agents.

Beqir turned to look at Raj. 'I had promised my crocodiles

some Indian meat tonight, but my Yankee friend insisted I keep you alive. He left the specifics to me, though. So, Mr Rana, I've chosen a special place for you: Burrel prison. You may have heard of it. I'm sure they'll look after you very well there.'

His eyes then settled on Geeta, who was six feet away from Raj, also on the floor and on her knees, her hands bound. 'You, Mrs Rana, are very lucky. I plan to keep you here with me at Beqir Mansion with all the comforts a beautiful woman like you should have. And I'll be there by your side.' With a sinister smile, he added, 'Every night.'

Though battered and bruised, Raj mustered up his strength and said, 'General, I am telling you once again, we are not RAW agents. I'm a stakeholder in Gef Bajrami's film production house and this is my wife. We're here just to make a travel documentary on Albania. I beg you, please check with Gef.'

The General's wicked smile didn't waver. 'Oh, I'm aware you have no association with RAW and are simple filmmakers, Mr Rana. Gef and I are friends, and he's made your status clear.'

'Then why are you doing this to us?' asked Raj.

'You see, when I was in college, I wanted to be an actor,' began Beqir. 'But my father, Major General Hoxha, forced me to pursue a military career. The actor in me never really left, though. Whenever I get a chance, I take on new roles. And the role I want now in Albania is as its NSA. For that I need to sacrifice someone to impress my President secure my role as his security advisor.'

Beqir giggled like a child, walked up to Geeta and began

playing with her hair. 'So now I am playing the role of a national saviour. You two are the villains, enemies of the state, and I am Albania's protector. Tomorrow the headlines will be screaming: "General Hoxha Saves Albania from Coup. Indian RAW Agents Apprehended". Maybe the subhead will be, "A grateful nation elevates its hero to NSA." How do you like that, Mr Rana?' The General fixed his eyes on Raj's blood-smeared face.

'The Yankee you speak about is nobody's friend. Today, he has advised you to sacrifice two innocent Indians for his personal ambitions. Tomorrow, he will sacrifice you for the very same thing. Just remember that.' Raj suspected that Beqir's Yankee friend was none other than Robert Sullivan, the US NSA and supposed ally of Beqir's.

Raj's words had struck a nerve. The General was no fool; he knew the inherent risks in allying with someone like Robert. But he couldn't show his fears to his captive. He slapped Raj across the face—hard. 'Don't you know who I am? Let anyone—you, her or the Americans—even think of betraying General Beqir Hoxha, and they'll find themselves in the lake with my crocodiles.' Gesturing to his guards, he said, 'Take them upstairs. Once the doctor has examined them, take Mr Rana to Burrel and her to the penthouse.'

Before walking out, he paused at the door and said gently to Geeta, 'Better get cleaned up before dinner.'

A doctor and a nurse were waiting on the second floor. The doctor checked them both. After the nurse bandaged Raj's wounds, the pair of them left. A guard remained outside Raj's room and the other took Geeta to the penthouse on the third floor.

Though wounded and hurting, Raj's mind was working overtime. He realised Robert Sullivan had advised the General to sacrifice them for gaining Metta's trust and getting the role of the NSA. He also knew Burrel was not a place for humans. If he had to succeed in his mission, he had to get out of the Burrel, come what may. As the night dragged, he also worried for Geeta.

Come dawn the next day, Raj was bundled into a van. The drive was long. One guard sat with him in the back while another took the passenger seat next to the driver. As the van drove down the long and winding road, Raj noticed the never-ending canal running parallel to the road. Beyond it, grasslands stretched out till they touched the distant mountains standing tall against a background of a vast blue sky. Tall black pine and chestnut trees dotted the plains. Raj sat silently, his eyes devouring everything as his brain recorded every detail.

After a three-hour drive, the van stopped in front of a massive greystone building. The wrought-iron gates were crowned with a sign: Burrel Prison.

The guards escorted Raj out of the car. The director of the prison, Khabib Zane—a tall, beefy, bald man—was already waiting for them. 'Welcome to Burrel, Raj Pratap Rana,' he said.

Without further ceremony, he handcuffed Raj and led him towards the prison gates. The moment they stepped inside the gates, Raj was hit by the strong smell of fresh blood. Its source was a slaughterhouse off to the left.

'We feed our inmates well, Mr Rana,' said Zane as he guided Raj to a corridor with damp walls. He reached out to touch one of the walls and said, 'The only problem here is the plumbing, Mr Rana. I am told the ceiling in the general population cell is leaking, so please don't mind the damp.'

Once inside the prison, Zane handed him over to the supervisor in the administrative block, who asked Raj to strip and take a shower. He was then handed the prison uniform and escorted by a guard to the jail clinic for a medical examination. All had been routine up until this point, but just as the guard entered the clinic with him, Raj's demeanour shifted. He began mumbling and shaking his head.

'What? What are you saying?' asked the guard.

Raj did not respond to the guard but continued shaking his head and murmuring. The guard quickly assisted Raj onto a bed and alerted the doctor. 'He was okay till a few minutes ago but now, suddenly, something seems to be wrong with him.'

The doctor pushed the guard aside and began inspecting Raj. He scrutinised his eyes, his throat, all the cuts and bruises on his face and body.

He turned to the guard. 'Inform Mr Zane that this man is showing early signs of PTSD. For the moment, I'm going to administer a sedative. Get a stretcher and shift him to a private cell. Don't house him with the general population; he won't endure the night. Keep him under round-the-clock observation for a week and then bring him to me. I will give you a clearer picture then.'

The last thing Raj remembered before he blacked out due to the sedative was Geeta's face. She was reaching out to him through a mist as her voice echoed: 'Help me, Raj.'

12

IT WAS 8 A.M. ON 3 JUNE when Dhariwal walked into DD's office and showed him an article that Gef had sent. He had already forwarded Gef's message earlier that Raj & Geeta had been arrested. The article read:

'RAW Agents' Raw Treatment in Albania' read the headline. The article continued: 'Military police apprehended two RAW agents who were planning to orchestrate a coup in Albania. The arrest took place outside the Tirana Sheraton Hotel where they were staying, and they were taken directly to General Beqir Hoxha's camp office in Lin. "After a six-hour interrogation, one of them has been sent to Burrel Prison, while the other has been kept under house arrest for further questioning," said General Hoxha. The Albanian intelligence department has taken over the case and are investigating the matter. When questioned as to how the Indian has been sent to Burrel without a trial or a conviction, the General said, "These are RAW agents. Investigations will take a long time. Till then if we keep them in a local jail, there are chances they will be extracted by RAW. I have taken special permission for keeping the agent in Burrel."'

Dhariwal pointed at another smaller article, which read: 'General Beqir Hoxha has been made the NSA of Albania, effective today. President Tefik Metta announced the change of role this morning. The army will now be headed by General Pasha, formerly second-in-command to General Hoxha. Sources within the General's office suggest this promotion is in recognition of Hoxha's pivotal role in thwarting an imminent coup by RAW.'

'What happened in Tirana, Ajit? How come Gef did not see this coming, or is he a part of this betrayal?' asked DD.

For perhaps the first time, Dhariwal looked a little lost. 'Everything was going as per the plan, sir and suddenly the General changed his mind. Even Gef is clueless. In fact he believes he is also being watched, so I have told him to be careful. But Adia Markova called this morning. She told me that General Hoxha is being guided by Robert Sullivan and it was his idea to sacrifice "some Indians" to achieve his goal.'

DD sighed. 'And he did achieve his goal. Beqir is the NSA now. Robert's plan worked.'

'My first priority right now is to get them back, sir,' said Dhariwal.

'And how do you plan to do that?' asked DD.

'I'm sending Sniper in. AV and Lala will be on standby. But we need some ground support.'

'Can't Gef help?'

I advised him not to get involved. If Beqir discovers that Gef is helping us, we'll lose our only contact in Albania. We need to think of someone else. I'm inclined to approach Hector.'

'And what will you tell Hector when he asks you who Sniper is?'

'I'll have to take him into confidence and tell him that Raj & Geeta are indeed RAW agents and that Sniper is also one of them and is being sent to extract them and his help is needed. After all we are doing all this for him."'

'Good. I think Hector will buy that,' said DD. Just as he was about to continue, Shiva walked in. 'You may want to see this,' he said, switching on the TV.

It was the morning news. 'And for news from the Balkans, General Beqir Hoxha has become the National Security Advisor to the President of Albania, Tefik Metta,' said the anchor. As per our sources, he was instrumental in nabbing two RAW agents suspected of planning a coup in Tirana. General Hoxha stated that the authorities were still collecting evidence to confirm this.'

'The opposition will surely enjoy this. But more important is what do we tell the head of RAW?' asked DD

'He knows he has not sent anyone to Tirana for a coup. We will say Tirana is playing games and ask him to investigate. That will keep him busy,' replied Dhariwal.

'But our assets have got exposed this time, Ajit.'

'Not really sir. A film producer and his wife have been jailed. I will ensure a counter release that Beqir did this to get promoted. Through Hector, we will put pressure on them as well using the human rights organisation in Albania.'

'This has become a little messy,' said DD.

'I agree,' said Dhariwal.

'Anyway, for on-ground support, contact your friend Eyal. He will give Sniper a team to operate in Tirana.'

Eyal Shabbat was the NSA of Israel and the ex-head of Aman, the Israeli military intelligence establishment. During his days as head of Aman, Eyal Shabbat had worked closely with Dhariwal. Over the years, they had become close friends and continued to help each other in matters of national security.

After Dhariwal left the office, he called Eyal from his car. 'Ajit, how are you?' asked Eyal who surprisingly sounded fresh.

'I need help with something critical,' said Dhariwal, not wasting a moment.

'Is this regarding the two film producers from India who have been arrested?' asked Eyal.

'Yes. How did you know?'

'I am at the airport waiting to board for New York and I saw the hourly team update report. Very sad, Ajit. When I saw the report, I immediately called my contact in Tirana, who said that the Indians were made scapegoats by Beqir and there is no truth to the story.'

'Who is your source?'

Eyal paused momentarily before divulging, 'Beqir's doctor. We're helping him and his family secure American citizenship.'

'Beqir and Robert are close. Couldn't the doctor have asked Beqir to help him with the citizenship?' asked Dhariwal.

'He did, but Beqir refused. Apparently, the doctor is privy to many of Beqir's skeletons, so Beqir will never allow him to leave. We've been monitoring Beqir's staff to get a weak link and discovered the doctor's ambition to migrate to America.

We just played on that. He has been giving us information for the last four years now and we have managed to move his family to New Jersey. He treated the Indian man before he was sent to Burrel.'

'Does he know the state of the woman?' Dhariwal asked.

'I asked him. He said she is being kept drugged on a tropane alkaloid called Devil's Breath and is now under house arrest at Beqir Mansion.'

'I need help from your team on ground in Tirana.'

'Planning on an extraction?'

'Yes.'

'Done. I will talk to my man there, Caleb Hulata, once I land in New York. His details will be with you this evening,' said Eyal.

Dhariwal's next call was to Sniper. 'Are you ready?' he asked.

'Absolutely,' said Sniper, who had arrived in Delhi the previous night as per Dhariwal's request.

'I'll meet you at our usual spot in thirty minutes,' said Dhariwal.

The usual spot Dhariwal was referring to was his mother's house in Janakpuri. In their younger years, Sniper and Dhariwal used to spend time together in the house, eating Dhariwal's mother's home-cooked food. After her death, Dhariwal had converted it into a safe house for the Panther's Ghosts.

Thirty minutes later, Sniper met Dhariwal. 'What's the plan? Is Gef my contact for this mission?' asked Sniper.

'No. I've told Gef to stay out of this, Arvind. Apparently he is being watched. He may even go away to Greece for some time, till the air clears.'

'So I make it to the rendezvous point on my own?' asked Sniper.

'No. Safi Doha will pick you up and take you to his home. He has rented a service apartment for three months.'

'He's in Albania?'

'For the time being, on a business visa. As for your travel documents...' Dhariwal handed him an envelope.

'And my cover this time is?'

'Dr Anil Verma, a psychologist who holds a master's in trauma treatment. You're also a certified trauma surgeon—a unique specialisation that focuses on the treatment and care of injuries, often life-threatening, that are caused by impact forces. You're pursuing a PhD on the subject, and you're required to intern at a reputed hospital and work on a specific case for three months. You've been sponsored by billionaire industrialist and leader of the opposition, Hector Dekovi, as part of an exchange programme with Tirana Medical Association, of which Hector is a director. You have a recommendation letter from Hector to the executive director of Tirana District Hospital, Dr Agnus Brovina. She's been told that you're keen on working with an acute trauma patient: trauma that results from a single stressful or dangerous event.'

'And who is this acute trauma patient?'

'Raj Pratap Rana.'

'What acute trauma is he in?' Sniper asked, alarmed.

'He isn't right now, but he will be by the day after tomorrow.'

'What are you going to do with him?' Sniper's voice was getting louder.

'Arvind, if I had any other way to get him out of prison, I would have done it, but he's in Burrel, and it's near impossible to extract him from there. The only way he can get out is if he is in an acute trauma state and needs immediate hospitalisation,' said Dhariwal.

'And how exactly are you going to put him in this state?' asked Sniper.

'The only way out is if he's critically injured.'

'And who the hell is going to inflict this critical injury on Raj?'

'Gef's associate Yuri Pinari, who is still a prisoner in Burrel. If Gef gives him the green light, he'll do what's needed.'

'You just said you told Gef not to get involved.'

'He won't be involved—not directly. Yuri will.'

'No. No way. What if the guys in Burrel don't shift him to the hospital? What if he dies?' countered Sniper.

'This is the only way ahead, Arvind.' Before Sniper could say anything, Dhariwal added, 'Even Gef seconds this. According to Yuri, Raj's mental health already seems unstable. I believe he keeps mumbling to himself. The doctor suspects it's an acute case of PTSD. If we don't get him out fast, that place will drive him completely insane.'

'No. There must be another way out. There *has* to be another way out,' said Sniper. His voice trembled with emotion.

'This is the way out. And you need to be strong,' said Dhariwal, holding Sniper by the shoulders.

The weight of the situation pressed down on Sniper. Although it upset him, he could see that Dhariwal was right.

With a heavy heart, he nodded in agreement and made his way out.

'All the best, Arvind,' Dhariwal called after him.

Sniper did not even bother to respond; he closed the door behind him.

Moments later, Dhariwal called Gef Bajrami. 'It's a go. Tell Yuri Pinari if Raj dies, I will kill him personally.'

'Yuri will manage it,' said Gef, and hung up.

13

IT WAS 6 P.M. ON 5 JUNE 2020. Sniper had just been picked up by Safi Doha from Tirana International Airport, and they were on their way to Safi's apartment, when Dhariwal called. 'Yuri will do the job soon. I'm hoping Raj will be shifted to Tirana District Hospital tonight. Once Raj is admitted, Safi will leak the news to the press confidentially. The matter for printing is already prepared and with him. It will reach the editors tomorrow morning. This will add to the pressure, and they'll be forced to move Raj out of the hospital. Once they do that, we'll make our plans. So it's safe for you to meet Dr Agnus Brovina on the 7th.'

Meanwhile, 60 miles from Safi's apartment, Yuri prepared himself for the assault. Since being diagnosed with PTSD, Raj had been isolated in a solitary cell. This having taken place as soon as Raj entered the prison, Yuri had no clue what Raj looked like. All he knew was that Raj was allowed out of his cell for only an hour, at 7.30 p.m., after the more high-risk inmates had gone back to their cells. Given Yuri's prolonged incarceration at Burrel, his unusual request to be outside late raised no eyebrows.

At 7.30 sharp, Yuri saw an Indian prisoner being brought out by two guards and made to sit in the open courtyard with the low risk prisoners. He slowly walked up to him, sitting down beside him. Murmuring to himself, Raj was sketching something on an A3 sheet of paper with a pencil. It was a drawing of the Presidential Palace, its grand interiors brimming with people in what looked like a banquet hall. There were cars, soldiers and lifeless bodies outside the palace.

The guards were engrossed in conversation. Yuri took the opportunity to lean towards Raj, snatch the pencil and stab Raj on the right of his stomach, making sure it was only a flesh wound. When a shocked Raj turned around to look at his assailant, Yuri landed a powerful blow to his temple, then hurled him into the barbed-wire fence separating the courtyard from the cell blocks. Raj slid down to the concrete. Yuri spat on him. 'Bloody Indian spy.'

The other prisoners stopped what they were doing, their attention captured by the commotion. While one set of guards grabbed Yuri and dragged him away, the others rushed to Raj's side. He lay motionless, blood pouring from his ear and stomach. His eyes had rolled back, his mouth agape. The guards shook him, but he did not respond. Alarmed, they swiftly rushed him to the prison clinic.

The doctor took one look at Raj and said, 'This man is critically injured.'

Khabib Zane, who had been alerted to the incident, rushed in. 'Will he live?'

'I think he is haemorrhaging, which is why he's bleeding from the ear. Rush him to Tirana District Hospital immediately. Otherwise, he's not going to make it,' said the doctor.

An anxious Khabib ordered an immediate transfer to Tirana District Hospital. He called the executive director of the hospital, Dr Agnus Brovina. 'Doctor, whatever it takes, please make sure he lives. If anything happens to him, General Hoxha will kill me.'

'What happened?' asked Dr Brovina.

'One of our prisoners, Yuri, suddenly turned into a nationalist and decided to attack this Indian prisoner because he is a spy. Yuri stabbed Raj in the stomach with a pencil and hit him so hard on the temple that he is haemorrhaging and bleeding from the ear,' said Khabib.

'I'll see what I can do. We'll rush him to the ICU on arrival and treat him as best as we can, Zane,' said Dr Brovina.

'Thank you. One more thing, doctor. Under no circumstances should anyone have access to Raj. Particularly the press. This has to remain highly confidential,' said Khabib.

'In that case, once he's out of the ICU, you'll need to move him somewhere else for the rest of his treatment. Reporters are always hovering around here for news,' said Dr Brovina.

'I'll work something out then,' said Khabib.

Forty minutes later, the ambulance carrying Raj arrived at Tirana District Hospital. He was whisked away to the ICU, where Dr Agnus Brovina examined him and recommended some immediate treatment. The rest would be decided based on the results from the MRI and the X-rays. By the time she left the hospital, it was 10 p.m.

An hour later, Gef called Sniper and said, 'Your boy made it. He's in the ICU in Tirana District Hospital. Dr Agnus Brovina is in charge. Apparently, he's stable and responding to the medication. All his tests have been completed and the reports are awaited.'

A relieved Sniper passed on the message to Dhariwal, who in turn informed DD. 'Good job. So he's out of Burrel. Now to get him back home,' said DD.

'Working on it, sir. I've arranged for all the papers for Arvind. He will be meeting Dr Brovina. I am given to understand she is susceptible to bribes. I'm hoping Arvind will do the job,' replied Dhariwal.

◎∭∽

It was 9 a.m. on 6 June 2020, and the director of Burrel Prison, Khabib Zane, wasn't having a great day. Worry knitted his brows together as he stood before General Beqir, who was reading the morning newspaper. Despite all efforts to keep the incident confidential, the paper blared the news about Raj.

'Attack on Indian in Burrel Challenges NSA's Allegations of Espionage' the headline read. 'Tirana's Human Rights Watch is expressing concerns over last night's incident in Burrel, where alleged Indian spy Raj Pratap Rana was attacked by his fellow inmates. Rana was jailed without a trial and kept in solitary confinement without any indication of violent behaviour. Sources from within the facility indicate that Rana was already suffering from PTSD on arrival, suggesting he endured mistreatment prior to his imprisonment. It is also being said that, under President Tefik Metta's directives, a coerced confession was extracted from Rana by General Beqir Hoxha and that the attack in Burrel was meant to silence Rana. Currently, Rana is in Tirana District Hospital's ICU undergoing treatment for haemorrhage. Incidents like this raise concerns about Albania's drift towards authoritarianism, casting President Tefik Metta in the role of not just a leader, but also judge and executioner. The presidential office has not issued a formal report at the time this report went to press.'

Beqir slammed the paper down. 'Lie after lie after lie!' he roared. 'The press is cooking up stories as usual. How the hell did they get wind of this, anyway?'

'Sir, the hospital must have leaked it. I had cautioned the executive director personally, yet it got out,' said Zane.

'Now they're even questioning the validity of the charges against the Indian. I'll be the subject of a media trial. The opposition has already started saying that Rana is an innocent man and that I put him in prison purely to get the NSA role. All the good PR I received has been washed away.'

Khabib hesitated, then drummed up the courage to ask, 'I understand, sir, but what would you like me to do?'

Beqir was about to respond, when his phone rang. It was Robert. He walked away to take the call.

'You've screwed it up, General. Was there any need to assault the guy? I told you not to let things escalate with him,' said Robert.

'Not my fault. Some joker in the prison did it. What's done is done. Now tell me—what should I do?' the General asked.

'Don't react. Move the Indian to a safe place where the press has no access. Then inform the press that the attack was carried out by a random rogue prisoner. Tell them you're concerned for the Indian's well-being, so you are moving him to an undisclosed safe location with medical facilities and a dedicated doctor. Tell them you've acted against the perpetrator as well,' said Robert.

'I'll move him to the Acapulco Grande after midnight without anyone's knowledge, when the media is gone. It's the family hotel so we'll make sure nobody gets to him. Also, I'll ensure Yuri spends another lifetime in solitary,' said Beqir.

'Good. Treat the Indian well and keep him out of everyone's sight. Once he is better, you can send him back to Burrel if you want. Do everything discreetly, please, for God's sake,' said Robert, before hanging up.

General Beqir called and briefed Dr Brovina on relocating Raj. 'Arrange a doctor who can stay with him 24x7,' instructed Beqir.

Dr Agnus Brovina stood at just five feet and had a full-bodied figure and a motherly disposition. She was known for always being jovial, but the last twenty-four hours had taken a toll on her, and now, after this last call, her disdain for General Beqir Hoxha had grown. Despite being the executive director of a government hospital, she was hardly treated like a doctor by most politicians, but General Beqir in particular treated her like a servant, always ordering her around. She had half a mind to tell him that she had no doctor to spare, but then she realised that if she did not arrange for a private doctor for Raj quickly, Beqir would force her to cancel her long overdue leave and ask her to do it herself. To start with she put a plan in place to move Raj discreetly out of the hospital and into the hotel. Instead of an ambulance, she decided when the time came, she would use her black tinted personal SUV to transfer him.

Then she rang her husband, and started venting, 'That screwed-up General wants me to find a private doctor for that Indian prisoner who got beat up in Burrel. If I don't the jerk will ensure my leave is cancelled till I find one.'

'Then assign someone,' said her husband.

'I would if I had someone to spare. I'm already running short of doctors for the shift. If I send someone to look after the Indian, I'll have to cancel my leave and go back on duty.'

Dr Brovina's husband was the owner of a small book shop and had no clue about hospitals and the politics that surround them. But he had a keen business sense. 'Hire a doctor from one of the private hospitals and send them to look after this Indian patient,' he told her.

'These private doctors are expensive,' she said.

'Why are you bothered about that?' said her husband. 'Send the bill to the director of Burrel Prison.'

14

IT WAS 9 A.M. ON 7 JUNE 2020. Dr Brovina had had a restless night as she had still not found a doctor for Raj. No one wanted to take the risk of treating a convict, who according to the jail doctor had been haemorrhaging. The private doctors were worried that if the convict dies under their watch, Beqir would punish them. Though Dr Brovina tried her level best to explain to them that the convict was fine and there was no haemorrhage, they just did not want to be associated with Raj. Especially if they had to live with the convict till he recuperated. Unable to get anyone, she had no choice but to continue keeping him in the ICU. By now, all his reports had arrived, and they revealed no critical concerns. The bleeding from the ear was the result of a burst artery, likely due to the blow to the head. A complete ICU had already been created in room 1306 at the Acapulco Grande, and all that was needed was a doctor, which was now becoming a headache for Dr Agnus Brovina.

It was this state of mind that made her react sharply to her favourite assistant, Olgheta, when she walked into the room the next morning. 'What is it?' she snapped.

Olgheta was taken aback by her boss's reaction, but she responded calmly, 'There is a doctor waiting to see you.'

'I don't have any meetings scheduled, though. Who is this?' said Dr Brovina.

'Dr Anil Verma, a trauma surgeon from India. He doesn't have an appointment.'

'Tell him I can't meet anyone today.'

Olgheta paused before adding, 'Just so you know, he is carrying a reference letter from Hector Dekovi.'

Dr Brovina jumped out of her seat. 'Hold on, hold on. Please send him in.' Hector was on the board of the Hospital, and if he found out that she had not even met his reference, she would have another issue to handle.

Olgheta returned with an elderly man. He stood at an imposing six feet and fixed his piercing grey eyes on Dr Brovina. His grey beard matched his grey hair. The man smiled and extended his hand to her. 'Dr Anil Verma from India. Mr Dekovi said you are the boss here and if you agree I can have an internship.' He handed over a letter to her.

The compliment worked. To hear from a doctor that Hector Dekovi had spoken so highly of her was indeed a big thing for Dr. Brovina. She smiled back, asked him to sit down and opened the letter

The letter read: 'Dr Anil Verma is a trusted associate of mine. He seeks a voluntary internship at Tirana District Hospital for three months, during which he would like to focus exclusively on and tend to a trauma patient. I would be grateful if you could accommodate him without delay. He is willing to pay a fee to the hospital; for the period of the internship. I have discussed the plausible fee, but please feel free to negotiate and arrive at a fee that is mutually acceptable. Given that this is part of an exchange programme, his feedback on our hospitality and our hospital will be crucial in determining how our doctors are welcomed in India. Sincerely, Hector Dekovi.'

Dr Agnus Brovina looked at Sniper carefully for a few seconds and frowned a little. Was it all aligning a little too perfectly or was it some divine intervention? Sniper could see the hesitation and a flicker of doubt in her mind so he quickly stepped in.

'There is no compulsion at all. If it is not possible, I will try at the Universal Hospital in Tirana, though Mr Dekovi said that this hospital is the most reputed and you are the best in the business.'

That did the trick. Dr Brovina looked at Sniper lovingly for a few seconds. Christmas had come early for her. Then she said deferentially, 'I'm extremely sorry to have kept you waiting, Dr Verma. I'm normally not like this, but of late, the pressure has been so much that I find myself slipping in my manners. Please forgive any discourtesy.'

'Happens to the best of us, doctor,' said Sniper gently. 'To explain further, as the letter in your hand indicates, I'm Dr Anil Verma. I hold a master's in trauma treatment and a certification as a trauma surgeon from the Washington State Medical Association. My thesis for my PhD revolves around the impact of trauma on long-term memory. The chance to intern at a reputable hospital and to closely monitor a trauma patient for three months is essential for my study. Hector Dekovi, who is a close friend, recommended you and this hospital.'

Dr Brovina's eyes brightened further. 'You're in luck, Dr Verma. We have a recent patient who has been diagnosed with acute trauma and he requires personal attention. He is an Indian prisoner from Burrel, and he will be shifted to a room in the hotel Acapulco Grande to avoid media attention. The room has been outfitted as an ICU. If you want, I could assign you to this patient, but you will have to stay with him in the hotel.'

'Perfect. As he's Indian, I can converse with him in Hindi, which may be easier for my diagnosis.'

Just then, Olgheta entered the room and handed Sniper an envelope. 'It's as you had mentioned, Dr Verma. I counted it,' she said.

With a gracious nod, Sniper took the envelope from her and handed it to Dr Brovina. 'Mr Dekovi mentioned a requisite payment. He didn't give me specifics, but hinted that it would be somewhere north of 45 thousand dollars.'

Dr Agnus Brovina almost fell out of her chair. That was more than her annual salary. As expected, the money did the trick. If there were any remnants of doubt in her mind, they melted away, replaced by a bright smile. 'Oh! That's so generous of Hector. Saves me the trouble of explaining it all.' She opened her desk drawer to store the envelope.

'Then should I consider the internship confirmed, Dr Brovina?' asked Sniper.

'Absolutely. I will issue the letter of appointment right away.' She looked at Olgheta and said, 'Ensure that all the documentation is complete and have Dr Verma's 360-day, 24x7 access card ready, please. He will need to be with the patient round-the-clock and should not be stopped by anyone at any time. Issue him a pass for his car too. And see to it that he's allocated the room adjacent to the patient's.'

Also, please hand over all of the patient's belongings and his drawings to the doctor so he can study them as well.' Dr Brovina looked at Sniper and said, 'When he was brought to the hospital, we found some A3 sheets with weird drawings in his pant pocket. It may help you understand his state of mind.'

She pushed two books of her letterhead towards Sniper and said, 'You can use my letterhead to prescribe medicines to the patient, Dr Verma. Just make sure you write your name and ID number below your signature. By tomorrow morning, everything you need will be ready. And you're not answerable to anyone but me.'

Sniper thanked her and got up to leave. As if it were an afterthought, he asked, 'What did you say the patient's name is?'

'Rana. Raj Pratap Rana.'

As soon as Sniper left, Dr Brovina said to Olgheta, 'Send a large bouquet of flowers to Hector Dekovi with a thank you card from me right away. And please inform Dr Juarez that I will be taking my scheduled leave for the next two weeks, starting tomorrow.'

Having dispatched her assistant, Dr Brovina dialled her husband. Her voice was laden with affection as she said, 'Honey, get us an early morning flight to Paris the day after tomorrow, and confirm the booking at the Alpine Cottages for ten days. I found the private doctor; he's starting tomorrow.'

Outside the hospital, Sniper got into the passenger seat of a black Mercedes-Benz E-Class sedan that Safi Doha had arranged. Turning to Safi, who was at the wheel, he said,

'Time to give Dhariwal an update.' Safi dialled and put the phone on speaker. 'We're all set,' said Sniper. 'Tomorrow onwards, Raj is in my care. I'll evaluate his condition and then we can finalise the extraction date. Please thank Hector for all his help.'

'Did you get to see him in the hospital? Is he fine?' asked Dhariwal.

'Dr Brovina said he was fine and out of danger, Raj is being shifted to a hotel, the Acapulco Grande, tomorrow. I'll update you when I have more details.' Sniper disconnected and turned back to Safi. 'Thank you for organising all this, buddy. Let's go home.'

'Don't thank me. All I'm doing is executing. Gef arranged for the car, the house, your papers as Dr Anil Verma and the money for Dr Brovina. Dhariwal got Hector to give us the recommendation letter,' said Safi.

'Everyone's playing a pivotal role here. I'll thank each one personally when I meet them. To be honest, I was worried she would ask to see my credentials and keep a copy of it. But it looked as though she was in a hurry, so escaped the scrutiny,' said Sniper.

'Back home, my father used to say, "If the intent is noble, the experience is divine,"' said Safi.

'I guess he was right. There is nothing more noble than getting Raj and Geeta out of this place,' said Sniper looking out of the window. Somehow he was suddenly reminded of his own extraction from the Quetta prison many years ago.

15

IT WAS NOON ON 8 JUNE 2020. The receptionist at Acapulco Grande handed over the keys to Sniper and said, 'Dr Verma, you have room 1307, and your patient is in room 1306.'

Sniper thanked her and took the elevator to the thirteenth floor. Instead of going to his room first, he went straight to Raj's, where a nurse was waiting to brief him.

'He is under sedation as he was agitated and restless last night. All his medications are here and so is the prescription. I've been giving him his medicines on time and making sure he eats and rests well. He keeps mumbling very often to himself but that is a symptom, it will take time for him to become calm. I'm handing him over to you now, Dr Verma,' the nurse said. She handed over a file and walked out of the door.

Sniper gingerly sat next to Raj on the bed, examining the injuries that marred his face: bruises, a gashed ear, a particularly dark bruise on the temple, indicating blood clotting. Raj did not show any recognition, but the moment Sniper held his hand, Raj's fingers curled around his tightly. A lump formed in Sniper's throat and his eyes welled up. 'I'm here, son. I'm here,' he whispered. When Raj's hand relaxed, Sniper walked over to his room. He wanted to inspect the room thoroughly but was worried that there could be cameras and seeing him inspect the room on arrival would have raised suspicions. He decided to inspect the room later.

The receptionist had given him a spare key for 1306 so he could come and go without disturbing Raj. And with his hospital access card, he could enter the hospital whenever he had to pick up medicines.

He changed into shorts and a T-shirt and then retrieved a beer from the minifridge and looked out at the city of Tirana from his window.

The Acapulco Grande was a rectangular building with a cold façade. It was anchored in the centre of the city and was about 18 kilometres from Tirana International Airport, or, as the locals called it, Rinas International Airport. He could see the National Art Gallery about 2 kilometres to the left of the hotel, and to the right was Tirana Ring Centre, the main shopping complex. All the hotel's rooms faced the famous Grand Park, a 289-hectare public park. It was known for its artificial lake and was a 7 minute drive from Saint Procopius Church. Among the lush sea of trees was the Presidential Palace, now called the Palace of Brigades.

After downing the beer, Sniper decided to take a tour of the hotel. It boasted three upscale international restaurants on the lobby level and a jazz bar on the rooftop. A spa and the Gold Coast Gym were on the mezzanine floor, while the exclusive Crystal Gaze Club faced the park and was accessible from both within and outside the hotel. An airport shuttle ran every hour between the hotel and the airport, irrespective of whether there were guests coming or going. The thirteenth foor was a special floor as most hotels do not have one. It was built on special instructions of Misha as it had only two rooms and the rest of the area was left as a massive lounge for Misha to entertain his mafia friends. Though reluctant to hand over his room to Beqir's patient, he had to agree as the orders had come from Tefik who was already irritated with Beqir's mess.

After an hour of touring the hotel, Sniper used the key card for 1306 to enter Raj's room. A creaking of the wooden floor accompanied his steps. So he tiptoed into the room as Raj was fast asleep. He sat on the bed beside Raj and scanned the room. His eyes travelled from the flat-screen smart TV to the minibar facing the bed. Nothing seemed out of place. He turned his attention to the coffee maker sitting next to a bowl of fruit on a shelf near the window to the right of the room. Everything was untouched. The leftmost corner had a black armchair and a narrow diwan opposite it. He scanned the ceiling, AC vents and the pictures on the wall to see if there were any signs of a camera, but found nothing. And Raj's hospital bed was in the middle of the room. He took a chance and bent close to Raj's ear and whispered, 'Raj, it's me, Sniper. I'm here to take care of you.'

There was a slight flicker of the eyelids before Raj opened his eyes. Sniper could see that there was still no recognition in Raj's eyes and realised that the beatings had affected his memory.

Sniper smiled at Raj and tried a new approach. 'Hi, I'm Dr Anil Verma. I'll be treating you, Mr Rana.'

Raj smiled weakly at Sniper and whispered, 'It's good to see you, Dr Verma.' Then his eyes darted, seemingly searching for someone. 'Where is my wife, Geeta?' he asked, the panic rising in his voice.

'She's safe and resting at home, Mr Rana. You also need to rest.' Sniper patted Raj's hand. He wasn't surprised that Raj remembered Geeta. Trauma does affect the memory, but some things remain indelible.

Raj gazed at Sniper for a while, smiling, and then said, 'Silence is the beginning of revenge.'

Sniper hadn't been expecting a response like that. 'What do you mean?'

Raj didn't answer. Instead, he closed his eyes, his breathing becoming heavy.

Perplexed, Sniper mulled over his friend's words for a while. Eventually, he got up and quietly walked out of the room.

Later, from his own room, Sniper called Dhariwal on his Thuraya. 'He's safe and with me. He's in room 1306. I'm in 1307.'

'How is he?' asked Dhariwal.

'His face has taken a toll, but he'll recover quickly. We spoke today. He asked about Geeta, but he didn't recognise me. When I was about to leave, he said something that's stayed with me. I don't know what to make of it, though.'

'What did he say?' asked Dhariwal.

' "Silence is the beginning of revenge." When I asked him what he meant, he closed his eyes and fell asleep.'

'I think he's exhibiting tangentiality. Acute trauma sometimes leads to tangentiality, where a person says things that are irrelevant to the moment but are related to something from their past. It happens when a person is experiencing high anxiety and is most commonly seen in schizophrenics. I think the beatings he received in Lin and

Burrel must be causing this. We need to get him back fast before he goes from bad to worse. I spoke to Eyal—he said to contact his man on the ground for help and assistance in the extraction. A guy called Caleb Hulata. I've sent you his details. He'll meet you at the café in the National Art Gallery. It's close to your hotel,' said Dhariwal.

After the call, Sniper took a shower, ate some Tavë kosi a baked dish of lamb, rice, yogurt, and eggs, which was the national dish of Albania. He then left the hotel to meet Caleb Hulata. Since there was enough time and the weather was good, Sniper decided to walk the 2 kilometres to the café. On entering, the first thing he did was look at his watch—it was 7.30 p.m. Then he looked around for Caleb and found him sitting in a dimly lit corner on the far left. Sniper walked up to him, extended his right hand and said, 'Nice to meet you, Caleb. Dr Anil Verma.'

Caleb was a barrel-chested man of five feet and seven inches. He had jet-black hair and a prominent nose. A thick moustache curled over his full lips. Caleb smiled and motioned for Sniper to take a seat. He shook Sniper's hand and said, 'Nice to meet you too, Dr Verma, please take a seat.'

Once they were seated and the waiter had taken their order, Caleb said, 'I am aware of your patient, Mr Rana, in 1306 at the Acapulco Grande, Dr Verma. I also know you're in 1307 and that you aren't, in fact, a doctor, but an agent from RAW. Eyal told me to help you with his extraction. What's your current strategy?'

Sniper liked people who were direct, to the point and transparent in their communication. He already had a favourable opinion of Caleb. 'Looks like Eyal briefed you well. Yes, we need your help with the extraction.'

'We? As per Eyal this mission was assigned to a single RAW agent, and that is you,' said Caleb.

'Yes, it was initially. But having realised the magnitude of the operation, I've enlisted a few close acquaintances—ex-RAW agents. One of them is already here. Officially, though, I'm operating solo,' Sniper clarified.

'I agree. This is not a one man job. In that case, I may have a mutually beneficial proposal for you, Dr Verma,' said Caleb, who had faced many such instances where the agency allows only one person but then you have to enlist your own resources to help you out at the local level when you see the magnitude of the job. If you go back to the agency and ask for more people, they say they don't have that many resources.

Sniper leaned back in his seat and smiled. 'Well then, let's hear it.'

'You see, my team and I have been here for the last year for a single mission: eliminate the fifteen kryes and Misha Perci, dismantle the drug cartel in Albania entirely and return home.'

'Why?' asked Sniper.

'Misha Perci is Tefik's brother-in-law, giving him considerable power in Albania. The fifteen kryes handle the drug supply, passing it on to Misha, who then distributes it across the globe. One of the major source of the narcotics for Misha is Iran, a sanctioned country. The vast revenue from this drug trade is used by Iran to fund the manufacture of their WMDs. As you know, the Iranian WMDs are intended for use against Israel. While we've made efforts to neutralise these WMDs in Iran, it's a cyclical process—they rebuild what we destroy. We now know the source of the money. If we stem that, Iran will not be able to rebuild the WMDs, at least for a while, by which time we will find a way to cut off the root in Iran as well.'

'We're familiar with Misha Perci and his drug distribution network,' said Sniper. 'India is also a victim of his trade. His distribution network is set up in Nigeria and is run through a logistics company owned by the Sandesars. Ever since Nitin Sandesar was implicated in the cybercrime incident against America, he has gone underground. So Misha is running the logistics piece himself. If you want to dismantle everything, then you not only need to eliminate the fifteen kryes and Misha, but you also have to destroy the entire distribution network set up in Nigeria.'

Caleb nodded, impressed.

'And I presume you're asking me to help you eliminate the kryes and Misha, and dismantle the Nigerian set-up,' said Sniper.

'Almost. We'll manage the Nigerian set-up. You help us take down the fifteen kryes and Misha, and you will have automatically helped yourself too.'

'How so?'

'With Misha and the kryes gone, Tefik will be a sitting duck for the opposition. They will pass a no-confidence motion and throw him out of power in less than twenty-four hours. The subsequent chaos is going to help us. Before a new regime consolidates power, you can move your man out. I will have the aircraft ready to transport you and your guy to Greece.'

'You're forgetting General Beqir Hoxha in all this,' said Sniper.

'What about him?' asked Caleb.

'He'll likely try and seize control, given he has the CIA's support.'

Caleb's expression grew concerned. 'We hadn't considered that,' he admitted.

Sniper mused for a moment, then looked at Caleb and said, 'The plan may still work out with a few changes.'

'Then let's flesh it out. Let's meet at my place tomorrow at 5 p.m. Though one of my team members will pick you up, I will still give you the address just in case something goes wrong and you have to make it on your own,' said Caleb as he wrote down his address on a napkin and handed it to Sniper.

'I'll see you tomorrow,' said Sniper. 'In the meantime, I'll brief my people in India, see if they're aligned too.'

⊙∰~

After returning from the café, Sniper visited Raj. He was awake and watching the news when Sniper entered the room. Without interrupting him, Sniper sat in the armchair and watched the news with him. The anchor was talking about an upcoming gala at the Palace of Brigades in honour of President Tefik and his wife as they intended to celebrate their platinum wedding anniversary with grandeur at the palace.

After a while, Sniper gave Raj his medicines. 'Feeling any better now?'

Raj had his medicines quietly and then said, 'The past, the present and the future ... everything—everyone—is connected.'

Once again, Sniper had no idea what to make of Raj's words So he shrugged his shoulders and said, 'All right then, buddy, shall we eat dinner?'

Raj's eyes lit up at that. Sniper pulled out two large portions of ferges, a stew made of tomato sauce, cottage cheese, green peppers and garlic, which was very filling but at the same time light on the stomach. He had bought it on the way back from the café. He set the stews on the table. Then he helped Raj to a chair and the two ate in comfortable silence. Once they finished, Sniper helped Raj back into bed, pulling the sheets up to Raj's chin as the room was cold.

That was when he noticed a few sheets of paper sticking out from under Raj's pillow. He remembered Dr Brovina's conversations with him on the drawings, so he gently pulled them free and laid them out near the window. Raj was already drifting off to sleep. The first sheet displayed numbers scattered among building illustrations with corresponding letters. Recognising the SPG codes, Sniper deduced that the letters likely represented building names, and the numbers denoted the distances between them. The second sheet had a sketch of a lake, large barracks next to it and an even bigger building with towers looming on either side.

On the third sheet, he found a pencil sketch of a palace, its expansive gardens buzzing with figures congregated in what appeared to be a banquet hall. Amidst the festivity, in stark contrast, was a man lying dead in one of the rooms close to the hall. There was also a barrack-like structure behind the palace with a few dead bodies housed in it. An underground passage connected this barrack to a distant chapel, labelled 'Blloku'. Nearby was a hospital, with a man and woman positioned beside a car.

Not able to make sense of the pictures, Sniper concluded that these could be memories from Raj's past, from when he was studying in Albania. He had no explanation for the dead bodies, though. Perhaps they were depictions of unfulfilled revenge, Sniper guessed. He took photos of the sketches and forwarded them to Dhariwal with a text message: *'He's been sketching these in the room. I think, the palace drawings were done in Burrel because I remember Dr Brovina telling me about them and they look much older than the other drawings.'* Later, he also called Dhariwal and told him about his conversation with Caleb.

As they were about to wrap up the call, a message flashed across Sniper's screen.

'General Beqir Hoxha would like to meet you at Beqir Mansion in Lin at 8 a.m. for breakfast. Your attendance is expected. Regards, Adia Markova, Secretary to the NSA, Albania.'

Sniper read out the message to Dhariwal. 'Let me see what the ass wants.'

'I've observed sociopaths long enough to know how their minds work. I think, he wants to meet and assess you. He'll want to check if you're a doctor or a plant of the Human Rights department. He'll ask you specific questions to glean as much as he can,' said Dhariwal.

'And?' asked Sniper.

'If he is insecure, he will threaten you subtly. He'll parade Geeta in front of you. It will be a message to you that he holds all the aces, in case you're a Human Rights representative.'

'Hmm ... I'm looking at this as an opportunity. I hope I get to see Geeta. I'm more interested in checking how she is than in meeting the General,' said Sniper.

'I hope she's all right,' said Dhariwal, unable to keep the concern from his voice.

16

IT WAS 5 A.M. ON 9 JUNE 2020. Sniper answered the knock on his hotel room door to find a tall man in his mid-forties standing outside his room. He had the air of a soldier—close-cropped hair, well-polished shoes—but the knife scar that ran from above his left eyebrow all the way down to his cheek made Sniper wonder if he had a rougher history.

'Good morning,' said Sniper.

The man with the scar did not bother with pleasantries. 'The General sent me. Let us go.' Then he turned and walked towards the lift. Sniper was ready, so he closed the door behind him and followed.

There was no conversation throughout the three-hour journey. Finally, at 8 a.m., the car pulled up to the porch of a palatial house. Adia Markova awaited them. 'Welcome to Beqir Mansion, Dr Verma,' she said warmly, and escorted him to a waiting area. 'Please be seated. The NSA will meet you in ten minutes,' she said before leaving.

Exactly ten minutes later, Adia reappeared and escorted Sniper to General Beqir Hoxha's office. The moment Sniper stepped into the office, Beqir got up from his chair, which was behind a huge wooden table, and walked up to Sniper with a big smile, his right hand outstretched. The room was dimly lit, heavy curtains blocking out the sunlight. The rich aroma of tobacco hung in the air.

'How are you, Dr Verma? Nice to meet you. Please sit.' Ensuring Sniper's comfort, the General pressed a discreet buzzer. In response, Adia entered, her presence almost ghost-like on the plush flooring.

'Yes, General?' she asked softly.

'We'll have our breakfast right here. Please inform the chef,' he said.

After informing the chef, as Adia lay the wooden centre table with place settings for breakfast, the General turned to Sniper.

'So, you're a trauma surgeon, Dr Verma,' said Beqir.

'That's right,' said Sniper.

'How much do you know about trauma, doctor?' asked Beqir with a smile on his face.

'Enough.'

The abrupt response took the General by surprise. He looked at Sniper from head to toe. 'Adia,' he said suddenly, 'please ask Mrs Geeta Rana to join us for breakfast.'

'Mrs Rana has been feeling unwell since yesterday. I think she may still be in bed,' Adia said politely.

'Nothing better than a hearty breakfast to cure any illness, isn't it, doctor?' Beqir said. Sniper just nodded. Beqir turned to Adia and said in a harsh tone, 'Tell her I'm expecting her. Now.'

Sniper recollected what Dhariwal had said about Beqir wanting to give him a message. He smiled at Beqir, then looked at Adia and said, 'I think the General is right. A short walk, some fresh air and a good breakfast is all you need. Tell her Dr Verma would like to see her.'

As Adia left, a butler walked in with the breakfast trolley. General Beqir observed him for a while and then turned to Sniper. 'So, Dr Verma. What is your thesis all about?'

'The impact of trauma on long-term memory.' Sniper was deliberately keeping his answers short, and it was having an effect on the General. He was not used to people treating him this way.

'How did you get the internship?' asked Beqir.

'Dr Hector Dekovi arranged it for me.'

'How?'

'He's the chairman of the board of Tirana District Hospital, so he approved the exchange programme,' replied Sniper, wolfing down his breakfast as the General watched in disgust. Beqir hadn't even touched his food.

'What exchange programme?'

'The WHO-sponsored exchange programme with India.'

'When was this decided?'

'Three years ago, when he came for the global psychology seminar hosted by India.'

'Why now? Why not before?'

'President Tefik Metta is anti-India and pro-China. He did not move on it for the last three years he's been in power. Now the WHO has asked what the reason is for the delay.' This hit the way it was supposed to.

'Yes, my President is pro-China. But not all of us are. Hector surely isn't.' Beqir had somehow simmered down slightly. He saw that Sniper had finished his breakfast, so he pushed his plate away too and asked for a coffee refill.

'Is Dr Agnus Brovina helping you?' Beqir asked.

'I hope so. Right now, she's on her annual leave. But she

has ensured I have access to other doctors, hospital facilities and the patient's medicines.'

'Do you know this patient of yours is a spy?' asked Beqir as he put down his coffee mug.

Sniper picked up his coffee mug, took a sip and answered, 'I don't decide my treatment based on a patient's profession. For us doctors, every human life is equal.'

As the General was about to retort, Adia walked in with Geeta. 'Mrs Rana, sir,' she announced softly as she guided Geeta to the table with Sniper and Beqir.

Sniper smiled at Geeta and reached out to shake her hand, but Beqir quickly intervened and said, 'She does not shake hands with strangers, doctor.'

She looked healthy and like herself at first glance, but a closer look revealed that her eyes were glassy and she was constantly licking her lips. For a moment their eyes locked, and Sniper thought he saw a sign of recognition there, but the glassy look returned in a flash.

The General also noticed Geeta's persistent dry mouth, so he offered her a glass of juice. 'Dr Anil Verma is here to treat your husband,' he said, anticipating some sort of reaction. All he received was a faint smile and a gentle nod from her. When Sniper turned towards Beqir, he could see a look of disgust in his eyes. But when the General caught Sniper's observation, his demeanour immediately changed, and he smiled. 'Dr Verma, I want you to cure Mr Rana. But once he is fully cured, I will have to send him back to Burrel. He has a penalty to serve for espionage, you see.'

'What's wrong with Mrs Rana here?' asked Sniper suddenly, catching the General off guard.

'Nothing. Why do you ask?' Beqir seemed a bit shaken.

Sniper looked at Geeta carefully for a few seconds, leaned forward and fixed his gaze on Beqir. 'She looks drugged.'

'Oh, yes. She's been given Devil's Breath,' Beqir said casually, as though it were perfectly normal to administer such a drug.

Devil's Breath is the street name for the drug burandanga, or what a doctor would call scopolamine. The drug is derived from nightshade plants and is considered among the world's most dangerous. Used as a sort of 'truth serum', it also incapacitates users by essentially ridding them of their free will.

'Why is she on scopolamine?' asked Sniper.

'I like my pets to be docile and subservient to me,' Beqir replied. 'I'm impressed with your grasp on pharmacology, Dr Verma. Perhaps you are a real doctor after all.'

Choosing to remain silent, Sniper simply returned Beqir's look.

Beqir dabbed at his mouth with a napkin. Then he dropped the napkin on the table, stood up abruptly, pressed the buzzer and said loudly, 'Adia, Dr Verma is leaving. Please escort him to his car.' He pulled Geeta up by the arm and walked out of the room with her. Adia quietly materialised again and walked Sniper back to the car.

On the way back, Sniper's thoughts kept going back to Geeta, the look in her eyes haunting him. Once he reached the hotel, he walked into Raj's room and found him watching television again. The anchor was talking about the forthcoming elections in Albania. A graphic in the backdrop showcased previous results juxtaposed against predictions for the coming elections.

Wanting to speak to someone and spit out all the anger inside him, he walked up to Raj and blurted out, 'I met Geeta today, and she's in a bad state. That bastard Beqir has turned her into a vegetable. There's so much Devil's Breath in her that she just follows him around like a lamb.'

Raj continued to watch the news for a few seconds. Then he turned to Sniper and said, 'One thing about them tables … they always turn.'

At first, Sniper thought Raj was talking about Beqir, but he realised that he was referring to the election table on the screen. Sniper shook his head in anger and frustration, pulled out his phone and called Dhariwal. He put the call on speaker and sat down with a bottle of beer.

When Dhariwal answered the call, Sniper began, 'I met Geeta today. Beqir is keeping her on scopolamine. It may have been used to get the truth out of her initially, but now he is using it to control her. She's walking around like a zombie.'

'If she had told him everything, Raj would not be alive. Something tells me she has not confessed anything. I know in the paras they train you to beat the lie detector, but I'm not so sure a person can beat a truth serum,' said Dhariwal.

'I don't know if she confessed or not, but what I do know is that we shouldn't waste any more time and we should extract Geeta along with Raj—ASAP.'

'Did she recognise you?' asked Dhariwal.

Sniper hesitated. 'I'm not sure, but I *think* she did, but it is purely my gut feeling.'

'That's a good sign,' said Dhariwal. 'Tell me more about this Beqir Mansion.'

Sniper explained the layout of the mansion in great detail and included directions to the house. 'There's a lake behind the mansion, so there must be a way to reach it by boat if you come from the other side,' he said.

After completing the call, Sniper and Raj sat down for a quiet lunch. Sniper was halfway through his meal when his Thuraya started buzzing. It was Hector Dekovi. He hit the speaker button and continued eating.

'Good evening, Dr Verma. How's your patient doing?' asked Hector.

'He looks all right and behaves coherently most of the time, but there are bouts of restlessness. His eyes exhibit constant movement, suggesting heightened brain activity, but the rest of him remains calm. The constant mumbling has stopped, but I think he is suffering from tangentiality—he responds to questions with irrelevant idioms and statements.'

Sniper was quick to realise that Hector was speaking to him like a politician talking to a doctor about his patient because he was worried their calls might be tapped, so he put Dekovi's mind to rest. 'The Thuraya phone I use jams calls for outsiders so don't worry and speak freely. Coming back to Raj, he keeps drawing pictures of things he's seen in Albania but adds gore and violence. I think he retains these memories because of his HSAM.'

'What's HSAM?' asked Hector.

'Highly superior autobiographical memory. Raj has had this since childhood,' said Sniper.

'Anything else?'

'His tangentiality seems to have come from acute trauma. He has fitful sleep, marked by constant eyelid movement. These are indicative of PTSD, as per Dr Brovina.'

'What did she say?'

'Though the test reports appear standard, she feels the hippocampus, the part of the brain responsible for memory and emotions, may have been damaged, which is why he is constantly muttering. Now with medication and a change of environment, the muttering has reduced a lot. But he needs proper care, therapy and handholding even after the extraction is completed,' said Sniper.

'Tell me what else do you want me to do to help Raj and Geeta get extracted?' asked Hector.

'I have a meeting with someone at 5 today to discuss an extraction plan, you could join in,' said Sniper.

'I can join the meeting, but then it will have to be held away from the city.'

'Where do you suggest?' asked Sniper.

'We can meet at my friend's place in Elbasan, which is an hour's drive from here,' said Hector.

'Understood. I'll inform my contact,' said Sniper before disconnecting. He quickly called Caleb to adjust the meeting details, then reached out to Safi Doha, brought him up to speed and asked him to join the meeting in Elbasan.

'I'll pick you up and we can go together,' said Safi.

Sniper declined. 'Caleb is arranging for my transport. I'll fetch you en route. He'll join us midway.'

17

IT WAS 8 P.M. ON 9 JUNE 2020 when Safi, Sniper and Caleb walked into the farmhouse of Hector's friend Dr Hussain Mema in Elbasan. The house was in a secluded area surrounded by dense woodland and was an hour's drive from Tirana city. Hector was already there. After a round of introductions, they all sat down to discuss the extraction plan.

'Gentlemen, before we begin, there's something crucial I need to share,' said Sniper. All eyes shifted to him. 'Robert Sullivan was the one who advised Beqir to sacrifice Raj and Geeta and become the NSA of Albania.'

'I know. I heard from Adia,' said Hector.

'How do you know Adia?' asked Safi.

'Adia is from my village. We both belong to the Mërtur tribe, and we're related,' Hector said. 'During the reign of the earlier President, Juan Bosco, it was discovered that the banks of the two Albanian rivers Nikaj and Mërturit had gold deposits, so President Bosco ordered gold panning in the region. Since the police were corrupt, President Bosco instructed the army to protect the riverbanks. General Beqir Hoxha, who was just a colonel then, was put in charge of the protection detail. It was there that he met Adia, a stenographer interning for the project. Attracted to her, he propositioned her, but she refused. Furious, he raped her in his office and threatened to kill her family if she ever opened her mouth. The eighteen-year-old girl was devastated and tried to kill herself, but I found out in time and prevented it from happening. I motivated her to take revenge instead. She agreed and decided to live the rest of her life nurturing one single goal: ruin Beqir Hoxha. As per my plan, I told her to get close to Beqir. Initially she was repulsed by the man but the will to take revenge was so strong that she overcame her dislike and got very close to him. Over time, she convinced him to give her a job. To her luck, he kept her as his personal secretary. As time passed, she won his confidence and trust and started advising him on various issues. Today, if Beqir trusts anyone, it is Adia. She has been my source inside Beqir's coterie for years now, waiting for the moment to arrive so that she can exact her revenge. So, I think we should include her as well,' said Hector.

Sniper addressed Hector. 'I am sure she will be a great asset. One thing we should be clear about is that Beqir enjoys American support. This puts us in a catch 22 situation. If Beqir is neutralised, Misha takes over and between him and Metta they become a strong force to reckon with. If Tefik is neutralised, the US will put Beqir in his place as the President. In both cases, you lose Hector. I got to know to know that you, Adia and Caleb have been planning to overthrow the government for a long time. But let me tell you, if the Americans support Beqir and Tefik falls, the US will put Beqir on the throne, not you.'

'We're aware. Like I said earlier, that's why we've been working confidentially,' said Caleb.

'So what are you suggesting?' asked Safi, who had been listening silently for some time.

'I am given to understand that Misha Perci regularly conducts a monthly meeting with all fifteen kryes—is that correct?' Sniper asked.

'Yes, as per our observations in the past, during the first week of every month,' said Caleb.

'Not any more. According to Adia, the next meeting will not be chaired by Misha. Beqir Hoxha has asked his number two, Joseph Lika, the man who picked you up from your house, to meet Beqir in Lin, to chair the meeting this time,' said Hector.

Caleb was taken aback. 'How come this sudden shift?'

'According to Adia, after becoming the NSA, Beqir wants to control the kryes. Robert Sullivan advised him to do so,' replied Hector.

'Tefik agreed?' asked Sniper.

'Beqir convinced Tefik of a potential conspiracy against him from one of the kryes. Tefik took the bait.'

'This changes our game plan. I should loop in Dhariwal,' said Sniper, pulling out his phone. Once connected, he briefed Dhariwal on their discussions, ensuring everyone was on the same page.

'Do you know the exact date of the next meeting, Hector?' asked Dhariwal.

Hector quickly called Adia and came back with the date: 'Fourth July in a remote village called Hoti, which is three hours from Tirana. General Beqir owns a huge hunting lodge in the forests there,' he said.

'Fourth of July is Independence Day in America,' said Safi.

'Beqir must have chosen the day to curry favour with his American master. He can tell him, "Robert, I've taken control of the kryes on the day of your independence,"' said Caleb sarcastically.

'What are Joseph Lika's credentials?' asked Sniper.

'Lika is the former head of the Albanian special forces, Batalioni i Operacioneve Speciale, or BOS. BOS is the most elite unit of the Albanian Army and is tasked with wartime special operations and peacetime counterterrorism. On orders from General Beqir, Joseph opted for voluntary retirement and is now Beqir's go-to man. If Beqir wants anything done in Albania, Joseph is the man for it. He operates with a group of ten battle-trained mercenaries under him. Beqir, when he was blind drunk, once told me that when given a chance, he'd replace Misha Perci with Joseph,' said Hector.

'So let's hear your plan, Arvind,' said Dhariwal.

'I had planned based on an anticipated series of events, but looks like the strategy will have to be tweaked. Please feel free to step in, folks,' said Sniper, continuing, 'To begin with, we will have to be shrewd like Robert and play Tefik, Misha and Beqir against each other.'

'How do we do that?' asked Caleb.

'We eliminate all the kryes, including Joseph Lika, when they meet at Hoti. But make it look as though Beqir orchestrated the massacre,' replied Sniper.

'But if we kill Lika, Robert will not believe Beqir did it,' said Caleb.

'If Beqir can sacrifice two innocent Indians to become the NSA, he is capable of sacrificing Lika to take control. It should look like Lika, on the instructions of Beqir, eliminated all the kryes and once that was done, Beqir eliminated his only witness, Lika,' replied Sniper.

'Whether Robert believes it or not, Misha Perci will surely believe it, and he will go after Beqir for murdering the kryes,' said Dhariwal, who understood Sniper's plan.

'And my plan is to take out Misha Perci during his fight with Beqir,' said Sniper.

'Assuming Beqir kills Misha, a livid Tefik will then go after Beqir,' added Safi.

'Yes,' Sniper agreed. 'At that juncture, I'll need help from two ex-RAW agents, who have worked with me before on other missions but are retired and work only for me on special assignments I give them. Dhariwal, if you could get them here for me asap, then I could use them to take out Beqir,' said Sniper. To avoid revealing too much about the Ghosts to Hector and Caleb, Sniper masked their identity, referring to them as friends and ex-RAW agents.

'Beqir's assassination will be a body blow for Robert who will then go after Tefik, assuming he did it,' said Safi.

'He may or may not, but without Misha, Beqir and the kryes, there will be utter chaos. Hector here will immediately move in and bring in the no-confidence motion to oust Tefik from power,' said Dhariwal.

'Yes. And in the meantime, we will extract Raj and Geeta,' said Sniper.

'Brilliant,' said Hector, beaming from ear to ear. 'In one move, we will have cleaned the country completely. A new dawn will break in the Albanian skies next month.'

'Great plan if executed to precision,' said Caleb. 'I'll

speak to Eyal and have a small team of Mossad operatives here in a week's time. We will need to do a recce of Hoti and make sure we are there well in advance. If we need to eliminate everyone, then we need to use C4s. We can't have a battle with fifteen kryes and their bodyguards with guns and knives,' said Caleb.

'I agree. What do you need?' asked Sniper.

'I need someone to take care of the logistics for me and my team.'

'I'll handle that,' said Safi.

'And I'll need local support to stay there with my team unnoticed.'

'Leave that to me,' said Hector.

'The arms, ammunition and execution I'll manage,' continued Caleb.

'I will have the ex-raw agents flown down whenever you want them, Arvind,' said Dhariwal. 'All the best, gentlemen.'

An hour later, when Sniper was back in Raj's room, he called Dhariwal.

'I've briefed the Panther. AV and Lala will be there soon. Commence with Strike 4,' said Dhariwal.

Sniper disconnected and walked over to Raj. He was still busy watching TV. Sniper handed Raj his medication along with a glass of water, and said, 'Have your medicines and hit the bed, buddy. We'll be out of here soon.'

Without protest, Raj swallowed the pills and got under the sheets. Sniper switched off the lights and was just about the shut the door behind him, when Raj said, 'It's time to leave this place and start something new, but don't forget the ones who stood by you. Especially the ones who never gave up on you.'

The room sank into silence. Smiling to himself, Sniper shut the door behind him and walked into 1307. For the first time since he had met him in Tirana, he felt as though Raj had made some sense.

'I think he's getting better,' he muttered to himself as he sat at his table and checked the encrypted message that Caleb had sent him. It was the Hoti attack plan.

Grabbing a pen and notepad, he called Caleb. 'That was fast,' he said.

'The one luxury we do not have is time, my friend. I just tweaked an earlier plan based on our discussions today,' said Caleb.

'Best you take me through it,' said Sniper.

Caleb delved into the specifics. 'Let me first tell you who is doing what in reverse chronology. My team and I will leave Tirana immediately after the Hoti attack on the evening of the 5th. These are Eyal's orders. Hector will have a jet on standby to take me and my team out of Tirana and into Greece. We will depart for Tel Aviv the same day. Safi will have to arrange the logistics to Hoti and then from there to the airport. Adia is the influencer—she will pit Beqir and Misha against each other after the hit. The Hoti attack will be executed by me and four of my boys, who are arriving tomorrow.'

'So far so good. Let's go through the Hoti attack plan in detail,' said Sniper.

'Hoti is a secluded village in the Malësia e Madhe municipality in northern Albania. The village has not more than seventy families, all old and all Catholic. The village is surrounded by glacial mountains and has snow all through the year. Beqir's shack is about 2 kilometres away and located in a valley, surrounded by a small but dense patch of Alpine trees that stretches over a three-kilometre radius all around the shack. The Alpine forests have mountains to their north, south and west, while the Cem River flows to the east. The river starts in the snow-capped mountains and travels through Hoti on to another village, which is six kilometres away. 900 metres above the shack, there is a church run by a local, Father Marasha Sardini. Around the church there are three two-storeyed hostels where young transitional Catholic deacons come for training.

'Adia has given me the complete specs of Beqir's lodge. It's big, but it's a typical hunting lodge with standard entrances and exits, so it's not difficult to figure out the pressure points in the structure. The entire underbelly of the shack is sitting on a linseed-coated wooden platform with iron legs. The shack flooring is three feet above the ground so that the wood doesn't get affected by the moist soil and snow. There is a large open compound surrounding the structure, 450 meters away, and at the end of the compound perimeter, facing the kitchen, is a clearing where they have built a helipad. Two battery-operated carts, which can carry about eight people each, including the driver, transport people from the helipad to the lodge.

'My team and I will land up in Hoti as newly recruited Catholic deacons and stay at the hostel. The paperwork we submit to Father Sardini will show that all of us have completed four years of study in theology at a seminary in Vladivostok in Russia and have been sponsored by the

Russian Orthodox Church to do a one-year transitional deacon training. Hector will manage the paperwork through his contacts. We will use that as our base.'

'Sounds like a workable plan. Please continue,' said Sniper.

'Once there, we will settle down and, at an appropriate time, place C4s all across the underbelly and detonate them using a remote charge.'

'You mean to say you will blast the entire lodge with C4s? I agree most of them will be killed in the explosion, but my experience with C4s tells me that the plan does not guarantee that everyone will die,' said Sniper.

'Adia has given me drone footage that General Beqir has of the entire area. Based on that, I plan to have one agent as a sniper. He will be perched up top in the hostel, where he'll have an elevated vantage point. Anyone trying to escape will either run through the front entrance or try and exit through the back. This guy will have a good view and a clear shot on both sides because of the height. The second agent is an explosives expert. He will place the C4s on all the pressure points so that when it explodes, it causes maximum damage,' said Caleb.

'How will he maximise impact?' asked Sniper.

'The C4s will be placed such that the explosion will take place on all four sides and below. The side explosions will ensure that the wooden walls cave in and the flames engulf the building. The explosion beneath the lodge will tear everything asunder, giving no chance for anyone to escape,' said Caleb.

'Got it,' said Sniper.

'The other two agents and I will be on ground. We will surround the shack and box everyone in. The agent who detonates the C4s will join us after the explosion. That way we can surround the entire building,' said Caleb.

'The explosion, followed by any gunfire, will attract attention. Being a valley, the sound will echo and reach Hoti,' said Sniper.

'Yes, it will. Here is where I've modified the plan a little. All of us will be in Albanian army fatigues throughout the operation. Once everyone is dead, the sniper and the explosives expert, who are also chopper pilots, will fly out with Joseph Lika's remains in Beqir's chopper. The third agent and I will use one of the battery-operated carts to reach the river. There, the fourth agent will be waiting with a ferry. He would have parked a Pajero in the other village near the river bank and then taken the ferry to pick us up. The three of us will ferry to the other village, and use the Pajero to get out of the village. We will call Father Sardini later and tell him we fled out of sheer panic,' said Caleb.

'I get it. You want the villagers to believe that everything was executed by Albanian soldiers,' said Sniper.

'Yes. When the villagers gather in the church compound, they will see the lodge ablaze, notice soldiers wearing Albanian army uniforms leaving by boat, and assume that it's Joseph Lika who is flying off in his chopper.'

'So when the investigations start, all the witnesses will testify that it was the Albanian army that attacked the lodge and killed everyone.'

'And with Lika's body not there, everyone will assume

he orchestrated it and escaped in the chopper.'

'Brilliant. When do you leave for Hoti?'

'The meeting is scheduled for 4 July in Hoti, so we will arrive a day earlier, on the 3rd, and leave the village on the afternoon of the 5th, saying we're afraid for our lives and have decided to go back to Tirana. We will head straight to Tirana International Airport. The sniper and the explosives expert will land on a vacant field 6 kilometres from the airport and take a car that will be waiting for them. Safi has to ensure the landing spot and the vehicle. Once we meet back up, we take the jet arranged by Hector out of Albania,' said Caleb.

There was pin-drop silence for a few seconds as Sniper ran through the entire plan again in his mind. Then he responded, 'Thank you for detailing this out, Caleb. It sounds easy when you narrate it, but I know how difficult it will be for you and your people. Thank you for everything.'

'We won't be seeing each other again here, so I'll see you in Tel Aviv next. My wife, Eva, and I would be honoured to host you for dinner,' said Caleb.

'I'll be sure to meet your lovely wife, Eva. That's a promise,' said Sniper.

Sniper called Dhariwal next, running him through the entire plan, so that he could brief the Panther. It was late by the time he was done—3 a.m. He switched off the lights, got into bed and murmured, 'Only three hours left to sleep.'

The moment the lights went out in 1307, a hooded figure standing outside stirred. He retrieved a compact camera-like device coupled with a voice recorder from beneath Sniper's door, pocketed it and walked towards 1306. Swiping a key card, he entered Raj's room.

◦∭~

At 6 a.m. on 10 June 2020, Sniper walked into room 1306 with two mugs of coffee. The room was still dark because the curtains were drawn. Setting the coffee mugs down on the table, he pulled back the curtains.

'Rise and shine, buddy,' he said, turning towards Raj's bed—it was empty. He walked to the bathroom and knocked on the door. 'Coffee's ready, Raj…'

The bathroom door swung open at his touch. Raj wasn't in there. Sniper ventured out into the hallway and looked around. There was no sign of Raj.

Sniper felt his mouth go dry as anxiety started building up inside him. He licked his dry lips, grappling with his mounting panic as he ran down to the lobby. In the next one hour he searched the entire hotel inside out and came up empty. Back in Raj's room, he looked for clues. He found pieces of duct tape below the bed. There were some signs of struggle as the table lamp had fallen off and only one shoe was there on the floor. He tried to recreate the scene in his mind. 'They attacked him when he was sleeping, duct taped him and tried to put the shoes on his feet while he was in bed but he struggled. The right shoe was flung when they must have tried to put it on his feet. It hit the lamp and the lamp fell down. Realising he was making noise, they must have carried him off. And if no one in the hotel raised any noise, the possibility was that it could either be Beqir himself or Misha. Taking a deep breath, he picked up the phone and dialled Dhariwal.

'Yes?' asked Dhariwal.

'Raj is missing,' said Sniper, not beating around the bush.

'What did you say?'

'Raj Pratap Rana is gone,' replied Sniper, his voice rising.

'And you don't know where?' asked Dhariwal.

'No. Initially I thought since he was getting better, he may have wandered off but a few things I saw in the room suggest he may have been abducted,' said Sniper.

'What things?' asked Dhariwal.

Sniper told him everything he saw and his analysis of the situation.

Dhariwal was silent for a moment. Finally, he said, 'Okay, let's think of our next move.'

'To start with, I'm going to make some calls. Then I'm going to scour every corner of Tirana,' vowed Sniper, chastising himself internally. After disconnecting his call with Dhariwal, he called Adia.

'Raj is missing from his room; I think he's been abducted and I think it's your boss who has done this,' said Sniper.

'My boss is down with Covid. He's been bedridden since yesterday. It must be someone else,' said Adia.

Sniper received similar answers from Hector and Caleb. Discreet enquires revealed that nobody, including Misha and Tefik, knew about Raj's disappearance.

Sniper rang AV and Lala. They had landed just that morning and were on their way to Safi's apartment.

'Could he have wandered out of the room?' AV asked.

'He's never stepped out of his room and that too so early. If the local teams do not know anything about Raj's disappearance, then there's only one team left, who could have done this: the Americans,' said Sniper.

'They have no reason to abduct him,' said AV.

Sniper was about to respond, when he saw an incoming call from Dhariwal on his screen. 'I'll talk to you later,' he said, disconnecting the call to answer Dhariwal's.

'I've informed the Panther,' Dhariwal began.

'What was his reaction?'

'Upset but maintaining his composure, as usual. He asked us to drop everything and focus on Raj.'

Sniper's voice took on a determined edge. 'Raj is my responsibility; I will get him back but Strike 4 will go as planned. You can tell the Panther that.' He hung up before Dhariwal could say anything.

Still bewildered by this turn of events, unable to understand what had actually happened, Sniper went back to 1306 and began inspecting every inch. Raj's clothes, socks, belt, undergarments ... everything was untouched in the cupboard. The drawers were empty, as they had been. His pad and pen and a UV torch were neatly arranged on the coffee table. He turned towards the unmade bed and pulled off the sheets. There was nothing there. He looked at the bedside table and his eyes fell on the A3 sheets that were sprawled atop a newspaper. The top sheet featured the sketch of the Presidential Palace. He lifted the sheets and was about to put them back on the newspaper after a cursory look, when his attention was drawn to the paper's front page. A photo of the Palace of Brigades took up almost a fourth of the page, and below it was an article.

'*President Tefik Metta and First Lady Teuta Metta*

open palace gates. The presidential couple will celebrate their wedding anniversary at the Palace of Brigades on 10 July. This will be coinciding with the annual Chamber Music Festival from 10–22 July, which will be conducting its inaugural session at the Palace in honour of the couple. Musicians and music enthusiasts from across Albania and beyond will congregate for the event.'

Sniper put the newspaper down and looked out of the windows at the Palace of Brigades in the distance. Then he folded the A3 sheets, pocketed them and resumed his inspection of the room. The bathroom's neat arrangement mirrored the bedroom's: Raj's toothpaste, brush, razor and comb sat undisturbed. The mirror was foggy, as though someone had had a hot shower, but the rest of the bathroom was cold. He pulled back the shower curtains and checked the floor; it was bone dry.

'How come the mirror is still fogged up when the entire bathroom is dry?' he thought as he walked up to the mirror and touched its surface with his index finger; it felt strangely oily. It wasn't moisture on the mirror—it was some sort of liquid gel. Something occurred to Sniper. He rushed to grab the UV torch from the coffee table, switched off all the bathroom lights and shone the torch on the mirror. Glowing in fluorescent green letters, a message revealed itself: *'Retribution is patient only till opportunity knocks.'*

Sniper walked back into the living room, spread the A3 sheets on the bed and went over the drawings in detail. After spending twenty minutes scrutinising them, he went back to the windows.

The park was bathed in the morning sun's rays. The light

streamed through the trees, landing in patches on the grass. Some were circuiting the park, while others sat on benches looking up at the orange sky, welcoming a new dawn. A short distance from the park was where the Acapulco Grande was, where Misha lived, and beyond the park, behind the verdant trees, Sniper could see the dome of the Palace of Brigades. His gaze flitted between it, the newspaper article and finally the sketches.

A wry smile crept across Sniper's face. He pulled out his cell phone to call Dhariwal. 'He played us.'

'What? Who played us?' asked Dhariwal.

'Raj. I don't know why, but I'm going to find out,' said Sniper.

'What do you want me to tell the Panther?'

'Tell him Strike 4 is on.'

STRIKE 4

THE RETRIBUTION

JULY 2020

THE TEMPERATURE IN TIRANA WAS a balmy 33 °C. Inside Safi's apartment, Sniper, Safi, AV and Lala watched the news. The anchor shared how Albania boasted the lowest coronavirus numbers in Europe. Footage rolled: Albanian nurses were boarding the national aircraft carrier, as the anchor added that an additional sixty nurses were being sent to Italy, badly hit by the virus, to assist in patient care. The health minister appeared on the screen and began to explain that the gesture would ensure solidarity and friendship between the two nations. He recalled times past when Italy had come to their aid during crises. New footage showed the minister shaking hands with the nurses as they boarded the plane at Rinas International Airport.

Lala switched channels. A psychiatrist was talking about the complex emotions of revenge and retribution that often plague the human psyche. 'In its raw form, retribution provides peace and contentment to the tormented. There's profound relief for a victim when they see their tormentors pay. And the scales of retribution tilt to joy and satisfaction for the victim, especially if their tormentor endures great anguish. But the inherent danger in revenge and retribution is continuing the cycle of violence. They aren't the answer.'

Lala nodded gravely.

⊙∭~

The day before, Caleb and his team had settled into the Hoti church hostels as deacons. They had been planning for Strike 4 for over twenty-three days, and the day for action had finally dawned. While thousands of miles away the Americans celebrated Independence Day, Caleb and his team prepared for the Hoti attack.

18

IT WAS 6 P.M. ON 4 JULY 2020, and Albania was facing two extreme temperatures. While Tirana was hot as sin, Hoti was biting cold. Sniper, his eyes still locked on the television screen, said, 'I understand where Raj is coming from. For revenge and retribution, the key quality is patience. One has to plan meticulously. Most importantly, one has to detach from emotional ties and anything that might hold you back from rendering that brutal act. I think that's why Raj left us. He must have assumed that if he'd told us his plans, we would have let emotions cloud everything and pull him back from his goal.'

'I don't know about us, but Dhariwal would have ordered him to come back. What I still haven't figured out is when during his stay at the hotel he became okay,' said Lala.

'I don't think he was ever not "okay". I think he planned this whole thing from the beginning,' said Sniper.

'Are you saying that he planned on getting caught, being sent to Burrel and then being rescued, and *then* waited for the opportunity to escape us to carry out his solo Rambo shit once again?' asked AV. He was still angry with Raj for doing a number on them.

'Yes. I agree with Sniper, and there's no point in getting

upset, AV. We'll get to the bottom of this when we find him,' said Safi.

'It's been twenty-four days since he disappeared, and we have absolutely no clue where he is. To top it, Sniper has to continue with the charade that he is in the room. He is lucky the housekeeeping is not insisiting that they clean the room. If they do, the entire shit will hit the ceiling,' said AV.

'I have managed that part well. I have strict instructions that no one will enter the room and traumatise the patient and the housekeeping is happy not to bother me. I have even ensured a padlock on the door stating he has started wandering,' said Sniper.

'Where do you think we'll find him?' snapped Lala who was also beginning to get irritated.

'I know the boy well. We'll find him when he wants us to find him,' said Sniper. 'Unless…'

'Unless what?' asked Lala.

'Unless,' continued Sniper, 'we start thinking like him.'

⌇

A hundred and forty-two kilometres away, on a mountaintop hidden among Alpine trees, the Israeli sniper Elijah looked through the scope of his Sako rifle. The Finnish olive-green Sako TRG-42 sniper rifle was a powerful one, with a range of over 800 metres. It sat on a folding stock.

Through his scope, Elijah spotted Joseph Lika stepping out of the chopper, shaking hands with the caretaker and getting into the battery-operated cart. Behind Joseph, two soldiers descended from the chopper and joined him. The cart promptly set off for the lodge. Elijah spoke into the lapel mike for Caleb and his Mossad agents—Isaac, Levi and Nathan.

'The Wolf has arrived. Has two guards with him and a caretaker,' Elijah reported.

'Roger that,' Caleb responded. He spoke into his lapel mic and addressed the explosives expert, who was wiring the C4s in the underbelly and sides of the lodge. 'Are we done, Levi?'

'Yes. I'm just waiting for the Wolf and his people to enter. Once they're in the lodge, I'll get out.'

'Got it. You come straight back to me,' Caleb said. He glanced at the evening sky, already cloaked in darkness, and then at his watch. It was 7.30 p.m. He ordered on his lapel mic for everyone to pull on the night-vision glasses and switch on their helmet cameras. Then he addressed the other two agents. 'Isaac, Nathan, assume your positions and wait for my instructions.'

Isaac darted through the Alpine forest and took up a position to the north of the lodge, while Nathan secured a spot to the west. Caleb maintained his southern vantage point, closer to the chopper and the carts.

'Exiting now,' said Levi as he left the underbelly of the lodge—Lika and his team had entered. Levi sprinted southward, where Caleb was. Once he reached, Caleb handed him an AK-47 and enough ammunition to go with it. 'Take the east side,' Caleb instructed. And with that, Caleb and his agents waited.

The village of Hoti in the Albanian Alps was 50 kilometres to the north of the city of Shkodër, in the upper part of 'Perroi i Thathe', or 'dry steam'. Caleb and his agents had taken a black Mitsubishi Pajero for their journey—a model often favoured by farmers. Safi had bought it second-hand and had paid with cash. On 3 July 2020, they had first driven to Shkodër city and then to a town called Koplik. From the town centre, they had driven another 50 kilometres to reach the Hoti valley, and another 10 to finally get to the church in the village of Hoti.

At Hoti Church of Sacred Hearts, Father Sardini greeted them with exceptional warmth. His hospitality wasn't solely because the five deacons were sponsored by the Russian Orthodox Church, but also because of the prosperity they brought to his church. He almost swooned when he saw the briefcase with 50 thousand dollars that the bishop had sent along with the deacons as a donation for Hoti Church. This money was over and above the one-month advance Caleb had paid for their board and meals.

With most of the youngsters migrating out of the village for jobs, there were just a few old people left in Hoti. Also, due to the piercing cold, even the church hostels were nearly empty as most deacons had left for the warmer areas leaving only the cook behind to take care of the newcomers with food and hot water. In short, Hoti was looking like a ghost town, but this worked well for Caleb and his men. That was all they needed. Caleb and his agents had done enough reconnaissance after their arrival and were well prepared for the Hoti attack. Being flanked by massive glaciers and 2,000-metre mountains, the valley looked like an amphitheatre, with the lodge and the helipad situated in the middle.

When Caleb called Sniper, the Ghosts, who had been waiting eagerly, crowded in front of Sniper's laptop.

'All right, we're in position and our cameras are on,' Caleb said. He relayed the access codes to Sniper, who logged in. In a few seconds, the Ghosts had access to five different views from the Mossad team's five different cameras.

'We can see what you're seeing, Caleb,' said Sniper.

'Good. We have Joseph Lika, his two guards, plus a caretaker in the lodge as of now. Adia called to say that the army chopper that brought in Lika has gone back for the kryes. It's an eighteen-seater, so they will arrive together. Don't expect any commentary once the movie starts,' joked Caleb.

'We understand,' said Sniper, impressed by the composure the Mossad agents were displaying. Turning to AV, he said, 'Connect Dhariwal and the Panther.'

AV called Shiva and gave him a unique set of codes—the Ghosts were planning on sharing the operation's live feed to a screen in the Panther's library. Ten minutes later, in 7, Lok Kalyan Marg, Shiva approached DD in his office. 'Mr. Dhariwal is waiting for you in the library, sir. Strike 4 has commenced.'

The Panther walked with Shiva to the library. Dhariwal was waiting. They settled side by side before the screen. Shiva assumed his customary position, standing three feet behind the Panther. DD used the SAT phone kept next to him and spoke to Caleb, 'I am personally indebted to you and Israel for this assistance. I won't forget what you're doing for us. And I assure you that we'll be there for you when you need us. All the best, boys.'

An emotional Caleb, who had never been addressed by his own Prime Minister in his twenty-year career, replied, 'We won't let you down, sir.' Then, as an afterthought, he added, 'Once this is behind us, I'd like to come and meet you.'

'You make sure to bring your family with you,' replied the Panther, as he braced himself for the events that would unfold in Hoti.

19

Thousands of miles away, the American Independence Day festivities were about to begin. Though not as elaborate as they had been in the previous years, because of the pandemic, it was still a national holiday, and some families had barbecues to celebrate.

In the village of Hoti, Caleb looked at the night sky and shook his head. The moon had disappeared behind dark clouds, plunging the valley into inky darkness. The only way they could see was through their night-vision goggles.

Within the warm confines of the hunting lodge, all the kryes had settled in, safe from the biting cold outside. Amongst friends and family they did not look menacing. In fact it looked more like a group of senior citizens meeting for an annual function. Joseph Lika, his two guards and the caretaker were playing the role of hosts to perfection. As instructed by Lika, the caterers had left, leaving only Joseph, his men and the fifteen kryes in the building. Everyone was in high spirits. Music was playing and drinks were being poured out. Thirty minutes into the party, everyone was singing old folk songs and thumping each other's backs in friendship and bonhomie.

Outside, in the darkness, Caleb spoke into his lapel mic, 'All set, boys?'

The young Mossad agents replied in the affirmative.

'Nathan, head for the other side of the river and park the Pajero there. As per the prescribed time, take a ferry and pick me, and Isaac. We will take the ferry to cross over and then the Pajero to leave the other village. If we all try to leave together from here in the Pajero, there are chances that we may be spotted especially after the explosion.'

'Okay,' said Nathan as he headed for the church to pick up the Pajero and drive off to the next village.

Caleb pepped the other three agents. 'A little bit of action will warm us up, boys,' Caleb said. He and his team were used to the cold. But even with three layers of woollen clothing, the cold was getting to their bones.

At 9.25 p.m., Caleb gave Levi the green light. Levi, without hesitation, activated the detonator. It only took two seconds—a subdued whoosh escalated into a deafening explosion. The hunting lodge's underbelly erupted upwards, while the walls imploded, trapping its occupants inside. Orange flames leapt twelve feet up into the dark sky in seconds. The reverberations of the blast lingered as Caleb and his team advanced.

Inside the cabin, when the C4s exploded, Joseph Lika and the caretaker had been in the kitchen, where the impact hadn't been as intense. Both were stunned and badly wounded, but alive. The caretaker pushed open the kitchen door and tumbled out into the compound. He limped towards the helipad with a Glock in his hand, where the battery-operated carts were parked.

Elijah looked through his rifle scope and saw the lanky caretaker desperately making his way to the helipad. He aimed his crosshairs and squeezed the trigger. The caretaker was still moving when the .300 Winchester Magnum cartridge made contact with his temple. His head exploded like a dropped watermelon, and his lifeless body was thrown into the surrounding bushes. Elijah moved the Sako and aimed at the lodge, scanning for any survivors.

Caleb, Levi and Isaac closed in on the lodge from all sides.

Many miles away, the Ghosts and the Panther watched Strike 4 unfolding scene by scene.

'These guys are good at what they do,' said the Panther as he watched Isaac, who was coming from the north. Isaac spotted a figure climbing out of the rubblet. 'Lika's alive—.' He lifted his AK-47 and fired two shots.

But both bullets missed their target, and Joseph, badly wounded and in a panic, stumbled towards the trees. He too had a Glock in his hand.

'Damn,' said Sniper as he saw Lika ducking and hobbling towards the forest.

'There is too much smoke. I missed him. He is heading for the trees,' said Isaac. Caleb, sprinted from the back of the lodge to the front to corner Lika. Just as he ran past the burning pillars of the entrance, Joseph Lika, who was half way into the woods, turned and fired. Caleb swivelled, but it was too late. The 9x19 Parabellum cartridge hit Caleb's chest and tore through his heart, killing him instantly.

There was pin drop silence in 7, Lok Kalyan Marg as the Panther saw Caleb's body crash into a tree. As the Ghosts watched Caleb on their screens, a sense of frustration was brewing inside them. The loss of a hero like Caleb was too much for them to take. They were experiencing a feeling of anger mixed with sadness.

Hearing the sound of the shot, Isaac, who was on the north side, turned and ran. He caught sight of Joseph Lika cut through the trees and head towards the helipad. As he chased Lika, he passed his boss's lifeless body, and a blind rage surged through him. He did not even aim—he just lifted the AK-47 to his hip and fired as he ran.

The bullets hit Joseph Lika's right leg, and he buckled. As he fell, the Glock flew from his hand and disappeared into the tall, dry grass. Within seconds, Isaac was on him like a wild predator on its prey. Joseph tried to get out from under him, but Isaac's size and rage ensured he was pinned down. With a swift move, Isaac wrenched Joseph's right arm backwards, snapping it at the elbow and dislocating the shoulder joint. Leaning close, he spat out, 'You killed my friend and mentor, and for that I'll make you pay, you bastard.' He drew his hunting knife and plunged it into Joseph's back. Joseph screamed in agony, but Isaac stabbed him again and again, rupturing his kidneys, as Lika's screams echoed through the night. Soon, he went silent.

By the time Levi ran up to him and pulled him off, Joseph's back looked like it had gone through a meat grinder. Levi threw the mutilated body over his shoulder and ran towards the helipad. After dumping the body in the cargo hold, he took the battery-operated cart and went back for Caleb. By that time, Isaac had regained some semblance of control. Levi & Isaac loaded Caleb's body gently onto the cart and drove him to the army chopper where Elijah was already waiting in the cockpit with the engine running. They lifted Caleb's body and placed it gently inside the chopper.

'The Hoti attack is done. Everyone has been terminated, and the Wolf is in the cargo hold,' said Levi to Elijah as he boarded the chopper.

'Where's Caleb?' asked Elijah.

Levi's's voice cracked as he pointed to the body bag inside the chopper and said, 'He's gone.' Then he looked at Isaac and said, 'We'll see you at the airport, Nathan is waiting with the ferry by the river. As planned, take the ferry and then the Pajero on the other side. Call Father Sardini tomorrow and tell him what Caleb told us to say.'

While the Ghosts watched the army chopper lift off with Caleb and Lika's bodies, their eyes welled up with tears.

Within ten minutes, the army chopper had left, the Mossad agents trying to control their tears and emotions as they piloted. 26 kilometres to the west of Tirana International Airport, as the chopper flew over the Adriatic Sea, Levi opened the cargo hold and pushed Joseph Lika's body out. The corpse hit the sea and within minutes got devoured by the ever-hungry shortfin mako sharks. Within seconds, Joseph Lika was only a memory and a name in the history of Albanian politics.

Back in Hoti, Isaac and Nathan followed the exit strategy. They left the battery cart by the riverside, and Nathan took the boat to the next village. There they got into the Pajero that Nathan had already parked in the woods and drove off to Tirana International Airport, where a private jet awaited them. On the way, Nathan informed the Ghosts about the loss of Caleb.

'We saw what happened, Nathan. Our condolences run deep. We're so sorry,' said Sniper.

'Caleb was a brave soldier and he died for his country. While his death cannot be publicly honoured in Israel, he'll live in our hearts forever,' said Nathan, his voice thick with grief. With that, he signed off.

At 7, Lok Kalyan Marg, a hush had descended. DD, Dhariwal and Shiva left quietly to their rooms without even shaking hands to celebrate the victory. To them, the Hoti attack was a successful mission, but Caleb's death cast a pall over their triumph.

Today, they had lost a warrior who had fought and sacrificed his life for their cause.

◎§§~

Thanks to Safi Doha's press briefs, which had reached almost every media house anonymously, the citizens of Albania woke up the next morning to the news of the tragedy in the village of Hoti.

On 5 July 2020, the morning papers carried the gruesome details of the deaths of the kryes.

'Kryes Massacred in Hoti,' one of the headlines screamed. The article read, 'Eyewitnesses recount a chilling narrative from the remote village of Hoti. The Albanian army, under the supervision of Joseph Lika, massacred the fifteen heads of the formidable Albanian mafia with one explosion. The kryes were called for a meeting in General Beqir Hoxha's hunting lodge in Hoti, where they were locked in and burnt alive. Villagers saw Joseph Lika leaving the compound with his soldiers in an army chopper. Other soldiers took a marine boat to the next village and escaped from there. The entire village and the valley are in a state of shock, but strikingly, at the time of this report, official channels, be it police or government, seemed unaware of the orchestration of this attack.'

Within an hour, the entire world learnt of the Hoti massacre. While most rejoiced and even commended General Beqir Hoxha on his bold move to eradicate the mafia, for Tefik, Misha, Robert and President Sani Abdullah in Nigeria, it was a massive body blow. They all had something to lose, and were furious with General Beqir Hoxha.

When Robert saw the news, he called General Hoxha in Tirana immediately. 'What on earth is this? Why did you do this?'

'I'm hearing about this for the first time from the media, Robert. I have no idea why Joseph did this or where he is,' said Beqir.

'What do you mean you don't know where he is?' asked Robert.

'The police found my chopper in an abandoned field close to the airport. There was blood in the cargo hold. Joseph has been missing since last night. His phone is dead, so there's no point calling him. I woke up to this news and now I will have Misha and Tefik baying for my blood while the rest of the world is sending me congratulatory tweets.'

'Could it be that Misha or Tefik did this for an ulterior purpose?' asked Robert.

'No. Killing all the fifteen kryes means cutting off both arms. Misha and Tefik would never do that, not under *any* compulsion. This has to be someone else's work,' said Beqir.

Before Robert could respond, Beqir said, 'I have Misha calling on the other line. Let me call you back.'

Beqir disconnected and picked up Misha's call. Misha did not even wait for a greeting.

'The moment you said you wanted to have a meeting with the kryes in Hoti, I knew you were up to something devious. But I never assumed you would do something like this. Beqir, if you think by eliminating the kryes you have cut off my drug supply, then let me tell you I will rise from the ashes like a phoenix and burn the hell out of you. I'm not afraid of your army, Beqir. Wait and see what I'm going to do to you,' Misha spat out.

⊙∭~

Misha spent the rest of the day alone, grappling with the impending nightmare of how he was going to manage his drug operations. Between fielding calls from anxious associates and clients, Tefik's revelation added another layer of anxiety. He had told Misha that there were rumours circulating in the drug circle that President Sani was planning to take over the supply chain. 'This will be a disaster for us, Misha,' Tefik had warned.

At 9 p.m., when the police commissioner called to say that they still hadn't located Joseph Lika, Misha was livid. 'I want him caught quickly, Commissioner, or your family will be paying the price!' he shouted, slamming the phone down.

After desperately trying to calm down, he called the senior editor of the *Albanian Daily News* and said, 'Let the people of Albania know that General Beqir is a murderer, and the

President has put together a special investigative team to enquire into this massacre. The SIT will be calling General Beqir Hoxha for questioning soon.'

Misha's next call was to Tefik's secretary. 'Fix a meeting for me with the President at 9 a.m. tomorrow.'

It was almost 11 p.m. when he finally walked out of the Acapulco Grande and got into his car. 'Take me to my sister,' he told the driver.

This was a habit he had developed when he was just seven years old. Every time he was upset, Misha would go to his sister, Teuta Perci. She knew how to console him. She was his strength.

∼⊙∭∽

Meanwhile, 60 kilometres away in Lin, silence rang through Beqir Mansion. The army was conducting their own search for Joseph Lika, but several hours had passed since the Hoti attack and the General still had no clue where Lika was. Amidst all this, everyone had forgotten about Raj.

While the General nursed a glass of whiskey in his living room, his mind raced to find an explanation for what had transpired in Hoti. He expected an attack from Misha soon, so he had stationed two soldiers with AK-47s at the main gate of the mansion, while four more patrolled the mansion compounds. Two personal bodyguards stood outside his living room and two more inside.

He looked at his watch—the day was over. It was 12.05 a.m. on 6th July 2020. Across from him, Adia Markova sipped the glass of wine he had poured for her. Adia studied the General and thought, '*For the first time, you are afraid.*'

Her thoughts were broken by the General's question. 'Adia, if I ask you a question, will you give me an honest, fearless answer?'

Adia shifted in her seat and looked him in the eye. 'I've been loyal to you for decades, and I have always answered you fearlessly and truthfully. Go on.'

'Do you believe Joseph killed the kryes?' Beqir asked.

'No,' said Adia, unflinching.

'Then who did this?' he asked, his eyes sharpening.

'The CIA. And I think they've eliminated Joseph Lika as well.'

'What? Are you saying you doubt Robert Sullivan? He seemed genuinely shocked when he called.'

'I think he's playing you. This is straight out of the CIA playbook. With the kryes gone, Misha will come after you. You will kill Misha, then Tefik will come after you. The CIA will kill Tefik, and you will be framed—with evidence. They took care of that when framing Joseph Lika. Then they'll orchestrate your ascent to the President's chair and make you their puppet for life. They just used you and then sacrificed Joseph at the altar. The Americans are puppeteers.'

Though General Hoxha was amazed by Adia's analysis, he was shocked that he had clearly been manipulated by Robert. A chilling realisation dawned on him: if they could eliminate the kryes and Joseph, they could eliminate him too if need be.

'So making me the NSA and asking me to host the meeting with the kryes was all part of the larger plan,' Beqir said.

'They made you the scapegoat, General. You were so

busy with your new role and your newfound power that you forgot to look over your shoulder,' said Adia, driving the suspicion deeper.

'What do you mean?' asked Beqir.

'The Indian RAW agent and the doctor are missing from the hotel and apparently even Misha is not aware of their absence. The housekeeping girl who I planted there told me.'

'Oh my god. What happened to them?'

'My gut says Robert is behind this also. I think amidst all these developments, he has taken away your trump card against the Indians. You will now be a puppet in his hands.'

This was a strategy she had thought of singularly after the Hoti massacre, something she hadn't discussed with anyone, not even Hector Dekovi. She hated the Americans and wanted to ensure that Hector became the President. For that, she had to sow discord between the chummy Beqir and Robert. The thought of the General plotting revenge against Robert brought a smile to her lips.

'I will show Robert who I am,' roared Beqir.

'That is exactly what you will not do. Keep Robert in the dark about your suspicions. From now on, you become the puppeteer.'

'Thank you, Adia. You're my only true friend,' said General Beqir.

~

In New Delhi, at 7, Lok Kalyan Marg, DD was going through some documents when Dhariwal entered his office. 'Any news of Raj?' DD immediately asked.

Dhariwal was expecting this question, so he was quick to respond. 'Twenty-five days and we have no clue, sir. But I'm here for something else.'

'Tell me,' said DD.

'I spoke to Hector Dekovi this morning. Apparently, Adia Markova called him late last night and spoke of some developments.'

'Such as?'

'Adia has convinced Beqir that Robert was behind the Hoti massacre and the disappearance of Raj and Sniper. Now Beqir is feeling friendless and isolated. On the one hand, he has Misha and Tefik, and on the other, Robert,' said Dhariwal.

'I don't think that's what Sniper had planned,' said DD.

'No, it wasn't. Adia had to improvise, given the circumstances. But my subject of discussion is slightly different, sir. With Misha planning to eliminate the General, and the General planning a counterstrike, Lin will be a battleground soon. Geeta is in danger there, so Arvind and I propose we extract her before any of this violence unfolds. We need your approval for the change in plan,' said Dhariwal.

'Go ahead. But tell Sniper not to stop his search for Raj,' said DD with a pained look.

Back in his car, Dhariwal called Sniper.

'Tell the Ghosts we have a go ahead from the Panther. All the best.'

20

IT WAS 11.30 P.M. ON 6TH JULY 2020. Shkodër, one of Albania's most dangerous cities, buzzed with tension. The majority of its population of 200,000 lived below the poverty line, so the city was a hotspot for crime. The city was rife with drugs and human trafficking. After the assassination of the kryes, the city had become a free-for-all for smaller gangs. Though the police tried to quell the anarchy, looting, rioting and arson ravaged the city.

In the midst of this madness stood one man who seemed untouchable—Gef Bajrami. He was revered as the one who supplied the gangs with arms. If he died, they would be stripped of their firepower. So while the city burned, Gef's bungalow in Shkodër remained a safe haven.

Which is why Raj chose to meet Gef there.

After travelling 86 kilometres from Tirana to Shkodër, when Raj reached Gef's residence, it was almost midnight. Gef had been told of Raj's visit in strict confidence by Raj himself. When Raj arrived, Gef walked out to personally greet his friend and business partner. 'Welcome home, my brother,' he said to Raj.

Raj gave him a broad smile. 'Thank you for meeting me, Gef. But before we discuss anything, I need to freshen up. I've been on the road and in hiding for twenty-five days now.'

After a hot shower and finally in a fresh set of clothes given by Gef, Raj was served a lavish meal. Raj was so famished that he made no conversation till he finished eating. Once they were done, sitting outside with a glass of Grey Goose in his hand, Gef asked him, 'For a filmmaker, you seem to have gone through hell. Where've you been?'

'Hiding from everyone till I got to you,' said Raj.

'Along with Beqir, you have RAW and the Indian NSA looking for you, brother. Anything you're not telling me?' asked Gef.

'My dad took a bullet for the PM, so I gues the orders must have come from there,' said Raj.

'Ah! Now I understand why they're so desperate to find you,' said Gef. He looked Raj in the eye and asked, 'You were never unwell, were you?'

'No. I was acting insane to get out of Burrel.'

'If Dhariwal had not asked me to get Yuri to beat you up, you would have rotted in Burrel. Why did you run away from the hotel? Dhariwal had made plans to extract you from here.'

'I know. They would have extracted Geeta along with me and sent us back. But I'd never be able to live with myself without taking revenge on Beqir. Especially not now, after what he's done to Geeta.' Raj was deliberately hiding the real purpose, which was Plan B as discussed with Dhariwal before leaving.

'You cannot fight him alone. You're a businessman, and he is an army general and the NSA of Albania.'

'Better to die trying than live with regret.'

'You know, your people are very upset with you for disappearing on them.'

'Sure, but this is *my* revenge and I want it done *my* way.'

Gef sighed. 'As you wish, brother. I'll support you as much as I can. Tell me what you want me to do.'

'To start with, you need to keep my whereabouts a secret from everyone, including my people, and let me stay in your guest house in Lin.'

'Everything will remain confidential and you can stay at my guest house in Lin.'

'Thank you. Now I want you to arrange for everything that's written on this list,' said Raj, handing him a sheet of paper.

Gef looked at the list and then called his assistant. 'Arrange everything and have it ready in the next fifteen minutes.' Then he looked at Raj and asked, 'Are you mobile?'

'No. I've been using public transport: bus, tram, metro, all that. And without tickets most of the time, since I ran out of money,' replied Raj.

Gef called out for his assistant once again. 'Have the items placed in the black Mercedes SUV,' Gef told him. 'Tank it up and hand over the keys to my guest here.'

He turned to Raj again. 'Your list says four Glocks and ammunition, three hunting knives, four sets of earpieces, some C4s, climbing ropes, night-vision goggles, four Kevlars and a rigid inflatable boat. You going to war?'

'Yes. My own personal war,' Raj said.

'He has mercenaries guarding the mansion and himself. Even with all these weapons, you cannot do it alone.'

'That's why I came to you. I need two of your best men to fight with me,' said Raj.

Gef laughed. 'You really are mad,' he said. Then he

shouted to his assistant, 'Give Raj the new RHIB and send the Arabs in.'

An RHIB, or rigid hull inflatable boat, is a high-speed, all-weather boat used specifically for covert operations by US Navy SEALs, and the Arabs Gef referred to were his two Arab bodyguards, young and ready to fight.

While the assistant organised everything Raj needed, Gef took his friend to his study. There, he reached into his desk drawer, pulling out a .25 ACP Baby Browning. Handing it to Raj, he said, 'In case everything else fails, the last resort.' He gave him ten boxes, each with six rounds, in a paper bag, adding an ankle holster.

Raj inspected the Browning, loaded it and then strapped it to his ankle with the holster. He had just about adjusted his trousers over the Browning, when the Arabs walked in.

'Meet Ahmad Idrees and Sabah Salahi,' said Gef, as Raj exchanged handshakes with the duo. They sat opposite him in single chairs.

'They're seasoned street fighters,' Gef said, looking at his boys with pride. 'Both are excellent with Glocks, rifles and knives. Salahi is a martial arts expert and Idrees is a sniper.'

Raj sized them up. Idrees was tall, broad-shouldered and built like a tank, while Salahi was of average height but wiry. He smiled at both of them and said, 'It's not often that I hear praise from Gef's mouth. So this must mean you're both very good. I trust we'll work well together.'

'We've been with Gef for many years. His allies are ours too,' said Idrees. Salahi remained quiet.

'We were in Greece till you called. We arrived at 9 last night,' said Gef.

'You drove?' asked Raj.

'No. We flew from Greece and landed in Sarandë Airfield, then drove here. Took us about five and a half hours in total.'

'Hmm… Sarande sounds like a good plan for me too,' said Raj.

'Once your war is over, call me, and I will send you my private jet,' replied Gef.

Though Gef requested Raj to stay the night and travel in the morning, Raj courteously declined. He did not have the luxury of time and had to reach his next stop, Gef's guest house, before dawn as he wanted to be in Beqir mansion before Beqir made plans to disappear to escape from Misha. As Raj readied himself to leave, Gef handed him a wad of notes. 'Keep this. You'll need it. If you want to attack the General, using the RHIB, going via the lake is a good idea. He won't be expecting you to come from there.' He hugged Raj goodbye.

By the time Raj, Idrees and Salahi left Gef's house, it was 3 a.m. on 6 July. They took the black Mercedes SUV, with the RHIB strapped to the roof and a trunk filled with enough weapons to start a mini war. Salahi was carrying his favourite—the SAKO TRG 42 long-distance sniper rifle—while Idrees was happy with the Glock. They had a 198-kilometre drive from Shkodër to Gef's guest house in Lin, and the Mercedes made it in two hours and thirty-nine minutes.

When they arrived at the guest house, it was 5.40 a.m., and the sun was already up. They saw two black Honda CR-Vs already parked in the compound outside the guest house.

'Are you expecting guests?' asked Idrees, as he pulled up to the porch and switched off the engine.

'No, but I can make a good guess as to who's joined us,' said Raj as they all climbed out of the Mercedes. The three men stood on the porch, facing the front door, separated from them by a flight of steps, and waited. Raj, who knew they were being watched, waited for the door to open, while Idrees and Salahi waited for instructions from Raj, slightly puzzled.

It took three minutes for Sniper to open the door and step outside. Behind him, Safi, AV and Lala appeared. The group stood outside the door, looking down at Raj, Idrees and Salahi. 'Why am I not surprised to see you guys here?' Raj said.

If our presence doesn't surprise you, maybe our anger will,' said AV, who looked furious.

'Good morning, AV,' Raj responded pleasantly. 'Are we going to stand here all day, or should we go in and talk?'

'You kept us on pins and needles for twenty-five days, and now you have the gall to teach us etiquette?' asked AV. Raj noticed that Lala, Sniper and Safi were quiet.

He looked at Sniper and said, 'I have an explanation.'

'We're listening,' said Sniper.

'I think we should go in and talk,' Safi gently nudged.

Sniper looked at Lala, who nodded in agreement. Without saying a word, Sniper turned and made his way back into the house, with AV and Safi on his heels. Lala waited for Raj. The moment he walked up the flight of steps, he hugged him tightly and said, 'They're just very upset. It's best to wait till their anger dies down. Then, apologise for everything.'

'I'll handle it, Lala,' said Raj, as he nodded to Idrees and Salahi, who followed them into the house.

The living room was large, accentuated by a high ceiling. Sofas and armchairs adorned the room, and the Ghosts settled in. Idrees and Salahi decided to stay away from the family fight, so they went up to their rooms on the first floor, away from the others.

'Where do you want me to begin?' asked Raj. He sat across from Sniper. The other Ghosts were on either side of him.

'Why don't you try from the beginning?' said Sniper sarcastically.

'All right. If it's the beginning you'd like, please be patient with me,' said Raj. 'When Dhariwal assigned me to Strike 4, Geeta and I did some preliminary research and found out that there was more than one player in Tirana. Our assumption that a simple coup would solve everything was deeply flawed.'

'What do you mean?' asked AV.

'Strike 4 was a linear plan that went like this. Dhariwal speaks to Gef about the coup. Gef influences Beqir. The General executes the coup. Tefik's government falls. Hector Dekovi takes over as President. Beqir becomes NSA. Hector is pro-India and Beqir is anti-China. After the coup, Albania and India rekindle their friendship, and Hector allows us military bases in Albania. I had no role in any of this.

'The envisioned net outcome was this: international issues sorted and China thwarted. With the Sandesars repatriated, back home, we shut the mouth of the opposition who has been going to town saying DD is doing nothing about criminals who commit crimes in India and escape to other countries, like the Sandesars. All's well that ends well.

'The problem was the linear thinking, which was an outcome of a lack of foot soldiers in Albania, who could have given us more intel. That would have helped us plan better.

'When I came here the first time to study the language and the culture, I did some research and found out that there were multiple players with multiple ambitions in Tirana. Mossad were planning to strike Misha and the kryes; Robert and the CIA were looking for ways to prop Beqir, their puppet, as the next President. Unaware of all this, Beqir and Misha were fighting to become the NSA, and parallelly, Xi was pulling strings on Tefik to exert Chinese dominance over Albania. And it was in this political climate that we were planning to orchestrate a coup. Our odds were slim given our lack of a strong ally in Tirana.'

The Ghosts had begun to understand the enormity of the situation, but they still weren't sure where it was all leading.

'Are you saying Dhariwal read the situation completely wrong before advising the Panther?' asked Safi.

'Not deliberately, of course. But due to our scant presence here, he knew only what Gef knew,' said Raj.

'If you knew all this then, why did you accept Strike 4 and come to Tirana?' asked AV.

'One thing that I agreed with Dhariwal on is that we have to change the leadership in Tirana if we're to corral China. To me that was more important. That's why I accepted the mission. I came to Tirana to find out how else we could dethrone Tefik and put Hector in his place. I am Dhariwal's Plan B.'

'You could have told us what you knew. We would have thought of another way,' said Lala, his voice tinged with frustration.

'I could have, but that would mean further planning and further delay. I believed that if I could come here, learn what I needed to and go back home with a practical Plan B solution, it'd be best for us all, but then we got abducted. After that, my plan was to somehow get out of Burrel, which Dhariwal made happen through Yuri,' said Raj.

AV was about to reprimand him, when Sniper intervened. 'I think I understand your point. What happened next?'

'When I came out of prison and into the hotel, I realised from Sniper's conversations with Dhariwal that the entire Plan A had failed and now the only mission was to get me and Geeta out. When I realised that Strike 4 was getting compromised, I decided to act unwell and take my time to solidify my Plan B. When I got to know that Sniper was going ahead with Strike 4, but in a new format I decided to come clean. Then I realised that the entire plan was based on a lot of assumptions, such as Misha being succssful in taking out Beqir, and Robert retaliating and taking out Tefik. As per my calculations, Mish would not have been successful, so I decided to execute my own Plan B.

'Which is?' asked AV.

'Execute Beqir and then proceed to assassinate Tefik,' said Raj.

'And you were planning to do this alone?'

'No. With the help of Idrees and Salahi,' replied Raj.

The Ghosts looked at each other in amazement and then turned to Raj.

'You did not learn anything from the Kathmandu mission is it? This lone ranger, Rambo shit is what you were told not to do. And you are once again repeating it,' said Lala.

'Would Dhariwal or any of you have agreed to assassinate Metta after what we all have gone through?' asked Raj.

'Never,' said AV.

'There you go. This is the reason why I chose to go alone. I was assigned to complete Plan B and I will not return without completing my mission,' said Raj firmly.

'It is this stubbornness that got you into Burrel,' said AV.

'No. It was the poor execution of Plan A that got me into Burrel,' retorted Raj.

AV shifted in his seat. 'But Dhariwal got you out of Burrel.'

'Yes. I knew Dhariwal would have realised his Plan A had failed and he had to get me out. But in Burrel, when I realised I was going to be placed with the general population, I knew I would not survive even 48 hours so I had to get myself into a private cell. So I feigned PTSD symptoms, hoping the staff would see that I was unwell and needed to be away from the other inmates. Soon I realised that PTSD was not enough to get me hospitalised—the only way out of Burrel seemed to be on a stretcher. When Yuri came to hit me, he told me he was Gef's friend and following instructions. He deliberately hit me in my ear & severed an artery so that the bleeding would be intense. Then they would be forced to take me to the hospital, thinking I was haemorrhaging,' replied Raj.

'So you were confident Dhariwal would get you out of Burrel. But how did you know you would be under Sniper's care?' asked Lala who was curious.

Raj held Sniper's gaze for a while. 'After my dad's death, I always considered Sniper a father figure. I knew that he would come for me, no matter what.'

'If you believed in him so much, why did you ditch him and disappear? He was devastated by your absence,' said AV.

'I left him a message. "*Retribution is patient only till opportunity knocks.*" It couldn't be a detailed one, lest it be discovered by our enemies, so I hid it using "sympathetic ink". I knew he will see through my message and know where I was headed, which is why I asked Gef for this guest house and why Sniper brought you all here. He knew I would come here because Sniper was the only one who knew I had stayed in this guet house during my first visit.

'So Sniper pushing Dhariwal to take approval from DD to extract Geeta was an excuse to meet you?' asked Safi.

'Not exactly,' Raj replied. 'While Sniper anticipated my arrival here, extracting Geeta could have been part of his plan as well.'

While the Ghosts looked at Sniper, AV asked him the difficult question: 'Is it true?'

Sniper looked at Raj with tears in his eyes. '"*It's time to leave this place and start something new, but don't forget the ones who stood by you. Especially the ones who never gave up on you.*" Those were your words the day before you left.'

He addressed AV next. 'Yes. That night, when he said this, I suspected he was looking for retribution. I suspected the illness was all an act. But I wasn't sure. When I saw the message he left for me on the mirror, I started connecting all the statements he had made to me over the previous few days. I knew then that my doubts weren't unfounded and that he was headed for retribution and he was going to execute Plan B. I did not want to ruin his plans, instead be a strength to help him deliver Plan B. So I went along with

Caleb and completed that part of the mission and then told Dhariwal that we need to extract Geeta, knowing very well that Raj is headed here.

'"We'll find him when he wants us to find him." That's what you told us when we were discussing Raj earlier,' said Lala.

Sniper nodded. 'Yes. When he took Gef's Mercedes, I knew he wants me to find him as I had put a tracker on all the cars belonging to Gef without anyone's knowledge. Raj also knew I would have done this, hence the moment the Mercedes moved, I was convinced it was Raj and he was heading here.'

'Anyway, what's important is that we're all together now. Let's put the past behind us and move forward. Strike 4 is incomplete without the execution of Plan B,' said Raj.

The Ghosts' gazes lingered on Raj for a moment, before they all nodded. The anger had disappeared from everyone's faces. The team was back together again.

'Do we inform Dhariwal?' asked Safi.

'I'll do it when the time is right. As of last night, I'd told Dhariwal that we're going dark till we extract Geeta because we don't want any leaks,' said Sniper.

The lack of sleep, the anxiety, the anger and then the final explanation—it was all too much for the Ghosts, who seemed to have hit their limit for the day.

'No more conversations around Strike 4 till tomorrow morning, boys,' said Sniper. 'Today we rest and recoup. Tomorrow, we plan with fresh minds.'

21

IT WAS 8 A.M. ON 7 JULY 2020, and the Ghosts were all gathered around the breakfast table.

Idrees and Salahi had bonded well with the group. As far as they were concerned, Raj, a businessman, was on a mission to rescue his wife, who was being held captive at Beqir Mansion. Sniper and his team were helping Raj.

Sniper sat at the head of the table with Safi, AV and Lala to his right and Raj, Idrees and Salahi to his left. Lala was trying to understand from Raj the concept of 'sympathetic ink' messaging.

'What exactly is it?' Lala asked.

'Have you heard of invisible ink? That's another name for sympathetic ink. It's invisible either on application or soon thereafter, and can later be revealed by using heat or ultraviolet light. I left a message on the bathroom mirror using this ink and Sniper read it using a UV torch.'

'What was the message again?' asked Lala.

'"*Retribution is patient only till opportunity knocks*,"' said Raj as he bit into a slice of toast.

'Nice quote. Your own or you borrowed it?' asked Lala.

'I borrowed it,' said Raj.

'All right, folks, let's get down to business,' said Sniper, getting everyone's attention. 'Raj, take us through your plan.'

Raj got up and walked over to the large coffee table, where he had placed a site plan of Beqir Mansion. It was a hand drawn plan based on his observations when he was held captive there. The rest was courtesy Google earth. He invited everyone to gather around him.

Raj tapped on the wooded area behind Liqeni Kroko and said, 'We will park the SUV about 150 metres from Liqeni Kroko in this forest. The woods run parallel to the outer bank of Liqeni Kroko. From here, we will use the RHIB to cross the lake.'

'As per the information given by Adia to Dhariwal, Beqir has increased the number of guards at the main entrance and around the compound because he's expecting Misha and his team to attack him from the main road. He's not expecting an attack from us, and that too from across the lake,' said Sniper.

Then he pointed to what looked like a large wooden shed on the inner bank of Liqeni Kroko, about 75 meters from the mansion. 'These are the barracks for his guards. According to Gef, there are ten men, including the two at the main gate.'

'What if he has added more?' asked AV.

'We'll find out only when we cross over. We cannot afford to draw too much attention to ourselves, so everything has to be done using silencers and, if need be, using hand-to-hand combat, in the worst case scenario,' said Raj. 'Our plan is to attack at 2 in the morning because by that time everyone will be fast asleep. Idrees and Salahi will take the residential section, as most of the guards will be there to protect Beqir. Their job is to neutralise the guards and then kill Beqir. I'll focus on the office tower because Geeta is on the top floor.' He looked at Idrees and Salahi, who nodded in agreement.

'That won't be an issue. I'll take Adia into confidence and ask her to keep the main doors of both towers open,' said Sniper.

'Once we're in, we'll have to play it by ear. Remember, our main goal is to get Geeta out and back to the boat. I'm hoping that Idrees and Salahi will manage to hold the guards, if there are more than expected, till I leave with Geeta and return here,' said Raj.

'Will three people be enough to handle all this? Why don't Lala and I come with you?' asked AV.

'The more of us there are, the easier it is for them to spot us. They are ten and we are three. Shouldn't be a problem if we take them by surprise,' said Raj.

'I agree with Raj,' said Sniper, though he had a worried look on his face.

'Why have you planned the attack for so late tonight?' asked AV.

'My horoscope for tomorrow morning says, "Go forth and conquer." So that's what I plan to do,' said Raj, winking at AV. 'Honestly, it's just that I want her out before Misha attacks.

'All the best. We'll wait for you here. In case you feel outnumbered, call. We'll be there in fifteen minutes flat,' said Sniper.

After the briefing, Raj, Idrees and Salahi went off on a recce. They pinpointed exactly where the SUV would be parked and once again ran through the entire Beqir Mansion attack in excruciating detail. They spent hours hidden in the tall grass in the woods, studying the mansion and the guards' movements. Finally, at 6 p.m. they returned to Gef's guest house, had an early dinner with the rest of the Ghosts and hit the bed to get some rest before they left for the mission.

Sniper sat alone in his room for a while and then finally picked up the phone and called Dhariwal.

'We found Raj,' he said.

'Is he okay? Where was he?' Dhariwal was anxious to know every detail, and Sniper did not disappoint him, relaying every last detail to him.

'He's just like his father, Veer,' said Sniper. 'So loyal to the nation that he will willingly die for it. We could not change Veer, and I don't think we can change Raj. He will not return till he completes Plan B.'

'Veer died because of his patriotism. I cannot let Raj do the same,' said Dhariwal.

'Neither can I,' said Sniper.

'Then what do you plan to do?' asked Dhariwal, unable to keep the worry from his voice.

'I plan to go to Beqir Mansion tonight. I won't tell Raj, but I'll make sure I'm there when he needs me,' said Sniper.

Dhariwal said nothing, deep in contemplation. Then, he said softly, 'You're my only friend, Arvind. Without you, I'll be alone. So make sure you come back in one piece.'

'I will, Ajit. I promise,' said Sniper.

His next call was to his wife, Bhavani, in Pune. 'How are you, my dear?' he asked when she answered the call.

Holding back tears, she responded, 'I'm okay. But how

are you? Are you okay? When will you come back?' After the loss of their three sons to the hands of terrorists, the mere thought of losing Sniper unnerved her. Every time he went on a mission, she feared for his life.

'I'm holding up. Everything's going according to plan. Raj was asking about you,' he lied. Since the Rana family had been close to Arvind and Bhavani, after the loss of their children, the couple considered Raj their son. Raj loved them and met them whenever he was in Pune. But ever since Raj became one of the Panther's Ghosts, Bhavani had hardly seen his face.

'Was he?' she asked, a smile in her voice.

'Oh, yes. He said that after this is over, he's coming home to meet you, his second mother,' said Sniper.

'Did he say that? Did he really call me his mother?'

'He did. You know how fond he is of you. He's always maintained that he has two mothers. One in London and one in Pune,' said Sniper.

Bhavani could not control her tears any longer. 'I miss my children, Arvind,' she sobbed. 'And I miss you. Promise me you will come back,' she pleaded.

'I promise,' said Sniper for the second time that night, unaware that AV had walked into the room to ask him something. AV quietly retraced his steps and left before Sniper could see him.

～

At 1 a.m. on 8 July 2020, Raj, Idrees and Salahi got ready to leave for Beqir Mansion. Before they got into the car,

Sniper walked up to Raj, held him by his shoulders and said, 'May Goddess Kali be with you throughout this mission and give you the strength and the wisdom to face your enemy fearlessly.'

Raj felt the weight of his words. He thanked him, hugged the other Ghosts and got into the SUV with Idrees at the wheel and Salahi in the back. Inside the car, the weapons and the necessary equipment had already been loaded and kept ready, and to its roof was fastened the RHIB. They left at exactly 1.05 a.m. with a promise that they would return to the guest house the next morning with Geeta. On the way, Salahi called Gef and brought him up to speed on everything.

'Go with God,' Gef said before hanging up.

Thirty minutes later, Raj and the boys were positioned on the outer bank. The SUV was well hidden. All three synchronised their watches down to the second and began surveilling Beqir Mansion using night-vision goggles. The intent behind the scrutiny was to see where the security guards were at the moment.

'I see four guys in pairs taking rounds of the compound. There is an eight-minute gap when all four are on the other side of the mansion. That's our chance to cross the lake,' said Raj.

'Got it,' said Salahi. He and Idrees pulled down the RHIB and dragged it to the water. All three got into the boat and waited for Raj to give the signal. The moment the four guards disappeared around the corner, Raj murmured, 'Let's go.' Idrees started the engine, and they shot across the lake.

Though the sound of the boat wasn't very lound, it carried to the guards, and they hastened to where the noise was coming from. But before the guards reached the lakeside, the trio docked the boat and raced towards the mansion. Taking advantage of the shadows cast by the mansion's tall walls, they blended into the darkness, waiting for the guards to arrive. Salahi had the SAKO ready, while Raj and Idrees were carrying their Glocks.

A minute later, the four running guards reached the now motionless boat. They looked around for intruders, eyes scanning the vicinity. Not seeing anyone, they slowly approached the boat with their AK-47s drawn. Salahi looked through the scope of the SAKO and squeezed the trigger. The bullet hit one of the guards in the back of the head. His head exploded, and he fell headlong into the water. Realising that their intruder was behind them, the other three turned towards the mansion walls, but Salahi was too fast for them. Before they could even raise their guns, the SAKO had fired two quick shots, one hitting the second guard in the chest, flinging him backwards into the lake, and the other making contact with the third guard's forehead. The fourth guard, while turning, had accidentally dropped his rifle into the water, so he reached down for it, desperately. Idrees, who had seen him drop his rifle while Salahi was firing, charged at him, a hunting knife in his right hand. The fourth guard, pulled out his pistol, cocked it and turned towards them, but by then Idrees was upon him like a tiger.

The guard could only watch, paralysed, as the glistening knife descended into his chest. Within a few seconds, it was done. The entire attack on the four guards lasted not more than a minute and a half.

Raj and Idrees pushed the bodies into the water. The

submerged corpses created a flurry of bubbles for a few seconds before quickly sinking into the depths of Liqeni Kroko. The scent of the blood woke the Nile crocodiles, who came swiftly for the bodies. Within minutes, four crocs had a man each between their jaws, and they disappeared into the water for a quiet meal.

Raj and Idrees walked back to Salahi and dialled Adia's number. She answered in less than a ring. 'Yes?'

'Four down, six to go,' said Raj.

'Geeta's in the penthouse in the office tower. There's a guard outside her door. There are two at the main gate and at the residential tower, there are two outside Beqir's bedroom, and there's one guard inside,' she whispered.

'How is Geeta?' Raj asked.

'I gave her a shot of physostigmine, an antidote for scopolamine, ninety minutes ago. The antidote must have started working on her body already, but it'll take another twenty minutes for her to come out of the drugged state.' she said.

'Roger that,' said Raj, and disconnected. He briefed the boys on his conversation with Adia and then said, 'You two take the residential tower; I'm going for Geeta. All the best.'

Inside the residential tower, the Arabs entered the living room first, just to make sure there was nobody there. Then they advanced to the bedrooms, along a corridor. Contrary to what Adia had told them, there were no guards outside any of the rooms, so they quietly started inspecting each bedroom one by one. Having searched two rooms, they were about to enter the third, when their attention was drawn to the sound of water trickling onto leaves. They quickly walked outside in the direction of the sound and found a guard standing in the garden outside the bedroom and relieving himself. Another was a couple of feet behind him, smoking a cigarette. The boys realised that the guards' lack of alertness made this a good time to attack. But before neutralising them they needed to confirm in which room Beqir was sleeping. Idrees, thinking quickly, took a very small stone and threw it at the door of one of the unchecked bedrooms. The moment the stone hit the door, the guards outside turned and ran towards the bedroom that was at the far end of the corridor. They hastily entered the room.

'That's Beqir's bedroom,' whispered Idrees, as he signalled Salahi to follow him. Glocks in hand, the boys moved stealthily, under cover of the dark, and reached the door in seconds. Salahi stood to the left of the door, and Idrees to the right. Leveraging his size, Idrees turned and smashed the door in with his right foot. As the door gave way, the guards inside, expecting eye-level threats, were surprised. Using the training they'd learnt on the street, the boys had dropped to the ground and fired upwards the moment the door caved. For a few seconds, the two guards had no clue who was firing and from where. That was enough for the boys to unload three shots into each of them.

The third guard inside reached for the pistol in his hip holster. He pulled it out, turned like a ballet dancer and aimed at Idrees, who had already stood up and was advancing. But he forgot about Salahi, who was still on the floor. As the guard lifted his pistol to fire, the Glock in Salahi's right hand bucked twice. The powerful shots hit the guard's throat, flinging him onto a glass table, which shattered as his lifeless form crashed into it.

Salahi stood up quickly and walked across to Idrees. 'Where is Beqir?' he asked.

Idrees inspected the entire room, including the bathroom, but came back shaking his head. 'He's not here.'

'Oh, I *am* here,' came a voice.

The boys spun around. Beqir was standing at the door with a sawed-off shotgun in his hand. They had been so engrossed in the fight that they never heard the main door open quietly.

'The question is, who are you?' Beqir asked.

The boys did not respond. They stared at him as their mind raced for a way to kill him. Beqir looked at both for a few seconds, then aimed and fired at Idrees. The 12-gauge bullet hit Idrees right in the chest, lifted him three feet in the air and sent him crashing against the wall. Salahi dived to the left, behind a wooden cabinet as Beqir turned the barrel towards him. Tears streamed down his face as he looked at Idrees's body, lying a few feet away from him. There was a gaping hole in his chest where the bullet had hit him at close range. He looked at his lifeless childhood friend and brother-in-arms and wept quietly as he hid behind the cabinet.

'There is no way out, Mr Whoever-You-Are. Your friend is as dead as a doornail, and you're next,' said Beqir.

Salahi was about to respond, when he heard the door opening and Beqir saying, 'Adia, thank God you're here. Summon the guards immediately. We have two intruders here to assassinate me. Misha must have sent them.'

'Sure, General,' Adia said.

Then Salahi heard two shots, and everything went silent. A few seconds later, he heard Adia's voice. 'The General is dead. You can come out now.'

Salahi hesitated a bit and then stepped out from behind the cabinet. His eyes went to the body of General Beqir Hoxha, lying in a twisted heap on the floor. Adia's first bullet had hit him in the right shoulder, sending him spinning. The second bullet had made contact with the side of his head. Brain matter seeped out of the gaping wound.

Salahi noticed the Winchester rifle in Adia's hand and nodded. Then he couldn't help but stare at Idrees.

'Make sure you give him a decent burial, please,' said Salahi, picking up Beqir's shotgun and loading the chamber. Then he muttered, a prayer in which he asked God to forgive Idrees for any sins he may have committed, and walked out.

Adia looked at her watch. It was 3 a.m. on 8 July, 2020. Then she looked down and spat on General Beqir Hoxha's corpse. 'You lived like a dog and died like one.'

She walked out of the room and went to the garage where a golf cart was parked. She drove it to the side of the bedroom, dragged Beqir's body on to the cart and drove off to the lake. At the lake, she dragged the body out of the cart and pushed it into the lake. 'You loved your pets very much. Rest in pieces with them,' she said with a laugh.

After sending Beqir into his watery grave, Adia headed to the General's office, sat at his desk and dialled a number from the General's cell phone. The call was answered almost immediately with a laugh.

'Yes, General,' said Robert Sullivan.

'This is Adia,' she began. 'The General is dead.' Robert

was well-acquainted with Adia, as she was the one who often connected the General to him.

'What? How? Who is behind this?' asked Robert, shocked.

'It was Misha Perci,' said Adia.

'Why?'

'Revenge for the death of the kryes.'

'Did the General actually have a hand in that?' asked Robert.

'I'm not sure. After the Hoti massacre, Joseph Lika has been missing. And the General did not deny it when I asked him if Joseph was instructed to eliminate the kryes,' said Adia. With that, she told Robert she needed to take care of logistics and hung up the phone.

A stunned Robert rushed to the Oval Office and told Ann Wayne, 'I need to see the President now.'

Ann nodded, sensing Robert's urgency, and led him to the President, who was busy preparing a welcome speech for the Crown Prince of Saudi Arabia, who was arriving the next day.

'What is it, Bob?' asked President Hussain Akhmu, seeing Robert's flushed face.

'General Beqir Hoxha has been assassinated by Misha Perci. It won't be long before Beqir's army goes after Misha.'

'What about Tefik?' asked Akhmu.

'He's a shrewd man. To avoid civil unrest, he'll confine Misha to house arrest and order an investigation. This way he can tell the army that action has been taken and at the same time ensure Misha's safety from Beqir's loyalists,' said Robert.

'You seem to have lost your main man in Tirana, Bob. People are dying all over there and you seem to be only bringing me bad news all the time.' The President sounded irritated.

Robert gave Akhmu a frustrated look but kept his cool. 'Neither am I the President of Albania nor their NSA, hence I do not have control over the actions in their country, Mr President. Still I will see how we can salvage the situation.' Having given Akhmu an acidic retort, Robert got up and left the Oval office.

At that very moment President Akhmu decided: 'Its time to put this arrogant jerk in his place.'

22

IT WAS 1.30 A.M. ON 8 JULY 2020 when Raj walked up the four flights of steps to the penthouse. On the second landing, he spotted a guard, busy lighting a cigarette. Raj tiptoed up to him. He was just a few feet behind him when the guard sensed movement and turned. But he was too late. Raj plunged his bowie knife into his throat, ripping his vocal cords. Blood gushed out of the wound as Raj pulled out the knife. The guard cupped his throat, trying to stop the blood flow. He dropped to his knees and rolled over. Blood seeped from his body, trickling down the steps. Raj ascended the next flight of steps in seconds. In the penthouse, he found Geeta, alert and waiting. The antidote physostigmine had done its work. The moment Geeta saw Raj, she jumped up and ran into his arms.

'Thank God you're safe. I worried for you every minute,' she sobbed.

'Shhh … there's no time for talking. We need to get out of here. Can you walk?' he asked her.

She nodded, wiping the tears from her face.

'Come. Let's go then,' said Raj, taking her by the hand and leading her out of the penthouse on to the wooden deck outside.

Just as they stepped out, a garotte was looped around Raj's neck and a pair of powerful hands yanked him back, off his feet. He landed on his back on the wooden deck. Raj's assailant was unexpected: six feet four inches tall and extremely muscular—someone they hadn't accounted for. With one foot on Raj's back, the Albanian started tightening the garotte. Black spots started swimming before Raj's eyes, and he knew he was inches from death. Geeta tried to help, lunging at the Albanian, but weak from the drugs, she was no match for the huge man. He grabbed her by the neck and flung her aside, her head hitting the wooden railing, knocking her unconscious.

With only moments to act, Raj pulled out his hunting knife with his left hand, swung it behind him and plunged it into the ankle of the Albanian. The man let out a loud scream and let go of the garotte. Raj immediately yanked the noose off his neck, took a couple of deep breaths and stood. Blood from the slit ankle of the Albanian was spreading quickly, so when the man tried to stand, he stumbled and fell.

Raj slipped the hunting knife back into its sheath and went for the Glock, which was lying a few feet away from him. Noticing this, the man, who had managed to get back to his feet by now, kicked the Glock away from Raj with his uninjured leg and slowly moved towards him. As the man advanced, Raj leaned forward, pulled out the Browning strapped to his ankle holster and fired point blank at the guard's face. The .25 ACP cartridge hit the Albanian between the eyes from a distance of three feet, leaving a neat hole in his forehead. The Albanian stared into Raj's eyes for a few seconds before his own eyes turned glassy and he rolled over, dead.

Raj picked Geeta up, throwing her over his shoulder. Then he climbed down the four floors and headed for the boat, where he hoped the boys would be waiting for him. He feared the sound of the shot from his Browning would have carried across the compound as the night was still. *Someone will soon come looking for me.* Little did he know that between him and the boys they had cleaned up almost everyone. But the final and only two soldiers left guarding the main gate had heard the shot, as Raj headed towards the boat with Geeta.

At the lake, he placed Geeta gently inside the boat and called Idrees. The phone kept ringing, but there was no response. The same occurred when he tried calling Salahi. He thought for a second and then called Adia.

'Any idea where the Arab boys are?' he asked her.

'One is dead and the other left, asking me to give his friend a decent burial,' said Adia.

'Who is dead?' asked Raj in a panic.

'The big muscular guy is dead,' replied Adia.

Raj felt as though he had been punched in the stomach. A wave of grief crashed over him as he thought of Idrees's smiling face. He wiped the tears building in his eyes and said, 'Salahi is right. Give my friend a good burial, Adia. He deserves it. If I'm alive at the end of all this, I'll come and pray at his grave.'

'You do that,' said Adia, feeling the weight of his pain.

'Where's Salahi gone? After Beqir?' asked Raj.

'Beqir is dead. I shot him. I don't know where your friend went,' said Adia.

Raj thanked her, disconnected and waited in the boat.

Something told him Salahi would come. As he waited, he tried to revive Geeta. He was so busy trying to get her back to consciousness that he did not hear the two guards slowly approaching him. By the time he heard them and whirled around, the guards were hardly three feet from him. Both had their AK-47s pointed at him and Geeta.

'Who are you?' asked one.

'I came to take the lady,' said Raj, trying his best to keep them occupied till he could figure out an escape plan. Then, from the corner of his eye, he saw the familiar figure of a man with a grey beard moving stealthily towards them, a Glock in his hand. But Raj knew he had to keep a straight face for the guards scrutinising him.

'I think he is Misha's man. Boss said they will be coming,' said one guard to the other as they continued to train their guns on him.

'Are you?' asked a guard, taking one more step towards him.

By now the bearded man was almost behind them like a Ghost.

'No,' said Raj.

'Liar,' said the other guard, cocking his gun. He was about to shoot, when the bearded man shot one of the guards from the back.

The second guard whirled around, alarmed, and saw that the bearded man was hardly 6 feet behind them. He fired three shots at the the man with the beard. The first bullet missed, but the second hit the man in the stomach and the third in the left lung, puncturing it immediately. The man rocked back due to the impact of the shots and fell to his knees. Just as it seemed he'd collapse, with a loud roar, he lifted his rifle and fired a final shot that hit the guards right in the middle of the forehead, killing him instantly.

The Glock slipped from the bearded man's hand, and he fell headlong on the wet sand.

'Sniper, no!' screamed Raj, vaulting from the boat and running towards him, unaware that the first guard had somehow survived and was aiming at Raj's back.

Then the still night was shattered once again by a shot. Raj stopped in his tracks and turned around. The guard behind him toppled, half his face missing. Behind him was Salahi, holding Beqir's still-smoking shotgun. He had come running to the boat as he had heard the shots. Their eyes met for a second, and then Raj's attention snapped back to Sniper.

As blood poured out of Sniper's mouth, he looked at Raj with a wry smile on his face and whispered, 'I believe Veer died like this too.'

With tears streaming down his face, Raj placed Sniper's head in his lap. 'Don't go. Please don't go,' he begged.

'Raj,' Sniper whispered, drawing one last breath before going limp.

The night sky was filled with Raj's anguished cries as he looked to the heavens for justice. 'Why him, God? Why not me?' Salahi made his way over and held him tightly as Raj sobbed. Adia watched them from the window of Beqir's office with moist eyes.

Raj fought hard to regain composure.

'We need to leave,' advised Salahi.

Raj nodded, wiped his face and said, 'Yes, Dawn is breaking. 'Take Sniper and Geeta to Gef's guest house and hand them over to AV and Lala. They will ensure that they reach India. Sniper has a wife to mourn him, and Geeta a father to rejoice at her return.'

'What about you?' asked Salahi.

'I have work to do,' said Raj, his voice now cold, as he picked up Sniper's Glock and one of the guard's AK-47s and walked off towards the main gate.

Adia was by now waiting for him at the gate with a set of keys in her hand. She handed them over, pointed to the Range Rover parked in the corner and said, 'I can guess where you're going. May God be with you.'

Raj got into the car and dialled a number on his Thuraya. 'Target eliminated and extraction complete. Two casualties so far,' he said.

'Who all?' asked the voice on the other end.

'Idrees and Sniper,' said Raj, his voice choked with grief.

There was a moment of silence on the other end, and then: 'Where are they?'

'Adia will bury Idrees here. Geeta and Salahi are accompanying Sniper's body. They are on their way to AV and Lala,' said Raj.

'I will ensure they are brought back home. You take care.'

Raj started the Range Rover but sat there for three full minutes. Overwhelmed by a cocktail of sorrow, rage and frustration, he was transported back to when he had stood in front of his father's dead body in the cold morgue a few years ago.

'Everyone I love dies. I'm a bad omen,' he muttered.

Finally collecting the resolve, he hit the accelerator. The Range Rover jumped forward, leaving behind a thick plume of dust as he raced towards the Palace of Brigades.

Salahi could see the grief in the Ghosts' eyes when he arrived with Geeta and Sniper. Lala, devastated, hugged Sniper's body tightly as AV and Safi carried Geeta to a room upstairs. After making sure she was tucked safely into bed, they came down. As Safi sat next to Sniper's body, he was reminded of the multiple times he had saved the man in in the past. 'Why couldn't I save him this time?' he whispered to AV who was standing next to him.

AV who till now was controlling his emotions, let go of them and sobbed his heart out. 'He lived to get justice for his sons and died saving his adopted one,' said AV as his body racked with sobs.

After a few minutes, he took control of himself and turned to Salahi. 'Where is Raj?'

'He disappeared again. He asked you all to leave,' said Salahi.

'What's your plan?' asked AV.

'I've told Gef about what's happened. He's asked me to leave for Greece. I'll wait there for further instructions from Gef,' he said.

AV nodded. Salahi got up, bid farewell to everyone and walked out of the house. Before leaving, he turned around. 'Good luck.'

AV looked at Lala and Safi and said, 'Let's move Sniper and Geeta to the airport. The plane is waiting for us.'

Within minutes, they had loaded Sniper's body into one of their SUVs. When Lala and AV went up to fetch Geeta, they saw her stirring. They immediately washed her face with cold water and waited for her to regain her consciousness. The moment she opened her eyes, her first question was, 'Raj?'

AV explained what had happened and escorted her into the SUV.

~◦∭~

It was noon as the SUV made its sombre journey to the airport. A grief-stricken Geeta prayed in her heart that she would not lose Raj too. At the airport, the docking area for private planes was quiet and empty because most of the private jets owned by businessmen and traders had left Tirana, fearing travel bans and other restrictions as a result of the Hoti massacre. The Ghosts loaded Sniper's body into the waiting Learjet where an icebed had already been organised by Gef, and boarded the aircraft.

Then AV called Gef.

'We're leaving Gef, but without Raj. He's gone again. If he contacts you, which I know he will, tell him we cannot carry more grief in our souls, so to please take care of himself. We're praying for him.' AV signalled to the pilot, who gave him a thumbs-up and guided the jet towards the runway.

Just then, AV's Thuraya started buzzing. He looked at the screen and said to Lala, 'It's Raj.'

Lala immediately asked the pilot to stop the aircraft. As the Learjet came to a stop three feet from the main runway, AV answered Raj's call.

'Yes?' he asked.

'My battery is dying. You and Lala meet me at the chapel in Blloku at 5.30 p.m. today.' Raj was about to say something else, but the phone went dead.

AV looked at Lala. 'He wants us to meet him at a chapel in Blloku at 5.30 p.m. today. Where the hell is that?'

'I don't know,' said Lala.

'Wait, I've seen this word,' said Safi. 'It was in Raj's drawings, the ones Sniper showed us.'

'But where are the drawings?' asked AV.

'If we're lucky, Sniper may still be carrying them,' said Geeta.

The Ghosts immediately informed the pilot, who taxied back to the bay and opened the cargo hold, where Sniper's body was kept on ice. Geeta began searching Sniper's pockets. She finally found the drawings, wrapped in a polythene bag, in Sniper's back pocket. She spread out the pages. Safi pointed to a chapel-like structure. 'Blloku'.

'Where is it?' asked AV.

Lala traced his fingers from the chapel to the Palace of Brigades and stopped at a number. He tapped it and said, '8 kilometres from the Palace of Brigades.'

AV pocketed the papers. 'You and Geeta carry on,' he said to Safi. 'We'll see you later.' Geeta tried to protest and asked to be included but AV was firm that she leave with Safi

'Will we?' asked Safi.

'Will we what?' asked Lala.

'Will we see you later?' asked Safi.

'God willing, you will,' said Lala.

They all embraced, and while AV and Lala walked back into the terminal, Geeta and Safi flew off to Greece, where a commercial flight and a private jet was waiting for them. As Geeta and Sniper returned to India in Pavak Dahiya's private jet, Safi boarded the commercial flight to Pakistan.

23

IT WAS 12.30 P.M. ON 8 JULY 2020. Misha Perci watched his brother-in-law pace the library for a while and then asked, 'Do you have a plan, or should I tell you what I have in mind?'

Tefik had called Misha in for questioning, and they were in his library. 'Repeat what Adia said to you this morning,' said Tefik, ignoring Misha's question.

'She said Beqir Mansion was attacked early this morning, between 2 and 4 a.m. Four assassins entered Beqir Mansion, killed all the guards, assassinated General Beqir Hoxha in his bedroom and left. They did not touch her. Later, when she went around the mansion and the compound, she found dead bodies everywhere. She said that it was a complete bloodbath. Amidst all the chaos, the Indian girl also escaped,' said Misha.

'I don't give a shit about the Indian girl. What I want to know is who orchestrated the Beqir Mansion attack!' shouted Tefik, his eyes piercing through Misha.

'I don't know, Mr President,' said Misha softly.

'Ha! That's not what the CIA thinks, Misha. Robert called me this morning and told me that you orchestrated this,' said Tefik.

Misha Perci had never seen his brother-in-law like this, and for the first time he felt truly afraid of him. 'I promise you, Mr President, I had nothing to do with this. Robert is trying to drive a wedge between us. How has he concluded that I attacked Beqir?'

'The question you should be asking is not how he concluded this. The question that should be worrying you is why the CIA and the NSA of America believe you did it, Misha,' snapped Tefik, storming out, leaving Misha alone in the library.

Five minutes later, Tefik's secretary walked in. 'The President has instructed you to leave for the Presidential Palace to take care of the festivities personally. He has requested that you stay within the palace grounds.' The secretary walked out without waiting for Misha's reply.

○⟩⟨⟩∽

8,000 kilometres away in the Oval Office, Robert Sullivan sat before President Hussain Akhmu, who was waiting for Robert to respond to his question.

'If you are asking me whether after the assassination of Beqir, our plan in Albania has failed, the straightforward answer is yes. But we can always turn this around in our favour,' said Robert, a glint in his eyes.

'How so?' asked Akhmu grimly.

'If we support Hector Dekovi in toppling Tefik's government, we'll have him eating out of our hand,' said Robert.

Akhmu's eyebrows knitted together. 'Isn't that what Beqir had suggested in the first place? Then you dissuaded him and got the Indians put in jail. The FBI report says DD and Dhariwal suspect us of imprisoning the Indians. Beqir is dead, the Indians have escaped and now we're back to square one. Not to mention the fact that we've lost the trust of the world's biggest democracy.'

His frustration was evident as he continued, 'None of your plans have worked so far, Bob. The more I analyse your activities over the past few months, the more I'm convinced that your cowboy tactics are pretty myopic.' Akhmu had been waiting for a chance to lash out at Robert, especially after Charles Wood, the FBI director, told him in confidence that whispers within the White House corridors hinted at Akhmu being nothing but a puppet in Robert's hands. An African American from the Bronx, Charles had worked his way up from a beat cop to being at the pinnacle of the FBI, and he was a good friend of Akhmu.

Robert smarted at the insult. Though he kept his calm, the wooden smile on his face told Akhmu that the punch had landed in the gut. Robert's lineage was rooted in uneducated ranchers from Wyoming; only his father and he had broken that mould, pursuing education and a city life.

'My apologies for not meeting your expectations, Mr President. I'm sure you have a better solution to the Albanian problem, and I'm eager to hear it, sir,' said Robert.

Akhmu did not miss the sarcasm. He retorted, 'From now on, consult me before you decide anything, rather than informing me after you've failed. And now, as far as Albania is concerned, I recommend you put it on the back burner and focus on sorting out what's happening in Iran. The nuclear deal is back on the table, and I need a workable solution.' Then he called Ann and said, 'Send Charlie in.'

Robert understood that this was a signal that the meeting was over. As he walked out of the Oval Office, he began formulating a scheme to topple President Hussain Akhmu.

Back in the office, the President addressed the FBI director. 'What would you say if I told you I'm seriously contemplating making you my NSA, Charles?'

Charles was taken aback. 'I would say you're very kind and generous, Mr President. But what about Bob?'

'The world is vast, and we need our ambassadors everywhere. I'll station him somewhere good,' said the President.

'As you say, Mr President,' said Charles.

When Charles left the room, Akhmu swivelled his chair to take in the view of his beautifully manicured garden. He sighed heavily and called Ann in. As she entered, he gestured for her to sit, readying her for a dictation.

'Dear Bob,' he began. 'Having studied the intelligence reports that your team has put together on Iran, I have concluded it is imperative to have one of my most trusted people on the ground in Tehran. To this effect, I would like you to station yourself in Tehran by the end of this month. Effective immediately, you have been promoted to the position of "Chief Observer" for Iranian affairs. You will represent the Oval Office and its stances while stationed at the American embassy in Tehran. Best wishes for this new opportunity. Regards, Hussain Akhmu, President of the United States of America.'

'Bring this back to me to sign, give a copy each to both Robert Sullivan and the ambassador in Tehran, and file a copy in his personal dossier right away,' said Akhmu.

24

IT WAS 5.30 P.M. ON 8 JULY, 2020. Raj stood at a crossroads in Blloku and looked at the dilapidated chapel before him. There were creepers clinging to the walls and cobwebs everywhere. It was surrounded by a clearly neglected yard. The grass was almost ankle-high, and there was rubble from the broken compound walls lying everywhere. The entrance to the chapel was a small broken wooden door with the words 'Lummi kishëz, meaning 'Lummi Chapel', carved on it. The Lummis were missionaries who had settled in the east in the late nineteenth century. This was one of the few chapels built by them. Raj's eyes travelled to the two people standing ahead of him, also in front of the chapel. He pulled his cap down low and walked towards them.

'Good evening,' he said as he walked past them and pushed the door of the chapel open. It protested with a loud creak. There was barely any light inside. He took two steps down to the big hall in front of him, which had about two dozen wooden benches running on either side. Along the walls were large stained-glass windows. Once upon a time, they would have thrown vibrant colours into the room, but now, overtaken by creeping vines, they served as nothing but dirty glass panes that blocked the sunlight.

Layers of dust lay undisturbed and huge cobwebs crowned the high ceilings.

At the far end of the hall, on a wooden stage, was the altar. Behind the altar was a faded painting of Jesus, whose face seemed filled with sorrow. To the left of the altar was a massive brick wall, but to the right was a small door that led to a room. The room mirrored the chapel's general state of dereliction. Raj looked around the room and saw an old broken table, a chair next to it. Closer scrutiny revealed a door behind the table, cleverly disguised within the room's wood panelling.

Having studied the interiors of the chapel, Raj looked at AV and Lala, who had been standing at the entrance, and then sat down on one of the benches.

'What made you change your mind? I thought you liked going solo?' asked AV.

'Three people died for me. It took three deaths for me to realise that I am part of a team. I am truly sorry, AV. I really am.' Raj put his head in his hands.

'Better late than never, Raj,' said AV. 'Nothing you do will bring back Caleb, Idrees or Sniper. Let's look forward now and do what's best for our nation. But if vengeance for those we've lost is your sole goal, you can forget about Lala and me.'

Raj gave them a wry smile and looked down at his now battered shoes. 'Funny, a few years ago, when you guys were recruiting me as a Ghost, you wanted me in because my father had died on duty. You hoped I would realise his dream of making Strike 1 a success. At the time, I didn't join you all just to exact revenge for my father's assassination—I joined to see through an unfinished mission. The situation is no different today. I've lost another father figure in Sniper. And once again, I am not here just to avenge him, Idrees or Caleb. I am here to fulfil the task left undone by Sniper. If you want to help make Strike 4 a success, join me. If not, I'll go alone.'

AV and Lala were silent for only a moment.

'I'm in,' said Lala.

'And I've never backed out of a mission so far,' said AV with a smile.

'What's your plan?' Lala asked Raj.

In response, Raj walked up to the old broken table and chair and pushed them aside. He attempted to open the camouflaged door, but it resisted. Despite his efforts, it did not budge.

'Move aside,' said Lala as he walked up to the door. He positioned his heel next to the handle, just below the lock, then lifted his leg and kicked hard. The handle and the lock held on, but the old hinges gave way.

The door collapsed inwards and disappeared into a gaping hole just a foot beyond the threshold. Raj approached cautiously and shone his torch into the hole. It was a vertical tunnel twenty-feet deep, with iron stairs lining its side.

'I am going to go down those stairs. Once I reach the end, I will tell you if my plan is working or not,' said Raj.

'You be careful. If you find something even slightly unsafe, call out to us. We will find another way,' said Lala.

Raj nodded. He held on to the torch and began climbing down, mentally counting the steps: thirty-two in total.

At the bottom was another door. This one was not

locked. Raj turned the old brass handle and pushed the door open. A small colony of bats screeched, erupting out of the darkness, taking everyone by surprise. Raj shone his torch inside. A long, wide tunnel stretched ahead. He looked up at the others and shouted, 'My guess was correct. You can come down or wait up there.'

AV looked at Lala and said, 'You wait here. I'll go with Raj.' He climbed down and followed Raj, who had already ventured into the long tunnel. Before continuing, Raj started a timer on his cell phone. After a twenty-minute walk without any twists or turns, they reached another door, this one ajar. Pushing it fully open, they stepped into a small, four-feet-by-four-feet space that had rocky walls. There was an iron ladder here as well, which took them up a similar vertical tunnel. Thirty-two steps again. At the top was a trapdoor. When Raj reached the door, he checked the timer. He had taken twenty-six minutes in total, end to end.

Light filtered through the gaps made by termites in the trapdoor. He peeped through the gaps but could not see much. But he could hear the muffled sounds of people talking. That meant, his guess was right. There were guards in the room above. Then came the sounds of footsteps, a chair scraping against the floor and a heavy rifle butt hitting the floor. Raj figured it had to be an AK-47.

Raj waited a few moments, taking it all in. Then he descended a few rungs and said to AV, 'This tunnel leads to the guardroom behind the palace kitchens. And from the smell of food and the sound of utensils being washed, it looks like it is being actively used.' He looked at his watch. 'It's 7. I think the guard change happens now. Typical guard handover time is twenty minutes minimum, wherein they have tea together and exchange notes. The new shift prepares the dinner and leaves, while the old shift eats the leftovers and washes the utensils. After that, the guards go to bed. Since it's a twelve-hour shift, there should be two shifts: from 7 to 7. Judging by the sound of so many pairs of boots, I think we're talking approximately seven to eight guards per shift. If so, that makes it sixteen guards in total.'

Raj reset the timer. 'Now we run back and see how long it takes.'

Both ran back to chapel. He checked the timer—nineteen minutes, a good seven minutes faster than before. 'We'll have to do better tomorrow,' Raj said.

Once they were out, AV and Raj briefed Lala on what they'd found.

'We can't all risk going through this tunnel,' said Lala as the trio walked out of the chapel grounds.

'Absolutely not,' said Raj. 'One person has to come via the regular route and give us a signal as to when we can come out through the trapdoor.'

'And who should that be? Shall I?' asked Lala, as they climbed into the parked SUV.

'No. Gef,' said Raj, starting the engine.

Enroute, he made a call to Gef, and after a thirty-minute drive, he parked the car in front of a small cottage 19 kilometres away, on the outskirts of Tirana.

'What is this place?' asked AV.

'A village called Peza. When I was in Tirana for my studies, I bought this house through Gef. I used to come here on weekends to escape the city,' said Raj.

Lala looked around at the scenic landscape. The entire village was surrounded by rolling hills. Fields stretched across the valley as far as the eye could see. It seemed like a solitary tar road ran through the village, and an overladen minibus was ploughing down it. Raj walked up to the cottage, pulled out a bunch of keys and opened the door. Once inside, he gave AV and Lala a quick tour and said, 'We have four bedrooms here. I always pictured us all spending time together here.'

Lala could sense the melancholy in his voice. 'Let's focus on the job, Raj. There'll be enough time after that to grieve.'

Raj nodded and walked off into one of the bedrooms. At 8 p.m. came a knock on the door, and Gef entered with two large duffle bags. He shrugged them off before greeting the others and offering his condolences.

As they all gathered round the dining table, Gef asked Raj, 'So, what's the plan?'

Raj spread out an A3 sheet on top of the table and pointed at the chapel and the guardroom. He said to Gef, 'Remember Gregory used to talk of an ancient tunnel that leads into the Palace? Well, we found it. We inspected the chapel and Gregory was right, the tunnel runs from the Chapel to the guardroom in the palace compound. It's old, but usable. We'll be entering the compound through the tunnel. You need to make sure that you're in the palace at least an hour before.'

Raj turned to Lala & AV and said, 'Yuri's son, Gregory, is the CEO of our film production company and he is a regular visitor at the palace as he is making a movie on the President and his wife. He has a parking space behind the kitchen compound, where he parks his minivan with his filming equipment. It's only 90 metres from his parking space to the guardroom. Make sure the weapons and the ammunition are in the van and ready for use once we change.'

'Change?' asked Lala.

'You see, Gef will be in the palace as an invitee and Gregory will be there to do his shoot for Tefik's biography. But we can enter only as soldiers. So we need to enter via the guardroom, change into the guards' uniforms, get armed and then take their place,' explained Raj.

AV, whose confusion was written all over his face, interrupted. 'Raj, you have a plan in your mind. Unfortunately, none of us are privy to that plan. If you could first run us through it, then we'll be able to understand and even contribute to it.'

Raj took a deep breath and nodded. 'The plan is to enter the Palace of Brigades on the day of the presidential couple's anniversary celebration.'

'And?' asked Lala.

'And eliminate the President and Misha.'

A heavy silence filled the room. Then Gef ventured, 'You're a businessman, Raj, not an assassin.'

'Correction, Gef. I *was* a businessman. And after losing three close friends to this President, his brother in law and his general, I am now thinking, breathing and living like an assassin.

'Assassinating the President and his brother-in-law in his own palace is not child's play. This is the job of specialised mercenaries. We are just businessmen and friends with a few weapons. We don't have the special skills to take on such a job. Also, if anyone comes to know I was involved in the

President's assassination, I will never be accepted as an arms dealer anywhere in the world,' lamented Gef.

'Look, you may have professional reasons to keep Tefik alive. But I don't. And I'm doing this with you or without you,' said Raj.

Gef looked around the table. 'Since you guys have been so open with me and have treated me like one of your own, let me confess something.'

'What is it?' asked AV.

Gef looked apologetically at Raj and said, 'I am working with Mr Ajit Dhariwal, your NSA. He and I had planned to use Beqir to topple Tefik's government by orchestrating a coup. Our intention was to install Hector as the President and Beqir as the NSA. It would have ensured me a peaceful and prosperous life and India a good ally. And it would have also allowed me to have Yuri released. He could have been reunited with his family.'

'Then what happened?' asked Lala.

'Beqir got greedy and decided to become the President without a coup. He used the idea of a coup to frame you guys and become the NSA. Then he killed the kryes to weaken Misha, but that was his mistake. Misha killed him.' Look, I am sorry I hid all this from you as Dhariwal had a deal with me that I would keep it confidential.'

'Then why are you telling us all this now?' asked Raj.

'Because I am convinced that we are all going to die soon and I wanted to leave all my guilt here before that,' said Gef.

The Ghosts exchanged glances, their faces betraying no emotion. They were pleased that the Hoti attack was being perceived the way they wanted. But were not too happy with Gef's pessimism. Raj felt guilty about hiding his true identity and so many other things from Gef. But being a Ghost meant carrying the burden of a false life.

'So what are you suggesting?' asked Raj.

'I'm not suggesting anything. I'm just saying that I have no professional reasons to keep Tefik in power. I never thought of killing Tefik, but yes, I was always keen on eliminating Misha.'

'So, can we count you in?' asked AV.

'Count me in,' said Gef.

Raj looked at AV and Lala. Both nodded, on the same page as Raj. If India wanted to win this match, Strike 4 had to be modified. Unaware that Robert had been sent as a White House observer to Iran, the Ghosts were convinced that for Robert, losing Beqir would have been a setback, but the sly fox would turn to anyone, including Tefik, to get his pound of flesh in Albania. And the only way to stop the Americans and the Chinese would be to clean up Albania.

Acknowledging their consensus, Raj continued, 'Gef, I see that you've brought the weapons and the ammunition as I had asked, but I want you to arrange uniforms for all of us too.'

'By when?' asked Gef.

'By tonight. We'll be dressed as guards and carrying our AK-47s when we enter the tunnels from the chapel,' said Raj.

'I'll have to steal them from Gregory's theatre costumes. said Gef.

'We'll do it after dinner,' said Raj. 'AV, Lala and I will be dressed as guards and waiting inside the tunnel. Once you open the trapdoor in the guardroom, we will enter from there.'

'But how do I enter the guardroom and open the trapdoor?' asked Gef.

'Convince Gregory that a photoshoot with the entire Palace guard contingent is necessary for a good biography. Time it in such a way that they are all assembeled a little away from the guard room. While they are busy shooting, you open the door for us.'

'I can do that. It is a good plan Raj,' said Gef who was earlier worried as to how he would pull this off.

Raj addressed AV and Lala. 'Once we enter, we will need to fan out. With such a large function going on, no one will really notice us, but still to take no chances, cover yourselves completely with full sleeved uniforms and scarves around the neck. We will borrow some brown wigs from Gregory's store. Make sure the COVID masks cover you entire face, leaving just the eyes.'

Raj turned back to Gef. 'Get Gregory to ensure that the presidential couple are in one room for at least thirty minutes. The rest I'll take care of.' Then he looked at everyone and said, 'I'll give you all ultra-thin lapel mics and earpieces. Wear them at all times and just follow my instructions. Any questions?' he asked.

'When exactly do you plan to execute the palace attack?' asked AV.

'Tomorrow night,' came Raj's swift response.

After dinner, the Ghosts went to Gregory's costume shop and got well-fitting uniforms, neck bandanas, and well fitting brown wigs. They decided to park the SUV outside the chapel the next day—it was going to be their getaway car.

Back at the cottage, Raj handed over two vials of 40 mg

thallium to Lala and said, 'When Tefik and his wife are inside the library, there will be two soldiers standing guard outside. Mix the thallium into juice and give it to the bodyguards as though you are serving them a refreshing drink. It won't kill them immediately, but it will make them very sick on the spot. That should be enough for you two to move.'

He turned to AV, and said, 'Once I finish with Tefik, you make sure to move his body. Keep it some place where it'll be hidden initially but found eventually.'

He continued to Gef, 'When the time is right, you'll "discover" the body and raise the alarm. Make sure you announce it so that there is absolute chaos in the palace. We need that diversion to escape.'

Raj pulled out the sheet again, spread it on the tabletop and said, 'I will assassinate Tefik, Lala will poison the guards outside the library and AV will hide the body in such a way that it can be found easily later. We three will rendezvous near Gregory's van. Gef will enter the library, find the body, raise the alarm and create chaos. The guards will rush from the guardroom to the palace. We will go down the trapdoor and escape. The SUV will be waiting for us at the chapel. We'll head for Lin from there.'

'You missed Misha. What about him?' asked AV.

'Gef wants to deal with him as it is personal,' said Raj.

'He put Yuri in Burrel, and he ruined my business. I want to deal with him,' said Gef.

'All the best, guys,' said Raj, hugging each one of them in turn. 'AV, you can inform Dhariwal now if you want.'

AV nodded and made the call. 'Strike 4 is in motion.'

'It is about time you called. The Panther and I have been on pins and needles, with no communication from your end. Sniper had told me not to call you till you extract Geeta, so I kept quiet. Where is Sniper, put him on the line,' Dhariwal was sounding very upset.

AV waited for Dhariwal to let out his steam and then explained everything to him. At the end of it, when AV realised that there was no response from Dhariwal, he asked, 'Hello, are you there?'

'Yes, I am here. And my friend died there for me and my mission. I could not do anything to help him.' For the first time AV could hear Dhariwal crying and it was too much for him. Even his eyes welled up with tears.

Once Dahriwal had regained his composure he said gently but in a worried tone, 'I would not have advised the path you all have taken, but now that you have chosen it, tell me how I can support you'.

'Just pray for us, sir. I think in this mission that is one thing we need in abundance.'

'I will. Once you leave the chapel, call me. I will have the jet ready for you in Tirana,' said Dhariwal.

'No. Don't do that. Gef's jet will be waiting for us at Sarande Airfield. We will take that to Greece, and you pick us up from there. This way we will beat the search because they will expect us to fly out of Tirana,' said AV.

'Done,' said Dhariwal. Slightly tentatively, he asked, 'How is Raj?'

'He's changed,' AV whispered, walking out of the room. 'Sniper's death seems to have permanently erased the smile from his face. His boyishness is gone too. It's like he's matured overnight. With that deadpan look in his eyes, he comes across as a stone-cold assassin. Just the way Sniper was when he came back from Pakistan.'

'What else can you expect from a man who has lost his father, his mentor and his colleagues? Just bring him back safely, AV. His mother, Shanti, has no clue about anything so far,' said Dhariwal.

'Yes, sir,' replied AV. 'I'll do my best. In case we do not, tell Panther, it was an honour to be his Ghosts.'

'I will, AV. I will,' said Dhariwal.

25

IT WAS 7 P.M. ON 9TH JULY, 2020, and the palace guards had a small change in their routine. Unlike the regular drill, where the morning shift came back to the guardroom at 6.40 p.m. for the handover to the evening shift, today both shifts were asked by the film production team to assemble in the palace courtyard for a shoot with the presidential couple. The guards were looking their best, with well-ironed uniforms, shining brass buckles and polished shoes, holding freshly cleaned AK-47s. They stood in a group behind the chairs that were soon to be occupied by the presidential couple. The entire shoot was Raj's brainchild, and Gef had convinced Gregory that the shoot would help to portray Tefik as a soldier as well.

At exactly 7.05 p.m., Gef walked into the guardroom and lifted the trapdoor. Within a minute, the Ghosts were in, and in another two minutes, they had positioned themselves inside Gregory's van. After the photo shoot with Tefik and Teuta, at 7.30 p.m., all the guards returned to the guardroom. After a bit of friendly banter, while the morning shift guards remained in the guardroom the evening shift went off to their duties. At 7.35 p.m., the Ghosts left the van and entered the palace through the kitchen.

At 7.40 p.m., when Gregory returned to his van, Gef was waiting.

'Remember, please direct the presidential couple to the library and do a ten-minute shoot showcasing the President's affinity for history and literature. After the shoot, give them a five-minute break for touch-ups. Make sure you shoot them while they leave the library and walk together hand in hand into the presidential ballroom,' said Gef to Gregory.

'I'll do that. These are going to be brilliant shots,' said Gregory.

'Let me know before you start shooting, please. I'd like to be there to see it. Don't know if I'll ever get a chance to be so close to the the presidential couple again,' said Gef with a forced laugh.

At 8.30 p.m., Gregory called Gef and said, 'The President and the wife are coming down from their room. They'll be in the library in the next five minutes.'

Gef spoke into his lapel mic, 'The couple will be in the library in five minutes.'

'I'm making my way to the library,' came Raj's voice through the earpiece. 'AV, you be outside the room, but maintain some distance from their two personal guards, who will be standing around there too. Lala, you be near the door that leads to the kitchen. Guys, make sure the silencers are snapped on your Glocks and your Covid masks are in place. Remember the AK-47s are only for show. Do not use them under any circumstances.'

Once AV and Lala acknowledged the instructions, Raj asked them, 'And the thallium vials?'

'Yes, they're ready,' said AV.

'Are you carrying your rifle, Gef?' Raj asked.

'Yes. I have my SRS with me. It's dismantled and inside my violin case, I am walking around pretending to be one of the musicians,' said Gef.

The SRS is one of the shortest sniper rifles in the world. It's versatile and can be adapted for various missions, be it long or short range. The twenty-six-inch-long rifle was Gef's favourite companion. Having the SRS was like having three more shooters with him.

'You play the violin?' asked Lala.

'I played in high school, but now I play when the mood strikes me,' said Gef.

'You decided to carry a sniper instead of a pistol?' asked AV.

'Call it the idiosyncrasy of an arms dealer,' said Raj as he entered the library through a pantry door on the east side, from where snacks and beverages were served to people in the library. Once inside, he looked for a place to hide.

The room's blood-red interiors struck him the moment he entered. The opulent ambience, reminiscent of Windsor Castle, was intensified with a pervasive crimson. Gold and scarlet textiles graced the library's wall, punctuated by priceless paintings from Ruben and Fan Kuan. Plush red carpets blanketed the floor. Ivory pedestals with Asian and European artefacts stood everywhere. Wherever the carpets ended, glimpses of red marble emerged. Crimson drapes stood guard at the windows. Two big red-and-gold armchairs had been placed close together for the shoot, facing the windows.

Raj did not take long to decide where he would hide. He

stood behind the heavy red drapes in the far-right corner, diagonally behind the camera that was set on a tripod in front of the chairs.

Three minutes later, at 8.35 p.m., the door swung open, revealing the couple hand in hand. They were flanked by three bodyguards. Two stayed outside while one accompanied them into the library, showed them to their seats, and stood behind the camera. A few seconds later, Gregory and the cameraman entered. They bowed to the President's wife, shook hands with Tefik and took their positions behind the camera with their backs to the window. The photographer prompted them with cheerful exclamations of 'Cheese!' as he clicked pictures of them. Once that was done, he operated a video camera, and took shots of the room, the couple and the view from the garden. Within twenty-five minutes, everything was done, and the camera crew exited with their equipment, leaving Gregory and the bodyguard with the presidential couple.

'By when do you think the book and the video will be ready, Gregory?' asked Tefik.

'I'll show you the first cut rushes in early September, Mr President. Once you approve them, the book and the video will be ready for your signature by the first week of November. I recommend a Christmas launch, sir,' said Gregory.

'Good. That's a nice time to launch it,' said Teuta Metta.

'We'll give you two privacy for a few minutes to freshen up, and then I'll come to get you. Please make sure you two walk slowly when you're on your way to the ballroom please, Don't look into the camera. Talk to each other, laugh, smile—the aim is authenticity,' instructed Gregory. The presidential couple nodded in agreement, and Gregory left.

Everything was going according to plan until the bodyguard decided not to leave the room. Raj waited for a full minute, hoping he would leave, but when he realised that the guard had no such intention, he stepped out from behind the drapes. The time was 9 p.m. and the presidential couple were still sitting, facing the window, when they saw a presidential guard, his face obscured by a Covid mask, step out from behind the crimson drapes. The shock was written on their faces, and their eyes went wide. The bodyguard, who had his back to Raj, noticed the couple's expression and whirled around.

The guard had barely completed a 90-degree turn, when a 9-mm steel bullet released from Raj's Glock 18 hit him in the right temple. At close quarters, the impact was great. The bodyguard fell sideways onto the table in front of the presidential couple, toppling the teapot and cups onto the heavily carpeted floor. He was dead before his body hit the ground.

Raj pointed the Glock at Tefik, threw him a pair of handcuffs and said, 'Cuff the lady to the gold plated railing behind you.' He waited until Tefik had Teuta cuffed to the barrier that ran the length of the giant bookshelf behind the chairs. Then he gave him two square pieces of cloth and said, 'Gag her and blindfold her.'

Tefik complied without a word. Then he looked at Raj and asked, 'Who are you and what do you want?'

'I'm nobody,' said Raj, 'but I can answer your second question better: I want you dead.' He waited for the words to sink in, and then fired. The silencer-topped Glock 18 bucked twice in his hand as two bullets left the barrel and smashed into Tefik's heart. The armchair toppled with the impact, leaving Tefik lying on his back, his face a few inches away from his wife.

Raj confirmed that Tefik was dead and then walked out through the pantry door, leaving Teuta Metta, lying gagged and blindfolded next to her late husband, President Tefik Metta.

As he walked out of the pantry at 9.07 p.m., he said into his lapel mic, 'The husband is down, and the wife is cuffed. There's one dead rat inside. You can handle the two outside.'

AV took the cue and said to Lala, 'Get the juice.'

Lala had already got four glasses of mixed fruit juice ready on a tray in the kitchen. He called a waitress, who was serving drinks in the ballroom, handed her a glass of juice and pointed at AV, who was standing at a distance but in full view of the two guards outside the library. The waitress carried the tray to AV. She passed the two guards on the way, who smiled at her, hoping she would give them a glass too.

When she returned, Lala handed her two more glasses, pointed to the two security guards standing outside the library and said, '*Jepni lëng rojeve.*' Give the juice to the guards. She frowned at being asked to walk the same route twice for no apparent reason, but went across and served the guards anyway. They looked at her, smiled and then raised a toast to Lala, who responded with a smile and a raised juice glass. The thirsty guards gulped down the juice, unaware that each glass contained 40 mg of thallium. Five minutes later, the waitress went around collecting the glasses and disappeared into the kitchen. The moment the glasses arrived in the kitchen, Lala waited for the waitress to leave, then he wrapped the glasses in a tea towel and broke them by smashing them on the floor. Then he dumped the broken pieces into the garbage. 'Evidence cleared,' he muttered.

Then the wait began. AV and Lala watched the two guards. They seemed unaffected, and then, at 9.10 p.m., both guards started getting restless. The thallium had kicked in, working on their nervous system, lungs, heart, liver and kidneys all at the same time. Their stomachs started rumbling badly. As both of them started walking quickly but unsteadily towards the restroom, Lala and AV calmly walked forward and took over their posts. A minute later, they entered the library, moved Tefik and the dead guard into the adjacent cigar room, and moved the still handcuffed and gagged First Lady to the bathroom. Then they opened the library doors and walked off. They cut across the corridor, entered the kitchen and made for Gregory's van.

As they walked, AV said into his lapel mic, 'The husband and the rat are hiding in plain sight and the wife is in the loo.'

'Meet outside the van,' said Raj. As he walked up to the CCTV room on the first floor. There was only one man monitoring the cameras. Raj walked up to him and wrapped his arm around the man's neck from the back. He put enough pressure to ensure that the man passed out. Then he copied the footage for the entire day on to a USB stick and erased everything from the master file. Then he closed the door behind him and quietly left the building. As he reached Gregory's vehicle, he told Gef, 'You start exploring.'

Gef took the cue and strolled into the library like a visitor interested in looking at the president's books. Then he opened the cigar room and, waiting only a second, ran to the ballroom yelling, '*Presidenti është vrarë në bibliotekë!*' The President has been assassinated in the library.

Within minutes, a group of royal guards led by Misha Perci ran into the library and found the dead President and his bodyguard. Misha turned to one of the guards. 'Find my sister. Quick.' The guard first searched the room and then moved for the bathroom. 'I found her! She's alive!' he shouted, simultaneously activating his walkie-talkie. Immediately, an alarm went off.

⊙ʃʃ~

It was 9.20 p.m. when the guards in the guardroom jumped out of bed and ran towards the palace with their rifles. The moment they crossed the van, the Ghosts ran to the guardroom, opened the trapdoor and went through it, shutting it behind them. Unfortunately for them, one of the guards, while running towards the palace, thought he saw something from the corner of his eye. After a brief hesitation, he ventured into the guardroom and noticed a hastily discarded hankerchief over the trapdoor. It had fallen out of Lala's pocket while escaping. The guard lifted the hankie, inspected it and then opened the trap door. Cautiously, he descended the trapdoor's steps and ventured into the tunnel below. He pulled out his helmet light and strapped it on his helmet before walking down the tunnel. The light was bright, and it lit up the tunnel well. As the tunnel curved slightly, he could not see its full length, but he could hear footsteps ahead. Rifle in hand, the guard started running towards the sound.

The Ghosts, hearing the guard and noticing the light, raced down the tunnel, opened the door at the end, locked it from the other side and quickly climbed up the ladder that led to the chapel. Behind them, the guard came charging. He fired at the locked door, which gave way immediately, and climbed up to the chapel. Just as his head cleared the well and came up, a 9-mm steel bullet hit him right between the eyes, sending him crashing back into the depths of the tunnel, dead.

Lala holstered his Glock and looked at his watch. '9.50 p.m. Are we on schedule?'

'We are,' Raj confirmed as he got into the driver's seat of the SUV they had parked outside the chapel the previous night. AV climbed into the passenger seat and Lala got into the back. Raj started the engine and then called Gef. 'Goodbye, my friend. Until next time.'

'Until then,' Gef replied, disconnecting when he saw Misha Perci running towards the ballroom to quell the chaos.

It was 10 p.m., and there was a literal stampede at the Palace of Brigades as the terrified guests ran helter-skelter, fearing an attack by Beqir's men. Gef added fuel to the fire by insinuating to everyone that the attack could possibly have been by Joseph Lika, who was back to avenge his master's murder. Amidst the chaos, Gef quietly walked off to the van and waited. Gregory, who had found an opportunity to get an exclusive picture of the assassinated President, went about the palace, shooting both still pictures and videos of Tefik, his bodyguards and Teuta being assisted to her room. Once she had changed into simpler clothes, they escorted her out of the building to a safe house in Tirana.

By about 11.30 p.m., the tumult at the palace had subsided. The police and the army were there, and the forensics team was combing the entire area. The one big issue the police were facing was that someone had erased the footage for the entire day from the master files leaving them clueless as to who had executed the attack.

As the Ghosts raced towards Lin, Misha Perci alerted the police who had started putting road blocks all around the city. The Tirana International aiport, metro stations and bus stations were all informed that they should report if they found any kind of suspicious activity. Without a face or a camera footage, they did not even know what to tell the authorities. All they could say was, 'Stay alert.'

By the time the city was barricaded, the Ghosts had already left the city and were enroute to Lin.

At three minutes past midnight, Gef's Bombardier Global 7,500 lifted off from Sarande Airfield and headed for Athens. Raj put his hand into the side pocket of his uniform, pulled out the USB stick and handed them over to AV.

'You can use these to reflect on what we could have done better. Might help us the next time,' he said. Then he closed his eyes. Within minutes, he was fast asleep.

'He has started behaving like Sniper,' said Lala.

'I observed that too,' said AV, as he reclined the seat and stretched out.

'Should I call Shanti and tell her Raj will be coming home tomorrow?' asked Lala.

'Don't do anything till we reach New Delhi. You never know with him. He may disappear in Greece,' said AV.

'You never know,' repeated Lala, smiling as he looked at his sleeping friend.

He noticed a tear travelling slowly from the corner of Raj's eye, and said to himself, '*Welcome to the world of trauma, brother.*'

26

IT WAS NOON ON 10TH JULY. The Air India flight took nine hours and ten minutes to cover the 5,000 kilometres from Athens to New Delhi. By the time the Ghosts cleared the airport and reached 7, Lok Kalyan Marg, a full twelve hours had passed. While AV and Lala looked exhausted, Raj seemed surprisingly alert as they waited for the Panther in his study. A nervous Dhariwal was with them. He refused to sit down and kept pacing the room till the Panther walked in.

DD noticed the irritability written all over Dhariwal's face and said, 'My apologies. The German Chancellor's departure took longer than expected.' Then he looked at the Ghosts and said, 'Come, let's go to the Library.' Once inside the library, he walked up to each one of them, shook their hands, patted them on their backs and said, 'Thank you for your service.'

The mission had suffered too many casualties for anyone to celebrate, but there was a sense of relief in the Panther's eyes as he saw at least three of his Ghosts alive and standing in front of him.

Once they were seated with steaming cups of tea in their hands, DD took out three copies of the morning newspaper and handed them to the Ghosts.

'Albania Mourns the Death of its President, Tefik Metta.

'The citizens of Albania have lost their President and their National Security Advisor in a span of a few days. The turbulence reportedly began with an attack led by Joseph Lika, the right hand man of General Beqir, the National Security Advisor, on the fifteen mafia heads at a resort in Hoti. The attack occurred in the valley of Hoti a week ago, after which Lika went missing. Sources in the government, who would like to remain anonymous say that the President's brother-in-law, Misha Perci and the General did not see eye to eye on many things and there was a power struggle between them. They also said that in retaliation to the deaths of the kryes, Misha orchestrated the assassination of General Beqir Hoxha, at his residence in Lin. Recent eyewitness accounts suggest that it was Joseph Lika who returned to lead a retaliatory attack on the President, in his library at the Palace of Brigades. While none of the reports so far is confirmed, one thing we can confirm is the police reports, which say that once again, Joseph Lika has managed to escape the clutches of the law. Three guards were found dead in and out of the Library area and one missing. It is suspected that the missing guard may have helped Joseph Lika in carrying out the attack.

'Strangely, the vice president who was to take on the responsibility of the government and seven of the eleven ministers in the ruling government have resigned overnight, leaving the opposition stronger than the ruling party. In the absence of a leader from the ruling party, opposition leader Hector Dekovi has been unanimously elected by Parliament as the caretaker president till the elections next year. Under his directive, the police and the army are uniting in a concerted effort to track down the assassins.'

The Panther looked at the Ghosts and said, 'This victory is laden with tragedy. We lost Arvind, Gef lost Idrees and Eyal lost Caleb. But it is important for us to acknowledge that we saved two nations from going hostile. Today we have Hector, who believes in India and wants to strengthen ties with us. The Americans and the Chinese have been defeated strategically and phase two of OPOR has been demolished. President Hussain Akhmu has sent Robert to Iran on a punishment posting to please us, but we will not fall for such petty gestures from cunning foes. We will continue our work.'

'Strike 4 has been a successful false flag operation. I'm proud the Panther's Ghosts made it happen, even at the cost of their own lives for some,' added Dhariwal. 'Nobody else may know our victories and tragedies, but as long as we know we're doing this to make the world a better place, we will remain heroes in our own eyes.

'Go back to your families. Rest now. Till we meet again,' said the Panther.

'Till we meet again,' echoed the Ghosts.

They were just about to leave, when the Panther said, 'Raj, stay back, please.'

Once Dhariwal and the others had departed, the Panther walked up to Raj, hugged him and said, 'Somewhere in between, I thought I had lost you.' Then he guided him to the garden outside, where both sat on a bench.

'Is Dhariwal aware that you are the puppeteer in all this?' asked Raj, looking a bit more relaxed.

'What do you mean?' asked DD.

'I mean, does he know that you were pulling all the strings of Strike 4? Does he know I had your blessing for the Kathmandu mission? Does he know the modified Strike 4 plan where I would disappear was yours?' asked Raj.

DD held Raj's gaze for a while before answering. 'No. He still thinks he convinced me to have you lead this operation. In fact, he doesn't know that you were in touch with me throughout the Kathmandu romance. As far as Strike 4 is concerned, he thinks you modified the plan, and that he was the one informing me of your movements and activities,' said DD.

'Why did you keep this from everyone?' asked Raj.

'For two reasons. One, Ajit is very process-driven and would have preferred to prepare well before the Kathmandu mission. And something we did not have was the luxury of time. When you called from London and said Haji is returning to Nepal suddenly, I had no option but to let you go and do what you did. I know I overrode Ajit's authority and gave you the approval but, like I said, time was of the essence and you were the only rebel I could use.'

'And the second reason?'

'Ajit grew increasingly trusting of Robert—perhaps too much so. In the beginning, I also trusted Robert a lot, but over time, I learnt of his duplicitous nature. Had Ajit known of the twist in the plot and changes in Plan B, the news would have reached Robert as Ajit would have shared it with him with all good intentions, and Robert would have planned a countermeasure to derail Strike 4.'

'I never thought Robert would sacrifice us for his benefit,' said Raj.

'If you look closely, he too is a patriot. He did not sacrifice you and Geeta for *his* benefit. He did what he thought was in the best interest of his nation. And like they say, all's fair in love and war.'

'So just because we won you've forgiven the Americans? There's no value to Sniper's, Caleb's and Idrees's sacrifices?'

'I'm not God. I don't forgive or forget, Raj. Everyone will pay when the time is right. For now, Robert is suffering in Iran and Xi has been hospitalised again with another heart attack. These people, including Akhmu, should not be eliminated. They should live to fully experience the repercussions of their actions. Only then will the world understand and change.'

Raj noticed a fire in DD's eyes, but it faded as quickly as it had ignited.

'Was the Burrel episode planned?' asked DD.

'No. That one took me by surprise. Even at Lin, I thought I would be able to talk my way out, but I failed miserably. But then I knew Dhariwal wouldn't let me rot there, so I waited. As Plan B, I played the role of someone with acute trauma and PTSD to get out of there. Because I knew once I was out, you would extract me.'

'And why did you maintain the PTSD façade even after leaving the hospital and while at the hotel?'

'If you recall, being extracted then and forced to return to New Delhi wasn't our agenda. After our arrests, Dhariwal had decided to can Strike 4 and focus only on extraction. Even the Hoti attack was orchestrated to support the Israelis but also to create chaos and extract us out of Tirana. The only way to fully understand and modify the plans for Strike

4 with you was by persisting with my act. And then, once the kryes were eliminated, I knew I had to disappear to complete Strike 4. That's when I called you for guidance on my next steps. And you told me to leave the message for Sniper.'

The two continued to sit in the garden side by side, in silence, for a long time, reliving the past few months in their minds. Then DD asked, 'What's your plan?'

'I'll go to Earl's Court and meet Mom. It'll be a good break for me.'

'Good idea,' said DD. As if it were an afterthought, he asked, 'What about Geeta?'

Raj thought about this for a few seconds. 'I'll meet her when it's time for the next mission, sir. Please do give her my regards when you visit her at the hospital next.'

As he got into the grey Hyundai i10 that was waiting for him outside the PM's residence, he said to DD, 'Before I go to London, I want to go to Pune to meet Bhavani Aunty and spend a few days with her.'

'She'll love that. Arvind's demise has stripped her of her joy. The best thing you can do is spend time with her,' said DD.

Raj nodded. 'Goodbye, sir,' he said.

DD's hand rose in a parting wave as the i10 drove off. And as he walked back into his office, he whispered, 'Go with God, my son. Go with God.'

27

IT WAS 6 P.M. ON 20 AUGUST, 2020. A month had passed since Strike 4, and the Ghosts were scattered across the world. The Panther and Dhariwal were engrossed in national issues, and Hector had settled well into his new role as the President of Albania. There were only three players who were still restless.

One was Robert Sullivan, who was getting baked alive in a tent in the Lut Desert in Iran. The Lut Desert was hottest during the month of August, and the current temperature was 70.7 °C. Camouflaged as a desert safari team, he and his men were investigating specific coordinates provided by the CIA, suspecting an underground Iranian nuclear arms storage.

The other two players were parked in the front seats of a black Mercedes in an alley across from the Acapulco Grande in Tirana, monitoring the main entrance of the hotel. The reason they were here was because Gef had not lived up to his promise and Misha was still alive. When Gef called Raj and told him about it, Raj was upset. But when a week ago, Gef called and said he had information that Misha was in town, Raj flew to Tirana to help him neutralise Misha.

Once again without informing anyone.

After fifteen minutes of surveillance, Raj looked at Gef and said, 'I still can't get over the fact that a month has passed and you haven't been able to locate Misha.'

'I waited that night to get him with my SRS,' said Gef, 'but he never came out of the palace. In the morning, I was told that he'd gone missing from the palace the same night. You know how badly I want him dead. Teuta must have feared for his life and packed him off somewhere. But nobody seems to know where he is. Not even Hector. It's as though the earth swallowed him whole.'

They continued to wait a while longer, and then Raj said, 'And I *still* can't get over the fact that it's been a week of this bullshit surveillance all over Albania. I think he's left the country, Gef.'

'Where would he go? I've checked with President Sani. He's not in Nigeria. My contacts have scoured the rest of Europe and the UK. No sign. If he likes being alive, he'll never set foot in America, and he has no friends anywhere else. So where else can he be?' asked Gef.

'Let's go home and regroup,' said Raj, as he signalled Gef to start the car.

Within an hour they were in Raj's cottage in Peza. After a quick shower, they ordered some Middle Eastern food and decided to sit in the garden with their drinks. The cool air was invigorating, and the chilled Glenfiddich eased their nerves, helping them think better.

'If he's not in any of the places you mentioned, then he must be somewhere we least expect him to be,' said Raj.

'I agree. But knowing him well, he's not the type to land up in some unknown country and start a new life, especially when he fears assassination,' said Gef.

Silence fell between them as they thought hard. Then Gef looked at Raj. 'Teuta loves Misha and she knows his life in Tirana is in danger what with Hector in charge of the country. I am sure she has forced him to leave the country and if she has, then it would be to a place where she feels he will be secure. I think we should focus on her likes and dislikes and not his, when we shortlist the country Misha may have disappeared to,' Gef said.

Raj's gaze was fixed on the night sky, the stars shining brightly above them. 'Did Gregory not tell us once that the entire palace interiors were selected by Teuta?' he asked.

'Yes. She decided everything from floor to ceiling and replaced most of the original stuff,' said Gef.

'The library also?' asked Raj.

'Obviously.'

'The library looked more Chinese than Albanian.'

'Like a Chinese opium den.' Gef said with a chuckle. Then, a realisation dawned on him. 'You think the bastard is in China?'

'I don't know. But I can find out,' said Raj, as he stepped back into the house and dialled Dhariwal. 'Sir, could you please contact Ann Wayne for some intel?'

'What do you need?' asked Dhariwal.

'One, what did Akhmu and Robert last speak about. And two, which country has Robert been calling the most lately.'

'What are you up to now, Raj? Aren't you supposed to be chilling?' asked Dhariwal.

'Nothing, sir. Just clearing some confusion in my mind.'

Dhariwal called an hour later. 'I spoke to Ann. Apparently, Robert has been pleading with Akhmu to allow him to come back to Washington, but Akhmu has been firm about his decision. So now Robert has asked if he can go as the ambassador to China instead of rotting in Iran. Akhmu has told him he'll get back to him on that. Regarding the other query, well, his call records indicate frequent calls to Macau. He even visited the city a week ago,' said Dhariwal.

'By the way, Ann sent us the audio visuals of the conversation between Akhmu and Robert at the White House before he left for Iran. They were discussing Tirana. We have proof now of America's involvement, especially Robert's. I trusted the bastard. Anyway, you can check it out when you're back,' Dhariwal said.

'Don't waste your time on Robert sir. Screw him. He's not worth it. I'm leaving for London tomorrow to meet Mom,' said Raj.

'Give my regards to her,' said Dhariwal and disconnected.

When they ended the call shortly after, a smiling Dhariwal echoed Raj's sentiment to himself: 'Yeah, screw him.'

Raj walked back over to Gef. 'I've been thinking—Misha is an ambitious man. He will not waste his time hiding in China. He would prefer to be safe but be able to get back his lost narcotics business. And for that he needs to be some place safe and liberal.'

'And where do you think is this "safe and liberal" place?' asked Gef sarcastically.

'Macau.'

'Macau?'

'That's right,' said Raj.

'How do we confirm he's in Macau?'

'By going to Macau. Do you have any contacts there?'

'I have a French friend there,' said Gef.

'Plan the trip for when I return from London,' said Raj as he started laying the table for dinner. By the time they'd eaten and gone to bed, it was past midnight.

⊙∬~

Five thousand three hundred and thirty seven kilometres away from Tirana, DD was talking to someone on the phone, when Dhariwal walked into his office. DD gestured to a seat and mouthed, 'One minute,' and then continued his conversation.

'Thank you for everything, Vladimir. Hector Dekovi's your man in the Balkans now. I've spoken to him already. Take care.' He disconnected and turned to Dhariwal. 'Shiva has returned from China. Let's hear what he has for us.'

Once Shiva was called to the room, DD asked, 'What's the news from China?'

Shiva had completed his recce of Qincheng thanks to the warden, a close confidant of Paitoon. To go unnoticed, Shiva had disguised himself as a Pakistani journalist writing an article about the Changping District of Beijing. Having toured the famous Great Wall at Juyong Pass, Back Garden (White Tiger Gully), Natural Scenic Area and the Ming Tombs, he was escorted into Qincheng Prison by the warden without the knowledge of anyone in the government. Despite Paitoon's influence, a lot of money had to be paid, but he got exclusive access and found out which exact cell Paitoon's brother, Chin, was in.

Shiva shared all the details and played them the video he had captured discreetly using a button-camera on his shirt.

DD addressed Dhariwal. 'You two need to put together an extraction plan for Chin. Peng told Paitoon that if Chin is out of Qincheng and somewhere safe, he will ensure that Xi is out of power. I believe the Shanghai Cooperation Organisation meet is coming up, and Xi will be attending—he's feeling good enough to. Peng said he will use that period to orchestrate a coup and topple him.'

The SCO, an intergovernmental organisation founded in Shanghai, comprised eight member states including China, India, Russia, and Pakistan. Additionally, there were four observer states—Afghanistan, Belarus, Iran, and Mongolia—and six 'Dialogue Partners' like Armenia, Azerbaijan, Cambodia, Nepal and Sri Lanka.

'I won't use the Ghosts for this, DD,' said Dhariwal.

'Then whom do you propose?' asked DD.

'We will use RAW this time. The operation will require help from multiple quarters and could escalate into a war if there is a slip between the cup and the lip, sir.'

'I agree. Go ahead,' said DD. Pausing, he added, 'Where is Raj?'

'He was chilling with Gef in Tirana for a week, then in London with Shanti last week, but when I spoke to her last, she said he'd gone to the Himalayas to meditate. She mentioned he seemed more introspective and was a lot quieter. I think some yoga and meditation will help,' said Dhariwal.

'Let him be. He'll find his way back soon. Has Bhavani's monthly stipend been arranged?' DD asked.

'Yes, Raj has taken care of that. In fact, they stay together in Veer's bungalow now.'

'That's considerate of Raj. How is Geeta?' asked DD.

'She's recovering in Nainital. Her father is with her. He took a month's leave from ID and is looking after her, I believe.'

'Good to hear. All the best for China. Once the plan is ready, let me know,' said DD.

Dhariwal nodded, and both he and Shiva made their way out, leaving the Panther to himself.

28

IT WAS 4 A.M. ON 22ND SEPTEMBER, 2020 when EVA Airlines, carrying Raj and Gef, landed at Macau International airport. Raj was travelling on a Russian passport that Gef had made for him, taking on the persona of a spiritual guru, Swami Sadananda. His documents introduced him as a senior member of the well-known Bharat Hindu Samaj in Russia. The documents went on to say that the BHS worked closely with the Indian Embassy and had good relations with other Indian spiritual organisations in Russia. Swami Sadananda's purpose for visiting Macau was to enlighten its Indian community about the ten-thousand-year-old Hindu culture. Gef was travelling on an American passport as Benjamin Jefferson, who was in Macau to meet with one Ms Fanny Li for a public–private partnership venture.

Both Raj and Gef left Tirana using these new identities on the 19th , departing at 6 a.m. by Wizz Air and landing in Milan Malpensa two hours later, at 8 a.m. After a three-hour layover and an airline change, they took off from Milan on EVA Airlines at 11 a.m. and, after a twelve hour fifteen minute long flight, they landed at Taiwan Taoyuan International Airport, in Taipei at 6.15 p.m. local time.

And then, after a three hour, forty-five minute layover,

the same EVA Airlines flight carried them to Macau, landing five minutes before midnight. Their journey spanned twenty-two hours, two layovers and two separate airlines. When they stepped out of the plane, they were bone tired. But this exhaustion vanished upon seeing Gef's friend. His 'friend' turned out to be his former lover, Fanny Li, 'the free willed one' or simply put a person with a free spirit. Standing at five feet eleven inches, Fanny's flawless complexion was complemented by straight black hair, an oval face with a tapered chin, a straight nose and full lips. She possessed the elegance of a runway model and spoke with a sultry French accent.

Fanny was thirty years old and was half Chinese and half French. She was a director in the Department of Corporate Affairs, which came directly under the Governor of Macau. That helped them avoid the seven-day quarantine. Gef's initial interest in her was professional, due to her direct access to senior leadership in the Chinese government as well as to the governor. But over time, the friendship turned into love. Though they were distanced from each other because of their work, Raj sensed that they still had feelings for each other. They chatted in French throughout the thirty-minute journey to the hotel, with most of it being syrupy with love. They assumed incorrectly that Raj did not know the language. Fluent in the language, Raj was amused at the way she treated Gef like a child.

After dropping Raj off at the Pousada De Coloane, Gef went with Fanny to her house.

The Pousada De Coloane, a former manor house that now served as a beachfront hotel, boasted twenty-eight rooms, a swimming pool, an authentic Portuguese restaurant and a terrace for private fine dining. It sat on the Cheoc-Van beach located in the southern bay of Macau. The Pousada De Coloane was surrounded by verdant landscapes, with all twenty-eight balconies overlooking the sea, giving every guest a breath-taking sunrise and sunset view. The hotel was designed for those seeking respite from the noise of the city.

Though not under lockdown like other Chinese cities, Macau was almost dead in September. The gaming centres hardly had guests, and heavy rains were keeping people indoors. With barely anyone at the Pousada De Coloane, Raj was given VIP treatment. He was provided with an upgraded suite, a dedicated butler and access to a personal driver and vehicle. After a sumptuous dinner, Raj was about to retire for the night, when Fanny called him.

'*J'espère que je ne t'ai pas dérangé, Raj?*' she said breathily. Raj heard Gef tell her he doesn't understand French.

'I know. I am just having fun,' she said in French to Gef and giggled. She shifted to English and said, 'I hope I haven't disturbed you, Raj.'

'Not at all, Li,' said Raj.

A brief pause followed her words, and then Fanny's tone shifted to a more sombre note. 'One of Gef's men, a Tsinoy called Jude Hsiao, will come with two briefcases at 7 a.m. tomorrow.' The term 'Tsinoy' was used colloquially for Tsinong Pinoy, or Chinese Filipino.

'Thank you. I'll wait for him,' said Raj politely.

Another moment of silence passed. Then she said softly, 'You called me Li. It's been fifteen years since I've been called that. It is my surname and no one calls me by that name except my brother. From when we were toddlers he found that name easy to pronounce and always called me Li.'

'Where is he now?' asked Raj.

'In Qincheng Prison, serving a life sentence for treason,' she replied. Then she let out a dry laugh and added, 'We French are revolutionaries. He raised his voice against atrocities. So he was caught and put in prison without a trial. When the MSS came to take him away, he was twenty years old, and I was fifteen. I haven't seen him or spoken to him since.' She stopped and quickly changed the topic, saying, '*Bonne nuit, Monsieur Raj.*' Before Raj could respond, she disconnected.

⊘∬∼

Punctuality was important to Jude Hsiao, a notably fair, short and rotund Chinese Filipino man. When he knocked on Raj's door the next morning, it was 7 a.m., and Raj was about to sit down to breakfast. Raj welcomed him inside and extended the offer of breakfast. Jude refused initially, but when Raj insisted, he complied. After the butler left, they initially spoke about the weather, sightseeing and casinos. Once they finished their breakfast Raj said to Jude, 'Let's go through the items, please.'

Jude opened both briefcases. One had weapons and the ammunition that went along with them, while the other had a garotte, a hunting knife, night-vision goggles and a small box of C4. Jude reached into the side of one of the briefcases and pulled out a small envelope. Inside was an open ferry ticket from Macau to Hong Kong in the name of Joseph Lika and an open onward ticket from Hong Kong to Tehran in the same name. He pulled out a passport in Joseph Lika's name but with Jude's picture in it.

'This is for me. Let me know when to travel,' said Jude.

There was another envelope that contained a letter signed by Gef to the captain of a small cargo vessel in Macau. The letter read:

'Dear Capt. Parnell,

As previously agreed upon, I would appreciate your assistance in ensuring the safe passage of my spiritual guide, Swami Sadananda, to Shenzhen. Swami Sadananda will contact you directly, vide this letter. Thank you for accommodating this request during the pandemic.

Regards,
Gef Bajrami'

'Mr Bajrami and Madam Fanny will meet you for lunch here at 12.30,' said Jude. Then he thanked Raj for the lovely breakfast and left. With four hours to spare, Raj took a tour of Macau in the car provided by the hotel. Since it was raining, he didn't get out of the car, but he made certain to locate the jetty where he was to meet the captain of the cargo vessel.

At 12.30 p.m. on 3 September, Raj waited for Gef and Fanny in his room at the Pousada De Coloane. The couple did not disappoint him. They arrived on time. The trio settled down for a discussion over a simple lunch of soup and sandwiches that they asked the butler to serve, going on to request him for privacy, which he promptly gave them.

'Where do we start looking for Misha?' asked Raj.

'I made inquiries between last night and this morning. Macau is a small place, and anything new catches the eye, especially if you are here for the long haul. Apparently, Hong Kong billionaire Charlie Ho has been seeing a white-skinned blondie for a while now. The locals say he has come from Europe and is a drug dealer,' said Fanny.

Raj looked at Gef and asked, 'How are we sure that it's Misha?'

'We're not. But she has given her man a photo of him. He'll let us know soon,' said Gef.

'Who is Charlie Ho?' asked Raj.

'Macau has a number of licensed casinos, and they compete very hard with each other. The enmity between the owners runs deep, and they don't shy away from pulling the trigger. Initially, the local cops accepted bribes to mediate disputes between the warring owners, but of late, with a heavy crackdown by the Governor, the cops have moved out of the game, and the disputes are now being settled by a Hong Kong billionaire called Charlie Ho. The casino owners are petrified of him, because he is the brother of the boss of the notorious triad, 11k. They shoot your family first and then ask you questions. The casino owners pay him 10 per cent of their profits to maintain peace in Macau so that tourists feel safe and also to ensure no inter-casino rivalry. Last year, Charlie made 2 billion dollars. Now with the pandemic, tourism is almost dead, and the casinos are empty. With hardly any revenue coming in from the casinos, Charlie is now getting into drug trafficking. This European blondie is supposed to be his partner, according to my sources,' said Fanny.

'If it's Misha, then he is setting up his drug distribution network in Macau,' said Gef.

'Assuming it's him, where do we find him?' asked Raj.

'Charlie Ho has a guest house above the famous Portuguese boutique, The Tulips. It's on the Avenida da Praia Grande, which is in the heart of the commercial hub here in Macau. According to my source, his White paramour is staying there,' said Fanny. 'If my man confirms he is Misha, then we will put him under surveillance for a week to understand his routine. Then we'll know what to do.'

They spent the rest of the day in Raj's room avoiding shop talk, instead discussing their personal histories. While Gef and Fanny were completely transparent, Raj had a lot of secrets to hide but somehow managed to spin them a convincing story. Fanny was a little inquisitive when it came to Geeta, maybe because Gef had told her how he had gone to save her from Beqir, but Raj tactfully avoided a response.

Gef decided to take a nap, so Fanny sat in the balcony smoking a cigarette and watched Raj dismantle and oil the Glocks. Impressed, she remarked, 'For a businessman, you seem to know your weapons very well.'

Raj kept his calm and said with a smile, 'My father was in the police force, and I was tasked with dismantling and oiling his pistol and rifle every Sunday as a teenager.'

'I saw you handling the hunting knife and setting the loop on the garotte as well,' she said.

'Learnt that from him too,' he said calmly as he assembled the Glocks, loaded the bullets and put them in the case.

'What else do you know, Raj?'

'I'm a third-degree black belt in Shaolin kung fu and a martial art called kalaripayattu from the south of India,' said Raj, holding her gaze.

'You're a businessman and a movie producer, but you seem to have all the qualities of a commando,' she probed.

'My father wanted me to be in the police force, so he had me rigorously trained. Though it was years ago, you cannot unlearn certain things,' he said.

That convinced her. She sighed and said, 'My dad wanted me to be a ballet dancer. Instead, I ended up here.' She got up and stubbed out her cigarette. Then she got up, went to the turntable in the suite and put on a slow song.

'Dance with me, Raj. It's been ages since I danced,' she said, the setting sun throwing its golden light on her. Raj thought for a moment, then shrugged and walked up to her.

When Gef woke up, it was dark, and he could hear laughter coming from the balcony. He walked over and found both Raj and Fanny drunk, sitting on the floor and trying to sing 'Rhinestone Cowboy' by Glen Campbell. He smiled at them and said, 'I can sing better.'

That night Gef and Fanny slept in the suite on the double bed, while Raj took the single bed in the adjoining room. As he slept, he dreamt of a life he would never have with Geeta.

29

IT WAS 6.30 P.M. ON 8 SEPTEMBER, 2020 when Fanny's man reverted with his findings. It was confirmed: the European Charlie Ho was with, was Misha Perci.

Raj and Gef were thrilled with the news. Over the last five days, they had scoured the entire city looking for escape routes, in case they were boxed in by Charlie Ho's team. Disguised in helmets, they cruised Macau on a rented Kawasaki dirt bike, immersing themselves in the city's nooks and crannies. By the end of it, Raj's photographic memory had captured every last detail.

Fanny, Raj and Gef met at the Portuguese restaurant in the Pousada De Coloane that night. After dinner, they went to Raj's room to start planning.

'Here are the details and photographs of Misha,' said Gef as he spread out some pictures and documents from Fanny's source on the dining table in the suite.

There were photos of him at a café across from The Tulips, smoking weed outside his room in the narrow balcony above The Tulips, in the salon next to the café, and in a Mercedes van with Charlie Ho. Fanny mentioned that the last two shots were taken on Friday.

'You carry your Scout everywhere, but do you know

how to use it?' Raj asked Gef, pointing to the Stealth Recon Scout rifle.

'I've fired it once at short range, but I admit I lack the precision of a sniper. Given a chance, I'd probably be able to hit the body, but nothing more precise,' said Gef.

'Hmm ... which means you are at best a distraction. Now I wonder if you ever even considered killing Misha at the palace,' said Raj with a smile as he took the welcome letter from the General Manager which was lying on the table and flipped it. He began drawing the Avenida da Praia Grande. Then he drew The Tulips and, above that, the apartment where Misha was staying.

'I'll graciously ignore the palace comments and only say that you have a knack for drawing,' said Gef.

'And a knack for remembering everything too,' said Fanny as she watched him draw out the minute details in and around the Avenida da Praia Grande.

After completing the drawing, Raj pointed to the rooftop of the building opposite The Tulips, where the café was, and said, 'You'll have to shoot Misha from here.'

'When? Where?' asked Gef.

Raj looked at Fanny and said, 'According to your man, last Friday, Misha went to the salon and then left with Charlie in a Mercedes van. If that is a routine, then we know when to hit him.'

'How do we know he'll follow that routine?' asked Fanny.

'If he goes to the salon this Friday, then we can assume he'll go out with Charlie Ho that evening,' said Raj.

'Assuming he's going with Charlie, what do I do?' asked Gef.

'You'll aim for him from the rooftop and fire till you

hit him. Then you'll dismantle the SRS, throw it down this chimney chute and run,' said Raj, pointing at a big black chimney he'd drawn on the terrace.

'Run where? They'll know where the shots are coming from, so they'll rush up. What if they block the stairs, lifts and fire escape?' asked Gef.

'I thought of that. You won't run down. You'll run across to the other building, which is connected to this one with a concrete parapet. You'll come down the other building,' Raj said, tapping the drawing of the concrete slab connecting both buildings.

'And once I get down?' asked Gef.

'You'll take the rear exit, where Fanny will be waiting for you. You two will leave for her house and stay put there,' said Raj.

'What about you? What will you be doing?' asked Fanny.

'If Gef hits Misha, then I have nothing to do. If he doesn't, I have a lot to do. But we will take it as it comes,' said Raj.

'Why can't you be on the terrace firing at Misha?' asked Fanny, protective of Gef.

'I can, but the last time we spoke at the Palace of Brigades in Tirana, Gef said he wants to finish Misha himself. I'm just giving him a second chance. If you want him to chicken out, I'm okay with that,' said Raj.

'I'll do it,' Gef said hurriedly.

'Good. Any more questions?' asked Raj.

'When do you plan to do this?' Fanny had a worried look on her face.

'Friday.' said Raj.

'But that's tomorrow,' said Gef.

'You must be a certified genius,' said Raj, winking at Gef.

Gef was restless that night and couldn't sleep. Neither could Fanny, worried for Gef's life.

At 4.30 p.m. on 9 September, Misha walked out of his apartment building carrying an umbrella and entered the salon. It was raining heavily and Gef, who was sitting on the terrace in the building across the street, had covered himself with a large waterproof tarpaulin.

Gef spotted Misha and said into his lapel mic, 'He's just entered the salon.'

'I'm two blocks away from you, love. When do you want me to come?' asked Fanny.

'You reach the rear exit of the building next to the café at exactly 6.30 and wait for Gef,' said Raj, as he sat in the café nursing a coffee. There was only one other customer, and he was way in the back. The owner of the café sat behind the counter and couldn't see Raj unless he stood up.

'Are you sure he will come out at 6.30, Raj?' asked Gef.

'A hundred per cent,' said Raj.

As the clock ticked on, everyone waited. At 5.30 p.m., Misha walked out of the salon and entered his apartment building. At 6.15 p.m., he resurfaced on the covered balcony of his apartment with a rolled joint in his hand. He was dressed for the night.

'I see him,' said Gef.

'Wait till he comes down and then start shooting when I give you the signal,' said Raj.

At 6.28 p.m., the black Mercedes van rolled up in front of The Tulips. For a minute nothing happened, and then the rear window rolled down, and Charlie Ho flicked a cigarette onto the wet road. Within seconds, the window went up again.

At 6.29 p.m., Raj got up from the café and walked

towards the Mercedes. He was wearing a long black raincoat with the collar up. He also had on a black Covid mask and a waterproof cap. His hands were firmly inside his pockets. As he walked past, he bent down and attached a small brick to the back of the Mercedes, the door for the boot, and continued walking. A few steps away, he turned, crossed the road and walked back into the café and took his seat.

'What was that all about?' asked Gef.

Raj ignored the question and said into his lapel mic, 'Fanny, come to the meeting point and stay there.' A few seconds later, Misha appeared from the elevator of his apartment building. He stepped out into the rain with a large black umbrella and looked to his left. The black Mercedes van was parked ten feet away. He turned, and Raj pressed the button on the remote in his hand. There was a second's delay as the charge connected, and then the C4 exploded.

'Fire, Gef' said Raj, as he dived to the floor.

As the C4 ripped through the Mercedes and flung it five feet in the air, Gef started firing at Misha, who, shocked by the explosion, had fallen back onto the pavement. Gef fired about ten bullets at Misha as he got up and ran into his apartment building.

'Did I get him?' asked Gef.

'No. Run,' said Raj as he crossed the road and walked towards Misha's apartment building. The Mercedes had been blown to bits. The lifeless bodies of Charlie Ho and his three associates lay on the road, marred beyond recognition. Although the streets were practically empty, those present fled the scene, fearing another explosion or further firing from the rooftop.

As Gef dismantled the SRS, dumped it down the chute

and ran to the other building, Raj raced to the elevators of Misha's apartment building. He just caught sight of Misha going up. Opting for speed, he took the stairs to the second floor. Misha was running towards his room, but Raj was on his heels. As Raj rounded the corner, he was confronted with Misha holding up a pistol, aimed and ready.

'Who are you?' Misha asked.

Raj dived to the floor and came up shooting. The first bullet from his Glock hit Misha's chin, sending him spinning. The second bullet hit him in the kidney, and the third on the back of his head, splitting it almost in half, even as the lifeless body of Misha hit the corridor railing, hung there for a second and then toppled over onto the pavement outside.

Raj raced down the stairs carrying Misha's umbrella, exited the building with the umbrella covering him completely and kept walking northwards. In the alley behind him, Fanny, oscillating between crying and laughing due to the sheer relief and joy, had picked up Gef and taken him to her apartment.

Out on the rain-swept streets, Raj kept walking for another 2 kilometres till he crossed the Macau Tower Convention and Entertainment Centre and climbed the bridge over the City Canal. He came down on the other side and walked under the bridge, where he had parked his Kawasaki.

Changing into the dry clothes he'd stored in his bike, he threw the wet clothes and shoes into a dumpster nearby. Raj dismantled the Glock and threw its components into the canal. Then he pulled on a fresh pair of rain pants and a jacket over his clothes, put on his helmet and drove off to Pousada De Coloane for dinner.

30

IT WAS 6.30 A.M. ON 10 SEPTEMBER, 2020, Raj sat up in bed sipping a cup of tea and watching the morning news on Macau's most popular English channel, Lotus TV. Before going to bed the previous night, he had called Jude and told him to leave for Hong Kong at 11 a.m. and then take the onward flight at 2 p.m. to Tehran. A thrilled Jude was up and ready early in the morning for this holiday paid for by Gef and Raj.

In the room, Raj had had a good night's sleep and was well-rested as he listened to the reporter describing the shoot-out of the previous night on Avenida da Praia Grande.

'Last night,' the reporter began, 'the Avenida da Praia Grande transformed into a scene straight out of a Hollywood gangster movie. The owner of Café Song, the café opposite The Tulips, recounts bullets ricocheting off the pavements and a Mercedes van exploding in the middle of the road, killing Macau's biggest gangster, Charlie Ho, and four of his associates. An unknown assailant chased Misha Perci, an Albanian national and brother-in-law of the late President of Albania, Tefik Metta, up the stairs to his apartment above The Tulips and gunned him down. Perci's body fell to the sidewalk next to Ho's charred body. Perci had a chequered history with his involvement in drugs in Albania.

'The café owner, who was the sole witness, said that due to heavy rains, he could not see or hear much, but when he saw the number of bullets hitting the sidewalk, he realised it was an automatic weapon firing. Before that, the Mercedes van explosion came as a complete surprise. While he did spot an individual rushing into the building, the relentless rain prevented any clear identification. The killings of Charlie Ho, his associates and Misha Perci are a grim reminder of the '90s, when Macau was regularly rocked by gang wars. The police suspect this to be another gang-related incident but are not confirming anything till the investigation is complete.'

Raj muted the TV but left it on as he called Gef. 'Are you okay?' he asked.

'Absolutely fine. Fanny came just in time,' said Gef.

'I think you should leave tonight for Hong Kong, then fly off to anywhere except Tirana.'

'Fanny and I discussed this last night. We're taking the ferry to Hong Kong at noon and are flying from there to Cyprus. We'll stay put there for a week and then decide,' said Gef.

'Give my love and regards to Fanny and thank her for everything,' said Raj.

'I will. And you take care of yourself, please. Keep in touch, buddy. See you soon.'

◦∫∫~

In Zhongnanhai, 1,980 kilometres away, it was almost noon. Xi Wang had received news of Misha's death from the Governor of Macau and was waiting for the final police report, which was taking inordinately long. Reaching the end of his tether, he called Tony at noon.

'Find out who is behind Misha's murder,' Xi said, not waiting for a response before hanging up.

Three hours later, Tony called. 'I have some information, sir. This entire incident is a well-planned assassination and not a gang war.'

'Why do you say that?'

'The police found the dismantled pieces of an SRS, which is a sniper normally used in the Albanian Army. And the bullets retrieved from Misha have a distinct groove, aligning with the 9 mm calibre ammunition specially made for the Glocks used by Albanian Special Forces.'

'Are you saying the assassinations were carried out by Albanian Special Forces? Is Hector behind this?'

'No, sir. The police checked the exits out of Macau from last night till this morning. They did not find anything of interest there, so they're investigating another line. But I asked for both the airline manifest and the ferry exit lists and found one interesting name on the departure list.'

'Who is it?' asked Xi.

'Joseph Lika. He left Macau at 11 this morning by ferry to Hong Kong,' said Tony.

'Is he still in Hong Kong?'

'No. He left on the 2 p.m. flight to Tehran.'

'Shit. Now what will I say to Teuta?'

'If I may, Chairman, this is not the time to worry about

Teuta. It's more important to find out how Joseph Lika reached Macau, assassinated Misha and left for Tehran without getting caught.'

'And do you have an answer?'

'I think I have a theory, Chairman.'

'Stop with the suspense and spit it out, Tony. I'm on pins and needles here,' snapped Xi, irritated by Tony's storytelling.

'I think Joseph is working for the CIA,' said Tony.

'And why do you say that?' asked Xi with an exasperated look on his face.

'The CIA still loves Robert Sullivan, the ex-NSA of the US,' said Tony.

'But Robert was removed from the NSA post and was sent as a White House observer to Tehr...' Xi's voice trailed off. 'Robert is in Tehran. And he was close to General Hoxha.'

Tony nodded. 'Here's my theory, sir. Robert Sullivan orchestrated this entire thing from the start. He wanted to have General Beqir Hoxha as the President of the Republic of Albania so that America would have control over the Balkans. For this, he ensured the General became the NSA, and then used Joseph Lika to eliminate the kryes to make Misha powerless. His intention was to have complete control of Tefik and the nation. But it backfired when Misha assassinated Robert's man, General Hoxha. That ruined everything for Robert and Akhmu. Akhmu was furious with Robert for failing and sent him to Tehran as punishment. A humiliated Robert hit back. He used Joseph Lika to eliminate Tefik and Misha. Though he did not achieve anything for America directly, he did ensure that we lost control of Albania.'

'President Akhmu must be very happy. And who knows, he may call Robert back for achieving all this. We kept focusing on India and forgot that America is equally interested in our downfall,' murmured Xi.

'As always, Chairman,' Tony said, 'you are absolutely right.'

~

Back in Macau, it was 4.30 p.m. on 10 September. Raj paid his hotel bills, tipped his butler generously and asked the hotel driver to drop him at the Macau Outer Harbour Ferry Terminal. Once the driver left, Raj paid 500 Macanese pataca and took a *triciclos*, a bicycle rickshaw, to a lesser-known ferry terminal in Macau, located at Pier No. 11 at the Inner Harbour. The terminal was used to carry goods to Shenzhen, Jiangmen and Wanzai. Here he met Captain Parnell. Dressed in saffron and with a white turban and a white mask, he introduced himself as Swami Sadananda and handed over Gef's letter.

Captain Parnell welcomed Raj aboard his boat, which was carrying wood and furniture to a port in the north of Shenzhen. From there, Raj took a train to Fuzhou South, another train to Pingtan Station and then finally a ferry to Taipei Harbour.

It was late by the time he reached Taipei. Since flights to India operated only once a week and his was scheduled for the next day, Raj opted for a small motel near the airport. The next morning, he took a taxi to Taiwan's Taoyuan

International Airport, which was 40 kilometres west of Taipei in Taoyuan. Normally a busy airport, it was deserted now, with just two airlines operating due to the pandemic. Tiger Air Taiwan was operating within Taiwan, but it had hardly any passengers. Air Asia, an Indian international airline, flew to and from Taiwan once a week between Kolkata and Taiwan.

On Friday, 11 September, 2020, Swami Sadananda boarded the Air Asia flight from the Taiwan Taoyuan International Airport to Kolkata at 10.30 a.m. There were hardly any passengers on board, and with no other airlines operating, the flight took off early. Seven hours and forty-five minutes later, it dropped Raj at Netaji Subhash Chandra Bose International Airport.

He looked at his watch when he stepped out of the airport—it was 8.45 p.m. He made a call to Gef, only to have it answered by Fanny.

'Raj, did you reach safely?' she asked.

'*Oui, je l'ai fait,*' said Raj. *Yes, I did.*

There was a brief pause before she said, '*Donc tu parles français après tout.*' So you do speak French after all.

'*Oui,*' said Raj. '*Je vous remercie de tout de mon cœur. Sans vous, nous n'aurions rien obtenu. Merci, Fanny. Prenez soin de vous.*' I thank you for everything from my heart. Without you, we would have achieved nothing. Thank you, Fanny. Take care.' With that, he hung up.

Fanny looked at Gef's phone for a few seconds, smiling.

'Who was that?' Gef asked.

'Raj.'

'Raj? But you were speaking French,' said Gef with a quizzical look.

'There's so much we don't know about Raj,' said Fanny.

෴

It was 6 a.m. on 12 September, a day after Raj had landed in India. At 7, Lok Kalyan Marg, DD was going through the *India Times* newspaper in his garden as he sipped hot tea, when he came across an article. He smiled as he read the headline: 'West Bengal Chief Minister, Moushumi Banerjee, Says Corona is "Gone".'

He flipped through the sheets but nothing in particular caught his eye, until he reached the international news. His eyes fell on an article about Misha Perci's death in Macau. It read: 'Macau's police force has confirmed that the gruesome assassination of Misha Perci, the brother-in-law of the former Albanian President, the late Tefik Metta, was executed by Joseph Lika. Joseph Lika was the hitman of the late General Beqir Hoxha, who was murdered by Misha Perci. Lika had gone missing after the Hoti massacre in Albania, where he eliminated all the fifteen Albanian mafia heads in one evening. After the murder of his supervisor, General Beqir Hoxha, Lika resurfaced to assassinate former President Tefik Metta at the Palace of Brigades. Current President Hector Dekovi says he hopes the revenge killings are over with Misha's death and that Albania can move on to a better environment of peace and stability, which had disappeared during the reign of Tefik Metta.' DD finished his tea, then dialled a number.

'So, the Puppeteer has brought the curtains down on his show, I guess,' he said when the call was answered.

'Only for now, sir. When the master puppeteer pulls the strings, the Ghosts will rise again,' said Raj.

DD laughed. 'Glad to see your wit is back. Where are you?'

'Siddhashram,' said Raj.

Siddhashram was a legendary haven nestled deep within the Himalayas, home to siddha yogis, sadhus and sages.

'How did you manage entry there?' asked DD.

'My guru Swami Sai arranged it. I'm here for a week of meditation,' said Raj.

'When will you be back on duty?'

'Whenever the Panther calls, his Ghost will be ready, sir.'

EPILOGUE

THE CHAIRMAN OF THE PRC, Xi Wang, sat alone in his office, looking out of the window. His eyes were bloodshot; he hadn't slept. The very thought that he had become an untouchable in his own nation was eating him up. Internationally, he believed he could control perceptions: strategic investments in the US, in Europe and in influential human rights NGOs would likely prove effective. What he was worried about was the growing perception within China that he had run out of steam. Added to that was the new chatter on social media that he was actually responsible for the chaos in Albania. Investigations had revealed that the rumour had started in Qincheng Prison, and Xi was convinced that it was Chin's handiwork. Over the last few months, Chin had built a large fan following inside Qincheng Prison. Xi knew that if he did not move him out of there, a rebellion could break out within the prison walls, and there was a good chance that it would soon escalate outside too.

He called Tony and said, 'I think we need to move Chin out of Qincheng Prison.'

'Where do you plan to shift him, sir?' asked Tony.

'I'll let you know,' said Xi, hanging up. He switched on the television. The Prime Minister of India, Damodar Das, was being interviewed by a British reporter. DD was in the UK for discussions with the British Prime Minister, Joe Johnson.

'What do you think will be Chairman Xi's next move now?' asked the anchor.

'That is for my good friend Xi to decide. I cannot anticipate his thoughts or moves,' said DD with a smile.

'But you anticipated his moves when it came to the cyber-attack on BARC,' the reporter said with a smirk.

DD nodded. 'It's true that we were caught sleeping when the cyber-attack on the Mumbai electricity grid software happened. We learnt our lesson from that and built enough safety features around all our critical assets, so this time the firewall could not be breached. But we have no proof that China was involved in the attempted BARC attack. Since it is under investigation, I would rather not comment on it please.'

DD was countered by the reporter, who said, 'But the former NSA of America, Robert Sullivan, said very clearly that it was China's TAG-2 hackers who tried to sabotage your nuclear set-up.'

'America is a big country with highly advanced technology. They may have intel we don't. Yes, the US told us that TAG-1 hacked into our Mumbai electric grid and TAG-2 into our BARC set-up, but they have not shown us any credible evidence yet. Whatever they have is circumstantial and does not hold water in Indian courts of law.'

'I see that you are not mentioning China or Chairman Xi's name in any of your interviews or conversations regarding this massive cyberwar,' the reporter persisted.

'Like I said, why should I spoil his name? There is no proof that he did this.'

'A hundred and twenty nations are backing the proposed US-led sanctions on China, yet you maintain there's no proof of Chairman Xi's involvement?' the reporter said.

'The world anti-cyberwar task force is led by the US. If they have evidence that shows China was involved and if other nations want to act, then please ask them this question,' said DD, smiling politely.

'Are you at least willing to believe that there could be some connection, even indirectly, with China?' insisted the reporter.

'India has always stayed away from unnecessary politics, especially when nations go after each other. We are not part of any bloc and prefer to take a stand that is in the best interest of our nation and the whole world. At the same time, we know how to look after ourselves, and if we find proof of any wrongdoing on China's part, we will act firmly and decisively. But with regard to the US and the other nations, that's their prerogative,' DD said.

'So you're saying you are not part of the 120 nations,' pressed the reporter.

'No, we are not. As Mahatma Gandhi said, "Do not judge others. Be your own judge and you will be truly happy. If you try to judge others, you are likely to burn your fingers."'

'The American government has already shared enough proof with the International Court of Justice of China meddling in other nations' operations via cyber-attacks, and they are calling for a hearing next week,' said the reporter.

'Then I'm sure it will all be settled in the Hague, won't it?' said DD. 'You never asked me about our progress on green initiatives.'

'Any message for Xi?'

'Nothing political, but on a personal front, I would like to urge him to release Chin Luan Mao, who is rotting in Qincheng. Even if he is guilty of anything, there should have been a fair trial, and then punishment, if any, should have been awarded only after that. Taking his wife's brother, who is also her head of security, without any justification and putting him in the worst prison in China is unbecoming of the Chairman of the PRC. This is purely my view,' said DD.

The reporter was thrilled she had managed to get a bite from DD. She gave a knowing smile and said to her audience, 'Do not judge thy neighbours, and release Chin, says Damodar Das.' And with that, the interview ended.

Xi was not aware that Paitoon had entered the room and was watching the interview, so when he switched off the TV and turned, he was surprised to see her sitting on the small sofa by the door.

'How long have you been here?' he asked.

'Long enough to see a statesman still not utter the name of his enemy,' said Paitoon sarcastically.

'He's trying to take the moral high ground, and I could see right through his act,' said Xi.

'Forget about him and his morality. You have brought China down to the level of North Korea. We are isolated and humiliated, and like a coward you punished my brother for your failure,' Paitoon said, seething with anger.

Before Xi could respond, she walked off in disgust,

banging the door behind her. Xi pushed his chair back and stood, nearly toppling it over. His entire plan had failed, and now he was being treated like a pariah not only by the world, but also by his own wife. He knew very well that the Chinese were extremely proud people, and his citizens could rise against him soon if he did not do something.

Since the Chinese Communist Party had lost its right to impeach or vote him out as per the new resolution that he had made them sign, the only way to get him out would be to not extend his term in the coming session of the 20th National Congress of the party in 2026. He feared that Paitoon's father, a senior leader in the CCP, could even influence the Central Guard Bureau to arrest him. The CGB was responsible for the protection of senior party members and the Chairman, along with their families. The CGB selected and controlled the bodyguards, who were trained by the PLA.

His mind raced for a solution but came up empty. The phone's loud ringing interrupted his thoughts—it was Tony.

'I watched DD's interview. The situation does not look good for you, Chairman. If you don't do something quickly, between the US and Europe, you will cut off from every credible organisation in the world. If the Hague case goes against you, China will lose the UNSC seat. I am given to understand that President Akhmu is supporting Hector Dekovi in the coming presidential elections. In fact, all of Europe and Asia is supporting him. While OPOR has become a dream for us, this move also means we will be on our own. I believe Hector and DD have signed a deal wherein India is setting up its military bases not only in Albania but, with

Hector's influence, also in the rest of the Balkans too. This is perfect for DD and terrible for us, Chairman,' said Tony.

'India is a non-violent country. They have a policy of no first move,' said Xi.

'Not any more, Chairman, and you know that better than anyone else.'

'If he and Akhmu try anything, Vladimir will support me.'

'All due respect, Chairman, I doubt he will. DD and he have become very close. The two nations are bound by trade, culture, innovation and invention. Vladimir is very cunning. He knows which side his bread is buttered,' argued Tony.

Xi was surprised by Tony's political astuteness and equally irritated by how right he was. Unable to answer his questions, Xi snapped, 'Enough. My mind isn't working right now. I need to figure things out. I just need time to set everything right. Remember, we're the colossus China, not some small province like Tibet that can be attacked and annexed like we did them. And I took Tibet from right under India's nose. So the world knows they cannot write me off so quickly.' Xi disconnected. He sat still for a moment to calm himself, remembering his doctor's warnings after his heart attacks. As he closed his eyes and took deep breaths, a thought suddenly struck him.

He called Tony back. 'I know where to send Chin. Transfer him to Drapchi Prison.'

'In Tibet?' asked Tony.

'Yes. He'll be surrounded by the monks and nuns we jailed for treason. This will kill the brewing rebellion in Qincheng Prison,' said Xi.

Drapchi Prison, found in Lhasa, was the largest prison in

Tibet. Originally a military garrison, had transformed into a fearsome detention centre, notorious for its harsh treatment of Tibetan rebels and political opponents.

Xi ended the call and stretched his arms over his head as he looked out of the window. Behind him, there was a soft knock on the door, and Paitoon entered.

'What is it now? Xi asked, irritated.

'Nothing. I forgot my cell phone,' she said, reaching for the phone, which lay on the sofa near the door. She stepped out, closed the door firmly behind her and ran to her room. Once inside, she pulled out a Thuraya from her safe.

'They're shifting Chin Luan to Drapchi,' she said.

'When?' the voice on the other end asked.

'I don't know, but he won't last very long there. I need your help,' she pleaded.

'Leave it with me. I'll find a way to get him out.'

'Will it be soon?' she asked, holding back tears.

'I cannot promise you exactly when, but what I can promise you is that I will give this my all.'

'If you do, I will be eternally grateful. I have connections in Drapchi who can get your men inside,' said Paitoon.

'I will get back to you.'

⟡⟨⟨~

8,000 kilometres away, DD dialled Dhariwal and said, 'Meet me in my office. We have to get Chin out.'

Dhariwal's answer was immediate. 'Yes, Panther.'

ACKNOWLEDGMENTS

Writing a 'real–reel' book is not easy. But that makes it exciting, and this would not have been possible without the help of my editing team—a special thanks to Sanghamitra and everyone at the Scribe Crew for questioning us and helping us keep the adrenalin rush despite the twists and turns in the book.

We are eternally grateful to the Governor of West Bengal, His Excellency Dr C.V. Ananda Bose, for the foreword of this book and to Anish Chandy from 'Labyrinth' for making the Panther's Ghosts series happen. Thank you for standing with us, brother.

Finally, a big thank you to Westland Books for believing in us and trusting us with the next four books in the series. We promise not to disappoint you and the readers.